IS THE ECONOMIC CYCLE STILL ALIVE?

CENTRAL ISSUES IN CONTEMPORARY ECONOMIC THEORY AND POLICY

General Editor: **Mario Baldassarri**, *Professor of Economics, University of Rome 'La Sapienza', Italy*

This major series is a joint initiative between Macmillan, St. Martin's Press and SIPI, the publishing company of Confindustria (the Confederation of Italian Industry), based on the book collection MONOGRAFIE RPE published by SIPI and originated from the new editorial programme of one of the oldest Italian journals of economics, the *Rivista di Politica Economica*, founded in 1911. This series is intended to become an arena in which the most topical economic problems are freely debated and confronted with different scientific orientations and/or political theories.

Published titles

Mario Baldassarri (*editor*)
INDUSTRIAL POLICY IN ITALY, 1945–90

Mario Baldassarri (*editor*)
KEYNES AND THE ECONOMIC POLICIES OF THE 1980s

Mario Baldassarri (*editor*)
OLIGOPOLY AND DYNAMIC COMPETITION

Mario Baldassarri (*editor*)
THE ITALIAN ECONOMY: HEAVEN OR HELL?

Mario Baldassarri and Paolo Annunziato (*editors*)
IS THE ECONOMIC CYCLE STILL ALIVE?: THEORY, EVIDENCE AND POLICIES

Mario Baldassarri, John McCallum and Robert Mundell (*editors*)
DEBT, DEFICIT AND ECONOMIC PERFORMANCE

Mario Baldassarri, John McCallum and Robert Mundell (*editors*)
GLOBAL DISEQUILIBRIUM IN THE WORLD ECONOMY

Mario Baldassarri and Robert Mundell (*editors*)
BUILDING THE NEW EUROPE
Volume 1: The Single Market and Monetary Unification
Volume 2: Eastern Europe's Transition to a Market Economy

Mario Baldassarri, Luigi Paganetto and Edmund S. Phelps (*editors*)
INTERNATIONAL ECONOMIC INTERDEPENDENCE,
PATTERNS OF TRADE BALANCES AND ECONOMIC POLICY
COORDINATION

Mario Baldassarri, Luigi Paganetto and Edmund S. Phelps (*editors*)
PRIVATIZATION PROCESSES IN EASTERN EUROPE: THEORETICAL
FOUNDATIONS AND EMPIRICAL RESULTS

Mario Baldassarri, Luigi Paganetto and Edmund S. Phelps (*editors*)
WORLD SAVING, PROSPERITY AND GROWTH

Mario Baldassarri and Paolo Roberti (*editors*)
FISCAL PROBLEMS IN THE SINGLE-MARKET EUROPE

Is the Economic Cycle Still Alive?

Theory, Evidence and Policies

Edited by

Mario Baldassarri
Professor of Economics
University of Rome 'La Sapienza'

and

Paolo Annunziato
Research Department of Confindustria, Rome

St. Martin's Press

in association with
Rivista di Politica Economica,
SIPI, Rome

© SIPI Servizio Italiano Pubblicazioni Internazionali Srl 1992, 1994

All rights reserved. No reproduction, copy or transmission of this publication may be made without written permission.

No paragraph of this publication may be reproduced, copied or transmitted save with written permission or in accordance with the provisions of the Copyright, Designs and Patents Act 1988, or under the terms of any licence permitting limited copying issued by the Copyright Licensing Agency, 90 Tottenham Court Road, London W1P 9HE.

Any person who does any unauthorised act in relation to this publication may be liable to criminal prosecution and civil claims for damages.

First published in Great Britain 1994 by
THE MACMILLAN PRESS LTD
Houndmills, Basingstoke, Hampshire RG21 2XS
and London
Companies and representatives
throughout the world

A catalogue record for this book is available
from the British Library.

ISBN 0-333-61065-2

Printed in Great Britain by
Antony Rowe Ltd
Chippenham, Wiltshire

First published in the United States of America 1994 by
Scholarly and Reference Division,
ST. MARTIN'S PRESS, INC.,
175 Fifth Avenue,
New York, N.Y. 10010

ISBN 0-312-10380-8

Library of Congress Cataloging-in-Publication Data
Is the economic cycle still alive? : theory, evidence and policies / edited by Mario Baldassarri and Paolo Annunziato.
p.   cm. — (Central issues in contemporary economic theory and policy)
Includes index.
ISBN 0-312-10380-8
1. Business cycles. 2. Economic forecasting. 3. Economic indicators.   I. Baldassarri, Mario, 1946–   . II. Annunziato, Paolo. III. Series.
HB3711.I8 1994
338.5'42—dc20   92-21104
                                                                  CIP

Contents

1	Introduction *Mario Baldassarri, Paolo Annunziato*	3
	PART I: ECONOMIC CYCLE FLUCTUATIONS	9
2	Theory and Measurement of Economic Cycles: a Recent Debate *Marco Lippi*	11
3	On the Sources of Fluctuation of the Italian Economy: a Structural *VAR* Analysis *Paolo Onofri, Paolo Paruolo, Bruno Salituro*	33
4	New Measures of the Permanent Component of Output: a Multi-Country Analysis *Paolo Roberti*	65
5	The Real Business Cycle Theory *Giuseppe Schlitzer*	105
	PART II: CYCLE INDICATORS AND ANALYSIS	
6	The Use of Cyclical Indicators in Business Cycle Analysis *Paolo Annunziato*	139
7	Leading Indicators for OECD, Central and Eastern European Countries *Ronny Nilsson*	181
8	A Monthly Model of the Industrial Sector for Business-Cycle Analysis *Enrico Giovannini*	227
9	Business Cycle Analysis and Industrial Production Forecasts *Pietro Gennari*	257
10	Death and Rebirth of the Business Cycle *Innocenzo Cipolletta*	285
	Index	299

Introduction

Paolo Annunziato - **Mario Baldassarri**
Confindustria, Roma　　Università «La Sapienza», Roma

Interest in the analysis and measurement of economic fluctuations would appear to have its own cyclical trend, being strong and common during and after periods of considerable instability but more neglected during periods of continuous growth. Similarly, in the evolution of economic theory, periods of intense research into the origins of the cycle have alternated with periods of great confidence in the ability of economic policy to reduce economic instability. In particular, during the 1960s and the early 1970s the fiscal authorities of almost all the industrialised countries and international economic institutes were busily engaged in "fine tuning" the economy, in accordance with the dictates of Keynesian economics.

As regards the present day, we agree with Zarnowitz [2] when he notes that we are now living what can only be another period of disillusion in the ability of economic policy, be it monetary or fiscal, to stabilise the economy. This is proven by the onset of severe recessions in various parts of the world during the first half of the 1980s and the inability to invert the negative phase of the business cycle under way in the various industrial countries in these early 1990s. A consequence of the failure of old solutions develops into a need to research in more detail the causes of economic fluctuations and their measurement.

This collection of papers on the business cycle attempts to contribute to this process. However, the fact that attention is largely concentrated on recent developments in measurement theory and methodology should not be interpreted as an indication that the contemporary literature presented in this volume to a certain extent exhausts the topic. Business-cycle analysis almost coincides with short-term macroeconomics and has many common points with the economics of growth, money, inflation and expectations. The present volume inevitably and deliberately passes over many important aspects in order to provide more coverage of an empirical approach aimed at business-cycle measurement and analysis. In fact, all the works presented here strive to analyse and provide some indicators of the effect of exogenous factors (including economic policies).

The first section of the volume deals with recent developments in contemporary empirical macroeconomics and debates the observation that economic time series have a high degree of serial correlation, which means that any shocks to the series themselves are persistent. This evidence can be explained by assuming these series can be represented as non-stationary stochastic processes characterised by a stochastic trend. In this case, the traditional distinction between long-term trends, described by a deterministic trend, and short-term phenomena, represented by cyclical fluctuations around a trend, would furnish erroneous results. If there was an exogenous shock, the economy's growth path would be modified and the impulses would propagate via cyclical oscillations which would dampen very slowly, and generate a high persistence in the economic variables as a consequence.

Marco Lippi opens the debate by illustrating the various consequences deriving from the hypothesis that the important economic variables are generated by stochastic processes with trends that are either stationary or non-stationary (for example stationary in the first-order differences). It should be emphasised that many of the empirical results concerning the trend's variability are very dependent on the functional form which is traditionally used to represent the stochastic trend (a random walk). In fact the trend variability is not confirmed by the data when one assumes alternative dynamic forms. Moreover, on the theoretical plane, if one assumes that the permanent component represents the diffusion effects of technological innovations and the learning process of technical progress, the functional form obtained for the trend is anything but a random walk.

The paper by Paolo Onofri, Paolo Paruolo and Bruno Salituro and that by Stefano Fachin, Andrea Gavosto and Guido Pellegrini aim at identifying the nature of the innovations which generate the business cycle. Both the analyses attempt to isolate the supply shock effects from the demand shock effects by using structural VAR systems which place some restrictions on the basic macroeconomic relations and on the correlation between the different types of shocks. Onofri, Paruolo and Salituro explore the possibility that technical progress can be interpreted not only as supply shock, but also as demand shock through foreign demand. The influence of the foreign sector is reassessed in the light of the results obtained, suggesting that in an open economy the import of consumption models can be the channel through which stochastic growth is introduced.

The paper by Fachin, Gavosto and Pellegrini on the other hand confirms the significance of the supply shocks. The results they obtain in fact indicate that much of the variation in industrial production depends on these disturbances. The authors extend their analysis to the other major European economies: they find similar evidence in Italy, France and Germany while in the United Kingdom the permanent component explains the variability in industrial production to a lesser degree.

Giuseppe Schlitzer analyses the hypothesis that the permanent component of time series represents the supply shocks. The critical overview of more recent literature on the business-cycle reveals old problems which are still unresolved, namely, whether it makes sense to credit technology with the role of the primary source of economic fluctuations and whether it is correct to interpret the trend of Solow's residual in terms of changes in the state of technology. The author proposes considering some recent contributions which integrate the intertemporal stochastic approach with analysis of imperfectly competitive market forms. In this type of models, aggregate demand plays a greater role since its fluctuations can affect the level of economic activity through a shift in labour demand, which depends on companies' mark-up.

The second section concentrates on methods for measuring the business cycle for forecasting purposes. Paolo Annunziato's paper discusses the correct use of traditional cyclical indicators while Ronny Nilsson illustrates some applications of the method used by OECD to analyse cyclical fluctuations in east European countries. This method consists in identifying the time series which have recurring requences so as to use them to identify and predict the subsequent phases of the business cycle under way. By way of reply to the criticism of constructing a "measurement without theory", literature over the past fifty years has devoted considerable efforts to develop the theoretical bases of these indicators. Indeed they are proposed as an alternative to econometric models of varying sizes vis-à-vis which they still provide more reliable forecasts in the very short term. The latest advances in the real business cycle theory and in particular the development of stochastic growth models are an important step forward in understanding, interpreting and improving business-cycle indicators.

On the other hand, the excessive level of abstraction and inelasticity limits the use of macroeconomic models for short-term economic analysis. The macroeconomic model presented by Enrico Giovannini is instead directed at analysing the very short-term economic cycle, and is characterised by its use of monthly observations and information from business surveys. The model's endogenous variables for the Italian industrial sector are orders, inventories, industrial production and production prices. The author uses the model to verify the dynamic effects of demand and supply shocks on the endogenous variables, noting the high level of reactivity of industrial production to demand shocks (especially in the intermediate and investment goods sectors).

The methods for the short-term forecasting of industrial production are discussed in Pietro Gennari's paper which emphasises that better results are obtained with multivariate rather than univariate time series models. The author discusses problems regarding the use of electrical energy consumption and short-term economic-cycle surveys in this type of analysis.

Innocenzo Cipolletta closes the volume by surveying the main problems of business-cycle analysis in a paper which deals with the "cycle" of business-cycle theory, that is to say the fortune and misfortunes this approach has encountered over the years. In par-

ticular the author illustrates the debate about the separation of the cycle from the trend with the consequences the different options entail as regards the economic-policy choices.

The paper's objective is to emphasise that the economic system always experiences short-term movements, but then form and incisiveness differ with the economy's cyclical trends. The business cycle and the trend mutually influence one another just as short- and medium-term economic policies are not independent of each other: those who employ short-term policies to deal with short-term problems should ask what structural effects they may have and similarly those who propose structural measures should ask what effect they will have in the short-term. The author also analyses the forms of measures for correcting or mitigating economic fluctuations, pointing out that short-term policies are charged with reconciling the objectives of low inflation, maintaining the balance of payments and low unemployment.

BIBLIOGRAPHY

[1] ONOFRI P.: «Osservazione empirica e analisi economica: esperienze di indagine sulle fluttuazioni cicliche», presented at the workshop on *Giornate di studio su crisi della teoria e crisi degli indicatori*, Giardini Naxos, 24-25 October 1991.
[2] ZARNOWITZ V.: «Recent Work on Business Cycles in Historical Perspective: A Review of Theories and Evidence», *Journal of Economic Literature*, n. 23, 1985.

I - ECONOMIC CYCLE FLUCTUATIONS

Theory and Measurement of Economic Cycles: a Recent Debate

Marco Lippi
Università "La Sapienza", Roma

1. - Introduction

I shall begin by pointing out two limits of this review. Firstly, I shall not deal with non-linear theories of business cycles, i.e. with the attempts to show that simple non-linear equations can generate complicated fluctuations without any resort to exogenous shocks. I shall only focus on the debate that has taken place in the last decade within the so-called Slutzky-Frisch approach, in which fluctuations persist only because the economic system is continually hit by exogenous shocks. In spite of this limitation of the scope a complete review would have produced too long and perhaps not too effective a paper. My topic could therefore be made more precise as: demand and supply theories of the business cycles *and* the empirical analysis of aggregate variables. In particular, I shall deal with the debate which arose with the works published at the beginning of the eighties, in which the traditional decomposition of macroeconomic time series into a permanent and a transitory component was systematically questioned.

The reader should be aware that some technical detail will be unavoidable. Nonetheless, I will often resort to very simple examples or to intuitive explanations which, I hope, will clarify the matter also to readers who are not deeply acquainted with time series analysis.

As a final remark let me only observe that the present paper is problematic and that I do not pretend to give a complete account of the debate (1).

2. - The Traditional Decomposition Into Permanent and Transitory Component

Until the end of the seventies it was usual in macroeconomic or macroeconometric work to split aggregate time series into a non-stationary deterministic component, the so-called trend or permanent component, and a stationary residual, identified with the cyclical component. Let us consider, for example, the aggregate output, call it Y_t. This time series is evidently non-stationary both in the mean and the variance. The traditional model, applied to this case, is the following:

$$(1) \qquad \log Y_t = a + bt + C_t$$

where the variable C_t is a stationary variable, i.e. with mean and variance independent of t. The corresponding model in natural values is:

$$Y_t = e^{a+bt} e^{C_t}$$

which displays exponentially growing mean and variance.

More or less explicitly, the traditional decomposition is based on a very simple economic insight. The term $a + bt$ gathers all permanent changes taking place in the economy, like accumulation of capital, population growth, technical change; while C_t, by definition, represents the effect of all transitory causes of change. It must be pointed out that in the traditional model exogenous shocks affect only

---

(1) For quite complete references, see e.g. STOCK - WATSON [23], CHRISTIANO - EICHENBAUM [5], LIPPI - REICHLIN [14]. The opinions expressed here, with possible minor variants, are already contained in some papers coauthored by L. Reichlin and myself. I bear all the responsibility for the present version.

Advise: the numbers in square brackets refer to the Bibliography in the appendix.

the transitory component; indeed, the trend is a simple deterministic function of time.

It is hardly necessary to mention that the trend could be a more complicated function, e.g. a quadratic or even a polynomial of higher degree. However, this would not be of any importance to the present issue. The crucial feature of *(1)* is that the trend is utterly deterministic, while the stochastic element is totally concentrated in the transitory component. On the other hand, such a dichotomy is responsible for serious limits in the applicability of *(1)* to empirical variables. A simple example will suffice. Consider the population size and the elementary statement that its growth is proportional to the size itself, the proportionality coefficient containing a stochastic disturbance term:

$$P_t - P_{t-1} = P_{t-1}(k + u_t)$$

where u_t has zero mean and constant variance. Approximately:

(2) $$\log P_t - \log P_{t-1} = k + u_t$$

It can easily be shown that the solutions of the difference equation *(2)* do not agree with model *(1)*. This is a very important statement since it provides a deep insight into the turning point represented by works like Beveridge and Nelson [1] or Nelson and Plosser [17]. The proof of the statement is very simple. Let us start with a given period, $t = 0$ for simplicity, and apply iteratively *(2)*. We get:

$$\log P_t = \log P_0 + kt + u_1 + u_2 + \cdots u_t$$

Here, as in *(1)*, we have a linear function of time: $\log P_0 + kt$; however, the stochastic term in front of it is not stationary, its variance being increasing with t.

Therefore, as soon as a simple cumulative law, like the one in *(2)*, is introduced, model *(1)* reveals as inadequate. Notice, on the other hand, that the cumulative model *(2)* is a quite natural representation for many economic and social phenomena. For example, price changes in a mark-up model depend on the cost level, and a similar argument applies to productivity; to the latter we shall return later on in detail.

For the time being we can sum up the difference between the traditional model *(1)* and models like *(2)*, in which the variable turns out as the solution of a difference equation. In models like *(1)* a constant variance fluctuation is superimposed to a deterministic permanent component. On the contrary, in models like *(2)* no deterministic function of time can be determined so that the residual has constant variance. Moreover, whereas in model *(1)* the decomposition into cycle and trend is immediate and uniquely determined, the same does not hold in *(2)*. This identification difficulty has been the background of the debate we are going to deal with.

3. - «DS» Models for USA Output

The issue discussed above can be given the following alternative formulation. Given a non-stationary variable, how should we operate to turn it into a stationary variable? In particular, should we make use of a regression, the regressors being a constant, time and perhaps higher powers of the latter; or, alternatively, should we employ first or perhaps higher order differences? And what consequences would follow from a "bad" detrending? For example, if the data have been generated by *(1)* and we apply first differences, a stationary variable turns out:

$$b + C_t - C_{t-1}$$

Yet, in this case differencing, while reducing the component $a + bt$, to a constant has an undesirable effect on the component C_t. Indeed, the latter is already stationary, so that $C_t - C_{t-1}$ will possess a sizeable variation at the high frequencies. An example will suffice. If C_t were autocorrelation free, i.e. a white noise, the variable $C_t - C_{t-1}$ would be autocorrelated at lag 1, the autocorrelation being -0.5. Such an autocorrelation would be void of any economic meaning, being only due to the detrending procedure applied to Y_t.

If instead the data were generated by a model like:

(3) $$\log Y_t = \log Y_{t-1} + u_t$$

or, more in general, like:

(4) $\log Y_t = a_1 \log Y_{t-1} + a_2 \log Y_{t-2} + \cdots a_k \log Y_{t-k} + u_t$

with the condition $\Sigma \, a_i = 1$, then the application of the first difference would provide a stationary series without introducing spurious autocorrelations. In (3) this is obvious. In (4), introducing the lag operator L (remember that the operatore L is defined by $Lx_t = x_{t-1}$) we get:

$$(1 - a_1 L - \cdots - a_k L^k) \log Y_t = u_t$$

The condition on the sum of the a_i implies that $1 - L$ is a factor of the polynomial in L operating on $\log Y_t$; this means that the last equation can be rewritten as follows:

(5) $\quad (1 + b_1 L + \cdots b_{k-1} L^{k-1}) (1 - L) \log Y_t =$

$= (1 + b_1 L + \cdots b_{k-1} L^{k-1}) (\log Y_t - \log Y_{t-1}) = u_t$

i.e. that the model can be rewritten in the first differences of $\log Y_t$. If the polynomial in the coefficients b_i turning out on the left hand side has no root of modulus smaller than one then: 1) the variable $\log Y_t$ is non-stationary; 2) the variable $\log Y_t - \log Y_{t-1}$ is stationary; 3) the variable $\log Y_t$ cannot be reduced to a stationary variable by regressing on a deterministic function of time.

The variables generated by equations like (5), which therefore fulfill 1), 2) and 3), have been denominated "difference stationary", henceforth DS, whereas variables generated by models like (1) have been called "trend stationary", TS. Moreover, at the end of the seventies a statistical test (known as Dickey-Fuller test) aimed at discriminating between TS and DS models became available. More precisely, the test can reject the null hypothesis that the model is DS against the alternative that the model is TS.

The test was sistematically applied to USA macroeconomic data in Nelson and Plosser [17], and the result in most cases was that the DS model was not rejected. In a short time the traditional TS model was out of use in macroeconomics. At the same time, as we shall see below, the use of DS models produced a debate on the decompositions of the GNP into trend and cycle.

Before we go into this issue let us pause here to give a further clarification of the definition of DS and TS models, and to mention a different development of the criticism raised against the use of TS models.

As for the definition of TS and DS a very suggestive point of view is obtained by starting from the spectral density of the process $(1 - L)x_t$, where x_t here represents any non-stationary variable for which the application of $1 - L$ provides stationarity. Let $g(\lambda)$ be the spectral density of $(1 - L)x_t$. For the unskilled reader it will suffice here to bear in mind that the spectral density is a function defined in the interval $[-\pi, \pi]$, which takes on only non-negative values. The fundamental theorem of the spectral theory of stationary processes states that the process $(1 - L)x_t$ can be thought of as the superimposition of sinusoidal waves having all possible frequencies between $-\pi$ and π (2); the value $g(\lambda)$ represents the relative importance of the wave at frequency λ. For example, processes with no autocorrelation, i.e. white noises, have a constant spectral density; in other words, all frequencies are equally represented. Processes with strong positive autocorrelation have spectral densities concentrated at the low frequencies, and viceversa for processes characterized by a strong negative autocorrelation.

Now let us come to our point. If z_t is a stationary process and we consider the process $z_t - z_{t-1}$, the latter is still stationary, but with a special feature. The long waves have been, so to speak, cut away. Indeed, as the frequency of the sinusoidal wave approaches zero, the difference $\sin \lambda t - \sin \lambda(t - 1)$ tends to zero uniformly in t. In other words, the spectral density of $z_t - z_{t-1}$ vanishes for $\lambda = 0$.

Going back to the distinction between TS and DS processes, we can give the following definition. The non-stationary process x_t is TS

---

(2) See, e.g. SARGENT [22], pp. 256-65.

or *DS* according to whether the spectral density of $(1-L)x_t$ vanishes or not at $\lambda = 0$. In fact, in the *TS* case, applying the first difference reduces the non-stationary deterministic component to a constant, while the spectral density of $(1-L)\,C_t$ vanishes at zero (remember that C_t is already stationary).

As for the different development, I want to make clear that the rejection of *TS* models does not lead necessarily to the *DS* alternative. Rather, the *DS* model represents an extreme within a variety of models. In particular, interesting models have been put across, where the trend has a slope which is allowed to vary, even though not necessarily at every period, like in *DS* models. Such broken trend models are particularly suitable for the representation of important but sporadic events, and are consistent with the occurrence of higher frequency shocks (3).

4. - The Measure of Persistence of Shocks in a «DS» Model

As we have recalled above Nelson and Plosser employed a *DS* model to give a representation of the most important USA macroeconomic time series, in particular the log of the GNP. The latter will be denoted from now on with y_t.

According to a theorem which I can only mention here (4) under rather general conditions the variable y_t admits the following representation:

(6) $\qquad (1-L)\,y_t = b + u_t + a_1\,u_{t-1} + a_2\,u_{t-2} + \cdots$

(Wold representation) where u_t is a white noise. In other words, any stationary process can be thought of as a (generally infinite) moving average of a suitable white noise. The latter is the so called "innovation" of the process.

Representation *(6)* has been employed in Beveridge and Nelson [1], which is almost simultaneous and closely linked to Nelson and

---

(3) See, e.g. RAPPOPORT - REICHLIN [20], PERRON [18], HAMILTON [11], REICHLIN [21].

(4) See SARGENT [22], pp. 285-90.

Plosser's paper, in order to define a *measure of persistence* for the shocks hitting the non-stationary variable y_t. As we shall see, under particular assumptions the measure of persistence has an interesting relationship with the decomposition into trend and cycle. The measure is in any case interesting and has the following simple definition. It is possible to prove that the sum:

$$a(1) = (1 + a_1 + a_2 + \cdots) u_t = \left(\sum_{k=0}^{\infty} a_k \right) u_t$$

is the limit, for n tending to infinity, of the expression:

(7) $$E_t(y_{t+n}) - E_{t-1}(y_{t+n})$$

which is the difference between the expected value of y_{t+n} given the values of y up to t, and the expected value of the same variable given the values of y up to $t-1$. Now, looking at (6), the change of information occurring between $t-1$ and t is precisely u_t. The meaning of Beveridge and Nelson's result is therefore the following. The shock u_t causes a revision of the long run prediction of y_t equal to $a(1)$ times u_t. $a(1)$ is, by definition, the measure of persistence.

An interesting observation on the above definition is that if y_t is a *TS* variable, then the sum of the a_i vanishes. In fact, model (1) can be written as (remember that C_t is stationary):

$$y_t = a + bt + (u_t + b_1 u_{t-1} + \cdots)$$

and therefore:

$$(1 - L) y_t = b + (1 - L)(u_t + b_1 u_{t-1} + \cdots) =$$
$$= b + (u_t + a_1 u_{t-1} + \cdots)$$

which implies $1 + a_1 + a_2 + \cdots = (1 - 1)(1 + b_1 + b_2 + \cdots) = 0$.

This has a close correspondence to intuition. The shocks hitting *TS* models affect only the transitory component, and do not modify the long run prediction. The latter is based only on the trend $a + bt$. The measure of persistence therefore represents, so to speak, the distance of the model from the traditional one. The higher the persistence measure, the bigger the revision of the long run prediction due to a shock, the bigger the mistake we make by using the traditional decomposition.

From an economic point of view, the shocks of a *TS* model do not cause any permanent change in the economic system. Even though their effects last more than one period (due to the autocorrelation structure of C_t), their nature remains purely transitory. Instead, if the model is *DS*, the shocks do cause permanent effects.

Two observations are in order. The first concerns the size of the persistence measure. Evidently, if the $a(1)$ estimated for the real GNP had been nil or much smaller than unity, the whole issue would not have had any important impact. The reason for the interest of the profession in the topic was that according to Nelson and Plosser's estimation the persistence measure for the GNP was bigger than unity, namely surprisingly great. This means that the shock u_t forces a revision of the long run forecast which is greater than the shock itself. Such empirical results can explain the heated debate that followed and the considerable amount of energy spent in the argument up to the recent years.

The second observation concerns the general agreement in the interpretation of the shocks. Permanent shocks were interpreted in this literature as supply shocks, while transitory shocks as demand shocks. Such interpretations are not warranted in general. Nothing prevents one from thinking of shocks affecting technology and yet having only transitory effects, as well as shocks affecting demand with a permanent effect. Perhaps, to better understand the reason for such an agreement, the reader should keep in mind that this debate took place under the theoretical spur given by the "real business cycles" models, whose prototype, Kydland and Prescott [13], contains an attempt to explain economic fluctuations on the basis of an intertemporal general equilibrium whose most important source of fluctuation is a permanent shock to technology. The debate I am talking about concentrated on the importance of permanent shocks, while the identification permanent = supply, transitory = demand was never seriously called into question.

5. - «DS» Models and Decompositions Into Trend and Cycle

As I pointed out before, unlike *TS* models, *DS* models call for identification of the decomposition into transitory and permanent component. As in the above Sections, let y_t denote the log of the real GNP. Assume that y_t is *DS*. Then the trend must be a *DS* variable while the cycle is a stationary variable. If the latter are denoted by T_t and C_t respectively, a decomposition will be:

$$y_t = T_t + C_t$$

where T_t is non-stationary while $T_t - T_{t-1}$ is stationary with a positive spectral density at zero. Consider for example:

$$y_t - y_{t-1} = (1 + aL) u_t$$

with u_t white noise, $0 < a < 1$. A possible decomposition is:

(8) $$y_t - y_{t-1} = (1 + a) u_t - a (1 - L) u_t$$

where the trend is defined by the equation:

$$T_t - T_{t-1} = (1 + a) u_t$$

while the cycle is $-au_t$. Notice that *(8)* gives a representation for the first difference of y_t. Therefore also the trend and the cycle are in first differences (this is the reason for the operator $1 - L$ in the cycle component). Decomposition *(8)* is well known as the Beveridge and Nelson's decomposition. One can immediately see its particular feature. The shock hitting the permanent component is identical to the one of the transitory component.

Starting with *(8)* one can easily obtain an idea of the multiplicity of possible decompositions in the *DS* case. Suppose that v_t is a white noise process bearing no correlation with the processes T_t and C_t (this is equivalent to zero correlation between v_t and u_{t-k}, for any k). Let us take any moving average:

$$D_t = v_t + d_1 v_{t-1} + \cdots + d_s v_{t-s}$$

which is evidently a stationary process and consider the decomposition:

(9) $$y_t - y_{t-1} = [(1 + a) u_t + (1 - L) D_t] +$$
$$+ (1 - L) [- D_t - a u_t] =$$
$$= (T'_t - T'_{t-1}) + (C'_t - C'_{t-1})$$

where:

$$T'_t = T_t + D_t, \qquad C'_t = C_t - D_t$$

We have:

a) the process T'_t is still DS, i.e. is non-stationary, while $T'_t - T'_{t-1}$ is stationary. In fact, T'_t has been obtained by simply aggregating a stationary process to T_t.

b) the process C'_t obtained aggregating two stationary processes is stationary. Decomposition (9) is therefore valid;

c) decomposition (9) is no more so special as (8). Indeed, if we consider the Wold representations of $T'_t - T'_{t-1}$ and C'_t, their innovation is not identical. In both cases the innovation is obtained by complicated combinations of u_t and v_t, but such combinations are different, so that the cycle shock is different (non-perfectly correlated) from the trend shock.

In general therefore the cycle fluctuations and the trend fluctuations are generated by different shocks. The limits of this review do not allow entering in further details. What we want to retain is that for a given DS process there exist infinitely many decompositions into a transitory and a permanent component. The latter are not necessarily perfectly correlated.

Given a decomposition, the following formula holds:

$$\text{var}(y_t - y_{t-1}) = \text{var}(T_t - T_{t-1}) + \text{var}(C_t - C_{t-1}) +$$
$$+ 2 \,\text{covar}(T_t - T_{t-1}, C_t - C_{t-1})$$

To different decompositions there corresponds a different relative importance of the cycle (or, equivalently, of the trend) with respect to the total variance var $(y_t - y_{t-1})$. The result obtained by Nelson and Plosser was that given the estimated process for the American GNP, they were able to prove that for any decomposition the trend variance var $(T_t - T_{t-1})$, is overwhelming as a fraction of var $(y_t - y_{t-1})$.

The estimated model we are mentioning is precisely the one used in the example *(8)*. As specified above, $0 < a < 1$. Therefore we have a permanence measure greater than unity, in addition to the result mentioned just above, that the variance of the trend, though variable among the infinite different decompositions, is always considerably greater as compared to the variance of the cycle.

Lastly, coming to the economic interpretation, the relative importance of the permanent component was used by Nelson and Plosser as a strong support to the real business cycles theories, i.e. the theories explaining economic fluctuations mainly by permanent shocks to technology.

6. - The Debate on Nelson and Plosser's Results. Alternative Estimations

Nelson and Plosser's conclusions have been called into question by many authors, from many different viewpoints. Firstly, their model, on which their conclusions are grounded:

$$y_t - y_{t-1} = b + (1 + aL) u_t$$

is nothing other than an estimation based on the *ARIMA* procedure, which is a particular procedure, not the "true" model generating the data. Other models can be estimated using the same data and the results can be used to obtain conclusions on the relative variance of trend and cycle, or on the permanence measure. My reference here is for example to works like Harvey [12], Clark [4], Watson [24], in which unobserved (and uncorrelated) components models are employed. The latter are models whose basic feature is the opposite if compared to Beveridge and Nelson's decomposition . Let us consider here a very simple version. Let the trend be:

$$T_t = T_{t-1} + u_t$$

with u_t white noise. This is the process known as random walk. For the cycle consider the model:

$$(1 + aL + bL^2) C_t = v_t$$

assuming that v_t is white noise and uncorrelated with u_{t-k}, for any k. The process y_t is therefore obtained as the sum of a random walk and a stationary second order process:

(10) $$y_t - y_{t-1} = u_t + \frac{1 - L}{1 + aL + bL^2} v_t$$

The model *(10)* can be estimated. This means that the variances of u_t and v_t, and the parameters a and b such that the fit of the model to the data is optimal, can be determined. Notice that in this case the estimation provides automatically the decomposition into trend and cycle. Simple manipulations allow the determination of the measure of persistence. The results obtained by the aforementioned authors can be summarized as follows: *a)* unobserved component models like *(10)* are not outperformed by *ARIMA* models, used by Nelson and Plosser and other authors, as far as the goodness of fit is concerned; *b)* the resulting decomposition into trend and cycle is decisively in favour of a relevant transitory component; *c)* the measure of persistence is smaller than unity.

Results *a)* and *b)* are important and help establish that available data are typically insufficient to draw conclusions on the issues raised by Nelson and Plosser. Result *c)*, instead, is of little importance. As shown in Lippi and Reichlin [5], *c)* is a just mathematical consequence of the models employed.

Other important works in the debate are:1) Campbell e Mankiw [3], where the *ARIMA* procedure is applied to quarterly data, instead of the yearly data employed in Nelson and Plosser. This work confirmed Nelson and Plosser's results; 2) notice however that quarterly data are also employed in the work by Watson [24] mentioned above; 3) Cochrane [6], where a direct estimation of the measure of persistence, i.e. an estimation independent from the particular model chosen, leads to a very low value.

It must be pointed out that in this literature attention is concentrated very often on the measure of persistence while the main problem is the relative importance of the components in the trend-cycle decompositions. This may be explained by: 1) the trend component has been, with few exceptions (Nelson and Plosser's paper is among them) identified with a random walk; 2) on the other hand, it is possible to prove that given any decomposition of $(1 - L) y_t$ in which T_t is a random walk, the variance of $T_t - T_{t-1}$ is $a(1)^2 \sigma_u^2$, i.e. the measure of persistence squared, times the variance of the innovation of $(1 - L) x_t$ (5). In the next Section we shall discuss the identification implicit in assumption 1). In any case, given 1), the result in 2) above explains the shift of attention from decompositions to persistence measure.

7. - More on the Decompositions of a Given Process into Trend and Cycle

In Section 6 we have reported on works in which the process estimated by Nelson and Plosser is called into question. Different estimated processes can give rise to different decompositions. Now we shall go back to Nelson and Plosser's paper and to the argument employed to claim that if the process is:

$$y_t - y_{t-1} = b + (1 + aL) u_t$$

with $0 < a < 1$, then only some decompositions are possible, while the latter are invariably dominated by the trend. The argument is the following. Consider a decomposition:

$$y_t - y_{t-1} = b + (1 - aL) u_t =$$
$$= b + m(L) v_t + (1 - L) n(L) w_t$$

Since the degree of the polynomial $1 - aL$ is unity, then $n(L)$ must necessarily be of degree zero, i.e. it must be a constant, while

---

(5) See, for instance, COCHRANE [6].

$m(L)$ has a degree less or equal to unity. Therefore the decomposition is:

$$(m_0 + m_1 L) v_t + (1 - L) n_0 w_t$$

This is the basis for the subsequent analytical development. I claim that this basis is quite fragile, as it implies the assumption that cycle and trend must necessarily be finite moving averages (this is necessary to the argument above). If, instead, $m(L)$ and $n(L)$ were free of assuming any dynamic shape, e.g. containing an autoregressive part in addition to the moving average, the argument falls.

The criticism hinted above is developed in all details in Forni [9] and is implicit in an important paper by Quah [19] (based on a working paper circulated before 1990). The main result in Quah's paper is that given a real e, a decomposition can be found such that the trend (differenced) variance is smaller than e (6).

Bearing these arguments in mind the debate is brought back to its beginning. When we deal with a *DS* variable, there is an infinity of possible decompositions, in all of them the trend being constrained only by the condition that it must be another *DS* variable. If no theoretical information is available which leads to the identification of the trend, the whole research line we are describing appears to end in a blind alley. Moreover, with the results reported in this Section the measure of persistence also loses much of its interest. In fact, it can be shown that if the trend is not constrained to assume particular dynamic shapes (like the random walk), then an arbitrarily small variance of the trend is consistent with an arbitrarily great measure of persistence.

8. - Diffusion of Technical Progress and Permanent Component

Let us firstly recall that the economic interpretation given to the permanent component in the debate was mainly that of total factors productivity. When the underlying economic model is explicitly formulated, the output is represented by a standard production function

---

(6) For a similar result see also LIPPI - REICHLIN [15].

with a superimposed multiplicative term providing the productivity level. When the variables are transformed into logs such a term becomes additive and is usually modeled as a random walk, i.e.:

$$(11) \qquad \pi_t = b + \pi_{t-1} + \epsilon_t$$

where ϵ_t is a white noise. An equation like *(11)* possesses the cumulative property I mentioned in section 2. Nonetheless, *(11)* can give a good representation of productivity only in a world in which: *a)* there exists only one firm; *b)* there are no learning processes; every increase of the stock of knowledge is completely absorbed in a single period by the representative firm or, alternatively, by all the identical firms of the economy.

The choice of *(11)* is undoubtedly effective for econometric identification. However, the only economic meaning attached to it is the widespread assumption of the representative agent. In Lippi and Reichlin [14], we suggest a simple way to take into consideration diffusion and learning processes. In particular, we introduce for the productivity the model:

$$(12) \qquad \pi_t - \pi_{t-1} = b + a_0 \epsilon_t + a_1 \epsilon_{t-1} + \cdots$$

whose coefficients a_i fulfill the following properties: *a)* they sum to unity; *b)* the plot of their partial sums:

$$S_k = \sum_{i=0}^{k} a_i$$

has the *S*-shape typical of empirical research on technical progress (7).

A parsimonious parameterization of *(12)*, fulfilling *a)* and *b)* is the following:

$$(13) \qquad a(L) = a_0 + a_1 L + \cdots = \frac{a_0 \sum_{i=0}^{q} [1 + (1 + i) A] L^i}{1 - \alpha L}$$

---

(7) A standard reference is GRILICHES [10]; references to more recent work can be found in LIPPI - REICHLIN [14].

subject to:

$$\frac{a_0 \sum_{i=0}^{q} [1 + (1+i)A]}{1-\alpha} = 1$$

Empirical results obtained by *(13)* are encouraging, in that the model can easily compete with models in which the trend is a random walk; nonetheless the use of aggregate data seems to prevent the establishment of a clear hierarchy among different models.

9. - Multivariate Models

An interesting attempt to deal with the identification of the permanent component has been provided in some works in which the aggregate output is jointly modeled with another variable taken as a good representation of the cyclical component. In Evans [7] and in Blanchard Quah [2] bivariate models are estimated for USA output and unemployment rate. The approach is the so-called vector auto-regressive, *VAR*, where each variable is regressed on the lagged values of all the variables considered. Using standard vector notation:

(14) $$A(L) x_t = u_t$$

where in our case: 1) x_t is the vector whose first component is $y_t - y_{t-1}$, while the second is the unemployment rate, denoted by U_t; 2) $A(L)$ is a polynomial matrix in L, all the polynomial being of the same degree, with $A(0) = I$; 3) u_t is a vector white noise.

The next step consists in inverting $A(L)$:

(15) $$x_t = A(L)^{-1} u_t = B(L) u_t$$

Lastly, a criterion must be introduced to decide which one out of the infinitely many variants of *(15)* is endowed with economic meaning. The variants are:

(16) $$x_t = B(L) u_t = B(L) KK^{-1} u_t = C(L) v_t$$

where $C(L) = B(L) K$, $v_t = K^{-1} u_t$. Therefore the problem is transformed into that of identifying the matrix K. In Blanchard and Quah identification is achieved assuming that v_{1t} and v_{2t} are uncorrelated at any lag and of unit variance. The crucial assumption is that one of the shocks has no permanent effect on y_t, this is the demand shock. The other, being the only one to produce a permanent effect is identified as the supply shock. Although differing in this last identification step, both Blanchard and Quah's and Evans' papers provide results in which the demand component is very important.

Results in favour of a considerable importance of the transitory component are also found in a recent paper by Evans and Reichlin [8], where the multivariate version of the Beveridge and Nelson decomposition is employed. The authors show that the variance of the cyclical component is necessarily greater as compared to the univariate decomposition (this is a purely analytical result), and show empirical applications in which the difference is surprisingly great.

For the sake of completeness I will mention here another work in the multivariate approach, Lippi e Reichlin [16], where a problem already raised in theoretical work but never considered in applied analysis is studied for the models and data just mentioned. The problem is the following. As we have seen the model is identified by chosing a suitable K. Unfortunately, such an identification contains an unwarranted assumption. In fact, there exist infinitely many models consistent with *(14)* and the economic restrictions, in which the matric $B(L)$ is not obtained inverting $A(L)$. Such representations, the so called non-fundamental representations, produce different behaviors of the vector x_t as response to the shocks. These behaviors in some cases confirm, in other cases subvert the result obtained with standard representation *(15)*. This issue is rather complicated and I will limit myself to this short mention.

10. - Concluding Remarks

The paper has given a fairly complete and elementary review of the problems raised in the debate on the relative importance of the permanent and transitory components in the explanation of economic fluctuations. As we have seen, the issue can only be put into discussion when the permanent component is represented as a *DS* variable, whereas no problem arises when the latter is represented as a deterministic function of time. The use of *DS* variables, i.e. variables whose first differences are stationary, led to results which were strongly at odds with the traditional view, according to which the permanent component is a smooth variable while all short and medium run fluctuations are accounted for by the transitory component.

Several objections have been raised and some of them appear to be convincing. Firstly, alternative estimations have provided a good fit with a considerable importance of the transitory component. Secondly, as I pointed out above, the identification of the permanent component has been very often overlooked in this literature. If the trend is not constrained to assume a particular dynamic shape, then all the variance decompositions are possible *a priori*. Moreover, the consideration of diffusion processes for technical innovations suggests a process for the trend which is quite far from the random walk often employed as a model for productivity.

Undoubtedly, the debate reviewed in this paper has produced very important analytical progress. Nonetheless, in my opinion, the results are strongly limited by the use of aggregate data, by which the discrimination between rival models is often impossible.

BIBLIOGRAPHY

[1] BEVERIDGE S. - NELSON C.R.: «A New Approach to the Decomposition of Economic Time Series into Permanent and Transient Components with Particular Attention to Measurement of the Business Cycle», *Journal of Monetary Economics*, n. 7, 1981, pp. 151-74.

[2] BLANCHARD O. - QUAH D.: «The Dynamic Effects of Supply and Demand Disturbances», *American Economic Review*, n. 79, 1989, pp. 655-73.

[3] CAMPBELL J.Y. - MANKIW N.G.: «Are Output Fluctuations Transitory?» *Quarterly Journal of Economics*, CII, n. 4, 1987, pp. 857-80.

[4] CLARK P.K.: «The Cyclical Component of the US Economic Activity», *Quarterly Journal of Economics*, n. 102, 1987, pp. 798-814.

[5] CHRISTIANO L.W. - EICHENBAUM M.: «Unit Roots in Real GNP: Do We Know, and Do We Care?», *Carnegie-Rochester Conference Series on Public Policy*, n. 32, 1990, pp. 7-61.

[6] COCHRANE J.H.: «How Big is the Random Walk in GNP?», *Journal of Political Economy*, n. 96, 1988, pp. 893-920.

[7] EVANS G.W.: «Output and Unemployment Dynamics in the United States: 1950-1985», *Journal of Applied Econometrics*, n. 4, 1989, pp. 213-37.

[8] EVANS G.W. - REICHLIN L.: *Information, Forecasts and Measurement of the Business Cycle*, 21, OFCE, Paris, July 1992.

[9] FORNI M.: «Trend, Cycle and 'Fortuitous Cancellatins'. A note on Trend-Cycle Decomposition of Economic Time Series», *Ricerche Economiche*, vol. XLV, n. 1, 1991, pp. 115-9.

[10] GRILICHES Z.: «Hybrid Corn: an Exploration in the Economics of Technological Change», *Econometrica*, n. 25, 1957, pp. 501-22.

[11] HAMILTON J.D.: «A New Approach to the Analysis of Nonstationary Time Series and the Business Cycles», *Econometrica*, n. 57, 1989, pp. 357-84.

[12] HARVEY A.C.: «Trends and Cycles in Macroeconomic Time Series», *Journal of Business and Economic Statistics*, n. 3, 1985, pp. 216-27.

[13] KYDLAND F.E. - PRESCOTT E.C.: «Time to Build and Aggregate Fluctuations», *Econometrica*, n. 50, 1980, pp. 1345-70.

[14] LIPPI M. - REICHLIN L.: «Diffusion of Technical Change and the Identification of the Trend Component in Real GNP», LSE Financial Market Group, *Discussion Paper*, n. 127, 1991.

[15] — — — —: «On Persistence of Shocks to Economic Variables: A Common Misconception», *Journal of Monetary Economics*, n. 29, 1992, pp. 87-93.

[16] — — — —: «A Note on Measuring the Dynamics Effects of Aggregate Demand and Supply Components», forthcoming, *American Economic Review*, 1992.

[17] NELSON C.R. - PLOSSER C.I.: «Trends and Random Walks in Macroeconomic Time Series: Some Evidence and Implications», *Journal of Monetary Economics*, n. 10, 1982, pp. 139-62.

[18] PERRON P.: «The Great Crash, the Oil Price Shock, and the Unit Root Hypothesis», *Econometrica*, n. 57, 1989, pp. 1361-401.

[19] QUAH D.: «The Relative Importance of Permanent and Transitory Components: Identification and Some Theoretical Bounds», *Econometrica*, n. 60, 1992, pp. 107-18.

[20] RAPPOPORT P. - REICHLIN L.: «Segmented Trends and Non-Stationary Time Series», *The Economic Journal*, n. 395, 1989, pp. 168-77.
[21] REICHLIN L.: «Structural Change and Unit Root Econometrics», *Economics Letters*, n. 31, 1989, pp. 574-9.
[22] SARGENT T.J.: *Macroeconomic Theory*, Boston, Academic Press, 1987.
[23] STOCK J. - WATSON M.W.: «Variable Trends in Economic Time Series», *The Journal of Economic Perspectives*, n. 3, 1988, pp. 147-74.
[24] WATSON M.W.: «Univariate Detrending Methods with Stochastic Trends», *Journal of Monetary Economics*, n. 18, 1986, pp. 49-75.

On the Sources of Fluctuations of the Italian Economy: a Structural «VAR» Analysis

Paolo Onofri · Paolo Paruolo · Bruno Salituro
Università di Bologna

1. - Introduction (1)

The observation of a high degree of time dependence in macroeconomic time series is the starting point of much of the recent empirical macroeconomics. This dependence is translated into a strong persistence of the impulses imparted to time series. Indeed, it appears (2) that many time series can be adequately represented as non stationary stochastic processes. In other words the traditional view of a deterministic trend, resulting from long term phenomena, *vis-à-vis* cyclical fluctuations around it, would be a misleading simplification because, in reality, fluctuations would contain permanent components due to non-deterministic trends. Consequently the evolution of the economic system would be affected by impulses of different nature (possibly including either changes of regimes of economic policies or changes in the "rules of the game") which would shift the growth path through cyclical propagation mechanisms. These effects would impart a high degree of time persistence and would determine an hysteresis behaviour of economic time series.

---

(1) This paper is the outcome of joint research by the authors; P. Onofri and B. Salituro share the economic responsibility for the views expressed in the paper and P. Paruolo is responsible for the econometric approach. Specifically sections 4, 5, 7 were written by P. Onofri, sections 3, 6 and the *Methodological Note* by P. Paruolo and sections 1 and 2 by B. Salituro.

(2) For a different opinion see LIPPI - REICHLIN [10].

Advise: the numbers in square brackets refer to Bibliography in the appendix.

Such permanent components in fluctuations could be represented by stochastic trends. In trying to single out such components, many studies concentrated on the relative importance of stochastic trends versus traditional transitory sources of output fluctuations. Initially the analysis on the permanent and transitory components was carried out with univariate models; this approach, though, did not bring about clear-cut results and, in any case, was not able to discriminate among different theories of the business cycle. The most recent works followed the direction of broadening the spectrum of the macroeconomic variables under scrutiny, shifting to multivariate studies.

The multivariate approach allows the identification of several sources of output fluctuations, being able to distinguish, for instance, between disturbances which determine permanent effects (labour supply, technology, terms of trade, ecc.) and disturbances with only short term effects, traditionally interpreted as aggregate demand shocks. In this way it becomes possible to study the dynamics of the effects of the various impulses and their relative importance over time.

The main problem in this kind of analysis is the identification of the different shocks. Various authors, among whom Blanchard-Watson [3], Blanchard-Quah [4], Shapiro-Watson [13], have proposed methods to identify the structural innovations for systems with no long term relations among the levels of the variables. The set of restrictions used in such studies in order to identify the innovations can be given an explicit economic interpretation, contrary to the original approach proposed by Sims [14].

In case the levels of the variables are non-stationary and are tied together by long term relations (cointegration relations) it is possible to identify permanent and transitory stochastic components. Moreover this approach allows to investigate the adjustment process of the variables, when reacting to the different impulses, in order to attain the levels consistent with the long term relations (3). King-Plosser-Stock-Watson [9] use this approach to analyse the sources of the fluctuations of the American economy.

These above-mentioned approaches make up the bulk of the

---

(3) For an exposition of this methodology see WARNE [16].

so-called structural VAR analysis (4). In this paper, after introducing a very simple economic reference model with an aggregate production function, we will recall the results of a recent paper by the same authors, Onofri-Paruolo-Salituro [11]. In that paper, using a structural VAR system applied to non-cointegrated variables, we analised the role of demand and supply components in the fluctuations of the Italian economy. The obtained results will be compared with new findings based on a different system where we use implications derived from the assumption of balanced growth of the economy. The simple theoretical structure used in this model allows for the presence of cointegration; such a system is analysed using the maximum likelihood procedure suggested by Johansen [7].

The data are mainly time series from the quaterly national accounting system 1954-1989 re-elaborated by Prometeia, at first on yearly basis, for the period 1951-1969 (in a way compatible with the new ISTAT national accounts (1970-1989)), and subsequently on a quarterly basis, using previous time series of the national accounting system.

2. - A Simple Representation of Stochastic Growth

The reference model of our empirical investigation has been proposed by Shapiro-Watson [13] and King-Plosser-Stock-Watson [9]. Its long term properties derive from the neoclassical growth theory. Let us consider as a steady state production function a constant returns-to-scale Cobb Douglas function

(2.1) $$y_t^* = \alpha f_t^* + (1 - \alpha) k_t^* + \lambda_t^*$$

where y^* is the logarithm of output, f^* and k^* are the logarithms of labour and capital inputs and λ^* is the logarithm of total factor productivity (in other words of technical progress).

The above-mentioned papers refer to the balanced growth model presented by Solow [15], which implies, in steady growth conditions,

---
(4) See GIANNINI [6].

that consumption, investments and output, all in per capita terms, grow at a rate equal to the exogenous rate of growth of total factor productivity λ^*. The assumption of balanced growth entails also, in the long run, a constant capital-output ratio, $k_t^* = y_t^* + \bar{\theta}$; substituting in (2.1), one gets:

(2.2) $$y_t^* - f_t^* = \beta_0 + \frac{1}{\alpha} \lambda_t^*$$

where $\beta_0 \equiv (1 - \alpha)\bar{\theta}/\alpha$. Equation (2.2) shows that, under the assumption of constant capital-output ratio, the difference between the logarithms of output and labour input identifies a multiple of technical progress. Contrary to Solow's assumption, the non-stationarity of technical progress could be of a stochastic nature, that is one could assume the following generating process for technical progress

(2.3) $$\lambda_t^* = \beta_0^\lambda + \lambda_{t-1}^* + z^\lambda(L)\,\eta_t^\lambda$$

where z^λ is a stationary polynomial in the lag operator L. Such a process for technology is non stationary in the levels and stationary in the first differences, in other words it is integrated of order one, I(1); it reduces to a random walk with drift if $z^\lambda(L) = 1$. This equation describes the rate of growth of total factor productivity as a stationary process driven by the innovations η_t^λ.

The technical progress is driven by stochastic disturbances η^λ (assumed serially uncorrelated and with zero mean) which transmit their permanent influence to output, consumption and investments in the same amount. This implies that the consumption-output ratio and the investment-output ratio can be represented as stationary stochastic processes.

In order to extract the component due to technical progress from the time series of the Italian Gross Domestic Product (GDP), one can use the implication that in conditions of balanced growth, consumption, investment and income share the same stochastic trend. This entails, in the analysis of difference stationary time series, the presence of cointegration relations among the above-mentioned variables.

Other contributions to output fructuations from the supply side can emerge from movements of labour supply. In order to measure such contributions it is necessary to define the generating process for f, in analogy to what has been done for λ:

(2.4) $$f_t^* = \beta_0^f + f_{t-1}^* + z^f(L)\eta_t^f$$

In this way the set of real variables, no longer in per capita terms, will share two stochastic trends, which can be interpreted as the contributions to output fluctuations of labour input and of technical progress.

All the above remarks hold for a closed economy; in case of an economy highly integrated in the world market, permanent output fluctuations can also derive from shocks of international origin. In some cases one can think of supply impulses conveyed by changes in the terms of trade; in some other cases one can consider technical progress impulses transferred through world demand innovations. As far as the empirical analysis on Italian data is concerned, we will need to take these external conditioning factors into account.

Once the permanent components have been identified, the percentage of output variance that, in the short run, cannot be attributed to movements of the common stochastic trends and to permanent international effects will have, by definition, transitory nature and will be attributed to demand factors.

In order to analyze the transitory effects exerted on the output time series by demand components, one needs to define specific variables bearing nominal and real demand shocks. In Onofri-Paruolo-Salituro [11] we concentrated our analysis on international and demand components, letting the effects of supply-side disturbances emerge as "residuals". In this paper the emphasis is mainly on supply shocks, suitably conditioned to the evolution of impulses coming from abroad, leaving the effects of transitory disturbances as "residuals".

3. - The Econometric Framework

Given the nature of the assumed processes *(2.3) (2.4)* for technology and labour supply, the econometric analysis of GDP fluctuations can be inbedded in a vector autoregressive model (*VAR*), within which the innovations and the stochastic trends can be identified. The structural innovations underlying the variation in GDP are assumed to be linked to the innovations of the following stocastic model

(3.1) $$A(L) X_t = \varepsilon_t$$

where $A(L) = I - A_1 L - \cdots - A_k L^k$ is a matrix polynomial of order k in the lag operator L, and ε_t is a $p \times 1$ vector of i.i.d. gaussian variables $N(0, \Omega)$ (5). The VAR model (3.1) allows for both stationary and non-stationary processes; if, in fact, the roots of the characteristic determinantal equation $|A(z)| = 0$ are outside the unit circle in the complex plane the system is stationary; if some roots are on the unit circle the system is non-stationary and if they are inside the unit circle the system is explosive. The VAR model (3.1) defines therefore a fairly big class of processes with very different evolutionary properties (6).

The non-stationary case appears to be of special interest, given the observed non-stationary features displayed by most time series (7). In particular, roots at the point $z = 1$ are linked to a random-walk behaviour of the system, whereas seasonal stochastic non-stationarities are generated for instance by roots at the points $z = -1, z = \pm i$ (8). In this paper only unit roots at $z = 1$ will be considered, thereby excluding e.g. seasonal unit roots (9).

The autoregressive polynomial $A(L)$ can be decomposed as $A(L) = A(1) + A^*(L)(1 - L)$, thus focusing on the total impact matrix $A(1)$ of variations in X_t on future values of the system. It is easy to see that if $A(1) = 0$ then (3.1) can be rewritten as:

(3.2) $$A^*(L) \Delta X_t = \varepsilon_t$$

---

(5) We abstract here from the deterministic part for the sake of simplicity.
(6) The identification of structural unnovations is obviously connected to the assumed model, the choice of variables and the estimation method; how well VAR models of the type (3.1) approximate, for instance, non-linear processes is indeed difficult to establish.
(7) See ONOFRI - PARUOLO - SALITURO [11], ANSUINI - FORNASARI - PARUOLO [1].
(8) See ARDENI - PARUOLO [2].
(9) In the empirical analysis the seasonally unadjusted series were filtered through the seasonal moving average 0.25 $(1 + L + L^2 + L^3)$, in line with the findings of ARDENI - PARUOLO [2]. A constant was also included in the estimation of the VARs

If the polinomial $A^*(L)$ has all the roots outside the unit circle, then X_t is stationary in first differences, and admits the moving average representation:

(3.3) $$\Delta X_t = C(L)\varepsilon_t$$

The matrix $C = C(1)$ is the total impact matrix of ε_t on the first differences of the variables in the system (which are then cumulated in the levels) and is of full rank if X_t is stationary in first differences. The (infinite order) polinomial $C(L) = A^*(L)^{-1}$ satisfies the relation $C(L)A(L) = I$, from which one has $C(1) = A^*(1)^{-1}$. Specifically C is lower triangular if and only if $A^*(1)$ is also lower triangular; such a structure is exploited in the first model we discuss in order to identify one of the estimated systems.

On the other hand if the autoregressive impact matrix $A(1)$ is of full rank, the system is stationary in levels, and admits the moving average representation (3.3) with levels on the left-hand-side.

The matrix C in (3.3) contains the total multipliers of ε_t on the differences of the process X_t. The errors ε_t are here assumed to be linear functions of the $p \times 1$ vector of structural innovations η_t through $\varepsilon_t = F\eta_t$; the total impact effect of the structural innovations η_t is then given by CF, as can be verified substituting η_t into (3.3), which becomes:

(3.4) $$\Delta X_t = \tilde{C}(L)\eta_t$$

where: $\tilde{C}(1) = CF$. In the first model of this paper the structural innovations are identified imposing the diagonality of the variance covariance matrix $E(\eta_t \eta_t')$ and the lower triangularity of $\tilde{C}(1)$, see section 4; this latter condition corresponds to an analogous lower triangularity of the autoregressive impact matrix $\tilde{A}(1)$ in

(3.5) $$\tilde{A}(L)\Delta X_t = \eta_t$$

which is exploited in the estimation of the system.

The intermediate case between the stationary case in levels and in first differences is the one in which some linear combinations of the process are stationary in levels while the remaining ones are stationary in first differences. Such a case corresponds to the reduced rank condition of $A(1)$ (10) rank $A(1) = r$, i.e. $A(1) = \alpha\beta'$, α and β full rank $p \times r$ matrices, and the variables in the system are said to be cointegrated (11). In case of cointegrated systems, the process has a moving average representation *(3.3)* with, unlike the previous case, the impact matrix C of reduced rank $p - r$. Cumulating the first difference process one obtains the so-called common trends representation of the system

$$(3.6) \qquad X_t = C \sum_{i=1}^{t} \varepsilon_i + v_t = \beta_\perp \tau_t + v_t$$

where:

$$C \equiv C(1) = \beta_\perp \xi \alpha_\perp'$$

v_t is a stationary process and

$$\tau_t = \xi \alpha_\perp' \sum_{i=1}^{t} \varepsilon_i \qquad \tau_t = \tau_{t-1} + e_t$$

is a system of k random walks which make up the common trends in the system; the symbol $_\perp$ indicates the orthogonal complement of a given rectangular matrix a, i.e. a matrix $a_\perp$ such that $(a, a_\perp)$ is of rank p and $a_\perp a = 0$ (12).

The common trends representation suggests a different route in the identification of the structural shocks $\eta_t = F^{-1}\varepsilon_t$; $p - r$ of them, indicated as η_t^p, are cumulated in the trend components, while the remaining r innovations η_t^{tr} are transitory in the system. As equation *(3.6)* suggests, the permanent component is proportional to $\alpha_\perp'\varepsilon_t$; therefore test on the structure of $\alpha_\perp$ are indeed tests on the composition of the common trends in the system, thus allowing to evaluate which of the errors ε_t^i have a permanent effect on the levels of the

---

(10) Along with some additional conditions which rule out the presence of components integrated of higher orders, see JOHANSEN [7].

(11) See ENGLE - GRANGER [5].

(12) For a definition of ξ see e.g. the *Methodological Note*; the problem of inference on C is addressed in PARUOLO [12].

variables. In the following, for example, we test whether the hypothesis $\alpha_\perp' = (1, 0, 0)$ is compatible with the Italian data in a trivariate system with y, c and i; such an hypothesis corresponds to:

$$\alpha = \begin{pmatrix} 0 & 0 \\ 1 & 0 \\ 0 & 1 \end{pmatrix} \phi$$

where ϕ is a 2×2 arbitrary matrix. Likelihood ratio tests have been proposed by Johansen [7] for the latter formulation of the hypothesis, thus allowing to test for this specific structure of the common trends. The identification of the permanent (η^p) and transitory (η_t^{tr}) innovations is achieved here also imposing that η^p and η_t^{tr} be uncorrelated random variables (13).

4. - Demand- and Supply-Side Shocks: A Structural Non-Cointegrated «VAR»

In Onofri-Paruolo-Salituro [11] the analysis was based on the same approach outlined in section 2 with no reference, though, to implications from the assumption of balanced growth. In that paper it was assumed that deviations from long run output attributable to supply factors originated from shocks in λ and f. A structural VAR system made of five macroeconomic variables was estimated: the terms of trade (q) - to capture international supply shocks, world demand (d) - to capture international demand and technical progress shocks -, the GDP (y), the male unemployment rate (u) - to capture real domestic demand shocks - , and the inflation rate (π) - to capture nominal domestic demand shocks. In order to recognize the impact of labour input shocks, output was not expressed in per capita units. The likelihood analysis was able to reject the absence of cointegrating vectors in the six variables system $X_t = (d_t, q_t, y_t, f_t, u_t, \pi_t)$, while it did not reject it, consistently with theoretical assump-

---

(13) See the *Methodological Note*.

tions, when the system excluded f. The five variables system excluding f was used throughout the analysis.

The following restrictions on the long run interrelations among the innovations of the structural form ηi were imposed:
— q is affected y η^q but it is not affected by any other innovation;
— d is not affected by η^y, η^u, η^π;
— y is not affected by η^u, η^π;
— u is not affected by η^π.

In other words, in a small open economy, international variables are assumed to be exogenous, whereas, on the domestic side, aggregate demand shocks have no long run effect on output and nominal demand shocks do not exert any long run effect on real demand. The two domestic restrictions are more binding than the others, but still they are generally assumed as plausible. These identifying restictions correspond to the triangularity of $C(1)$ in (3.3), which implies also the triangularity of $\bar{A}(1)$ in (3.5).

Under the previous assumptions, the innovation η^y should contain all the supply innovations (originating both from technology and from labour input). Moreover, we can compare the effects of these supply disturbances on GDP with those exerted by other shocks, see the variance decomposition of Table 1 and the impulse response functions of Graphs 1 and 2.

TABLE 1

DECOMPOSITION OF THE VARIANCE OF y:
PERCENTAGE CONTRIBUTION
OF THE INNOVATION IN COLUMN (η^j) TO THE
EXPLANATION OF THE GDP VARIANCE

Quarters	η^q	η^d	η^y	η^u	η^π
1	3.2	8.9	60.4	25.8	1.6
4	3.1	19.1	47.9	17.6	12.3
8	6.5	15.8	53.7	10.5	13.2
16	9.5	13.7	60.0	5.8	10.9
80	17.4	7.6	70.1	1.4	3.3

GRAPH 1

RESPONSE OF THE LEVEL OF y TO SHOCKS ON SUPPLY (y), ON WORLD DEMAND (d), ON THE TERMS OF TRADE (q)

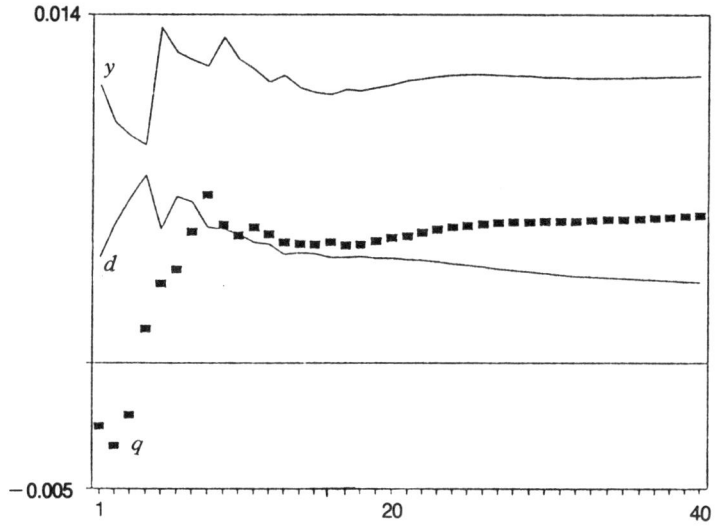

GRAPH 2

RESPONSE OF THE LEVEL OF y TO SHOCK ON SUPPLY (y), ON REAL DOMESTIC DEMAND (u), ON NOMINAL DOMESTIC DEMAND (π)

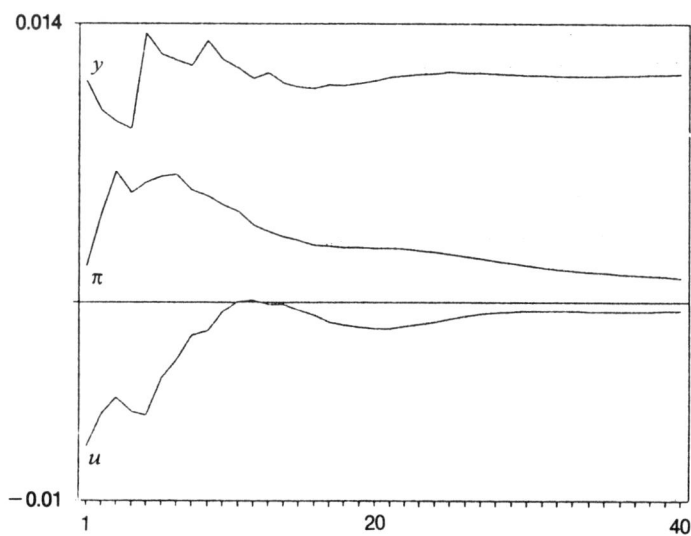

Conditionally on the assumed identifying restrictions, one can then consider the results as a description of the fluctuations of the Italian economy in the years 1960-1989. Within such a description, though the supply shocks play the most prominent role in explaining the variance of GDP, they cannot simply account for all the fluctuations of the Italian economy. Demand factors (hence policy variables) seem to have played a relevant role: their effects are constrained to vanish, but they do it slowly. On the other hand, international shocks, even if not negligible, do not dominate the domestic factors.

A cursory look at the time series of the real and nominal demand and supply innovations allows one to say that they do not contradict the common intuition.

As far as the supply shocks are concerned, it must be remembered that no distinction was made between the effects of technical progress and of labour input. As a result, Graph 3 appears less interpretable than the others. On the other hand, the graphical analysis suggests interpretations of the role of the shocks which might

GRAPH 3

DOMESTIC SUPPLY SHOCKS
(4-TERMS MOVING AVERAGE)

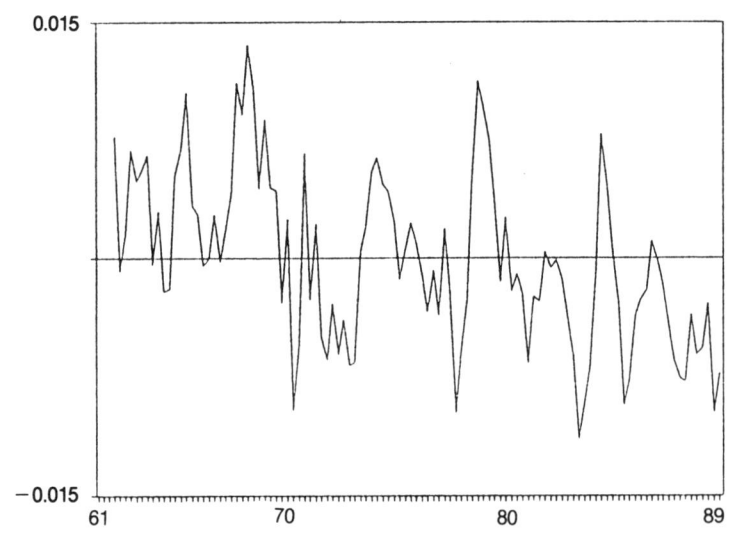

GRAPH 4

DOMESTIC REAL DEMAND SHOCKS
(4-TERMS MOVING AVERAGE)
NOTE: POSITIVE VALUES CORRESPOND TO NEGATIVE SHOCKS

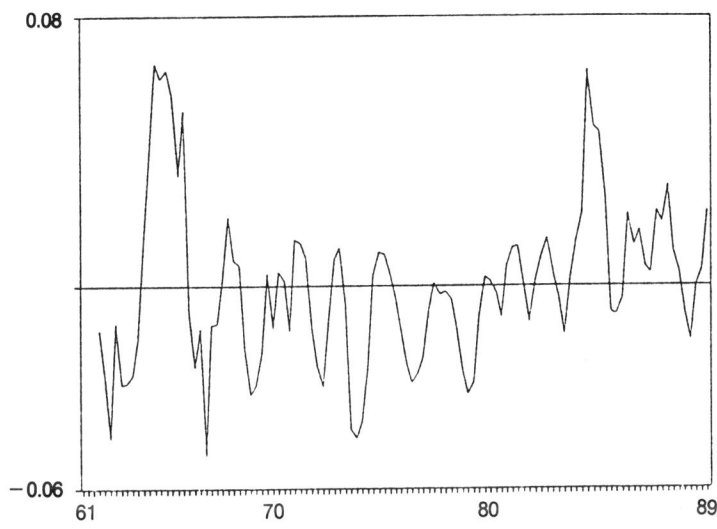

GRAPH 5

DOMESTIC NOMINAL DEMAND SHOCKS
(4-TERMS MOVING AVERAGE)

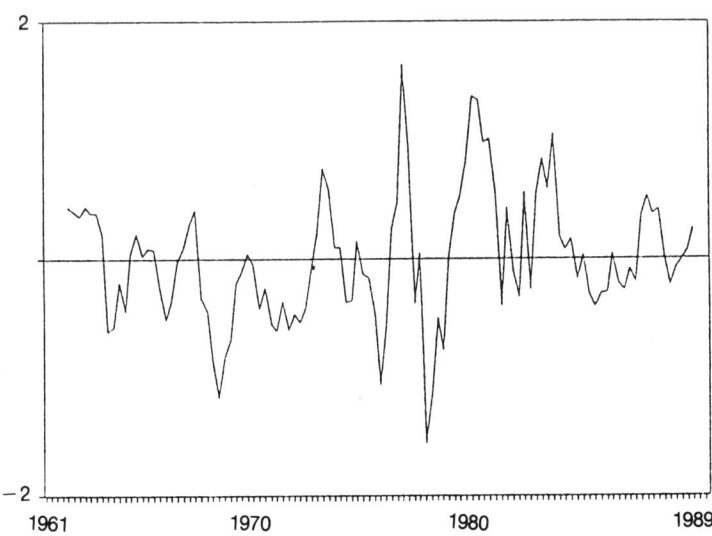

appear counter-intuitive. Considering, for the sake of simplicity, a decade as time unit for uniform behaviour, the sixties come out as rich in expansionary shocks both from the supply-side, and from the real demand-side; nominal shocks seem to have been mainly restrictive. This amounts to saying that expansionary real demand policies, with fixed exchange rates and surplus in the current account of the balance of payments, did not induce inflationary effects even in the presence of accomodating monetary aggregates.

In the seventies real demand impulses are seen to be still expansionary, whereas positive shocks from the supply side became minor episodes and nominal demand was characterized by strong positive and negative shocks.

Finally, in the eighties, the real demand shocks became negative though the public sector deficit increased quite substantially. In the decade of the economic adjustment, output fluctuations seem more tied to international fluctuations, and the high public sector borrowing requirements, financed by bonds, does not seem to have had an expansionary effect on output and inflation.

5. - A Different Approach

In the previous paper we have rapidly reviewed, we could not distinguish between supply shocks from technology and from labour input. On the whole, the supply shocks seem responsible for a large part also of the short run fluctuations. This strongly contradicts the traditional view of the short run fluctuations mainly imputable to demand shocks, thus suggesting we check its robustness through different investigation procedures.

Considering the neoclassical models of growth, we can exploit the implications of balanced growth in order to identify the contributions of supply factors to short-run fluctuations, according to a different line of approach. One implication of steady-state growth is the stationarity of both the consumption-output and the investment-output ratios. Given the non-stationarity of the aggregate series of output, consumptions and investment, such an implication means that cointegrating vectors are expected to exist among the three variables. In other words, it means that long run relationships should exist among the levels of the variables. The stylized economic system is thus characterized by a unique driving force, identified as a mixture of technical progress and labour input as defined by the stochastic processes outlined in the section 2.

As a first step in the analysis one can visually inspect the Italian times series for consumption, investment and output. Graphs 6 and 7 show the evolution, respectively, of the ratio of total consumption (households domestic consumption plus government consumption) to GDP and the ratio of total fixed investment to GDP, both in logs. The assumption of stationarity is openly contradicted. The non stationarity of the average propensity to consume in the last thirty years has been frequently emphasized. It is usually attributed to cultural, demographic and strictly economic factors. As far as the economic factors are concerned, reference is usually made to the growth of the ratio of household wealth to disposable income. Less attention has been paid to the investment-output ratio. In order to explain the non-stationarity of the investment ratio one may refer to institutional matters like house building laws and renting market regulations.

At first glance, one is thus tempted to draw the conclusion that Italy has not experienced balanced growth; nevertheless if one accepts the hypothesis that technical progress mainly affects the private sector of the economy, it might be pausible to calculate the same ratios with respect to private GDP. Moreover investment could be measured net of residential investment. Graphs 8 and 9 plot those new ratios, for which a simple eye-ball inspection does not allow one to reject the stationarity assumption, and hence the long-run balanced growth hypothesis. As a consequence, we shall focus our analysis on these variables.

In the theoretical model, the growth of population and of labour supply coincide, which means that, in order to isolate the exogenous impact of innovations in technical progress, it is sufficient to define the variables in per capita terms as shown in equation *(2.2)*. On the empirical ground, of course, labour supply and population do not coincide; their rates of growth may well diverge. Moreover the Italian economy has been experiencing cultural transformations which have produced long-run fluctuations of the partecipation rate. As a conse-

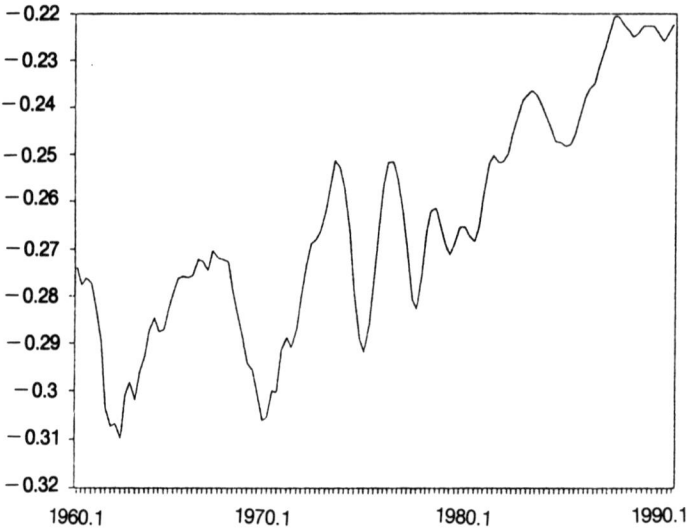

GRAPH 6

LOG OF THE RATIO OF TOTAL CONSUMPTION TO GDP

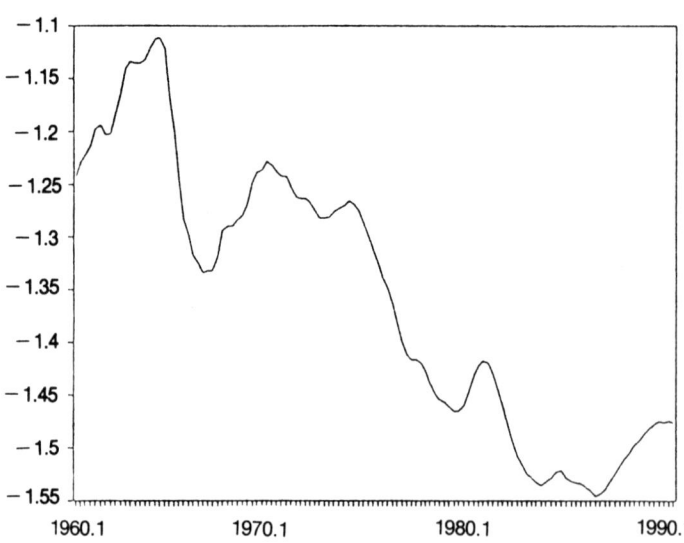

GRAPH 7

LOG OF THE RATIO OF GROSS FIXED INVESTMENT TO GDP

GRAPH 8

LOG OF THE RATIO OF TOTAL CONSUMPTION
TO PRIVATE SECTOR GDP

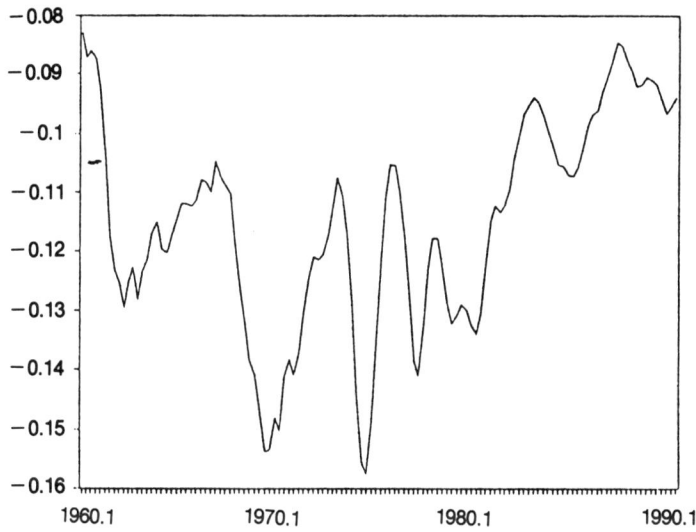

GRAPH 9

LOG OF THE RATIO OF GROSS FIXED INVESTMENT NET
OF RESIDENTIAL CONSTRUCTIONS
TO PRIVATE SECTOR GDP

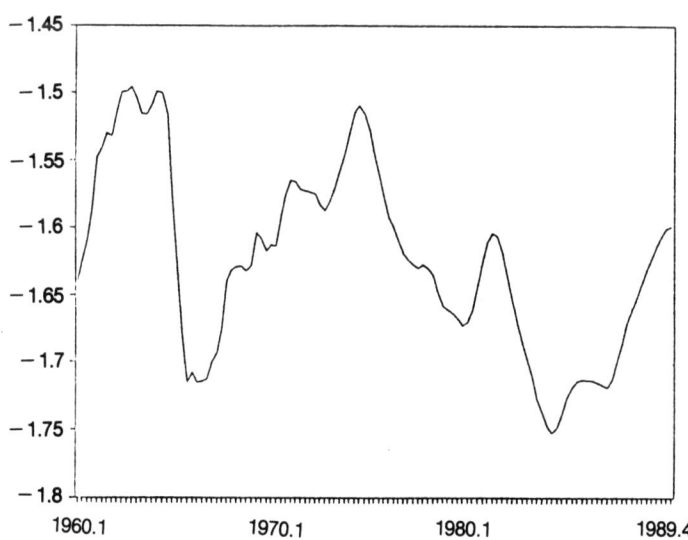

quence, the definition of the variables in per capita terms is not sufficient to single out technical progress effects; the partecipation rate, too, should be included, if one wants to check whether labour input shocks played any role in determining the fluctuations of Italian private GDP.

6. - Analyzing Supply-Side Effects in a Cointegrated «VAR»

Given the above premises, this section tries to address the issues of permanent versus transitory shocks in the system, rather than concentrate on the distinction between demand- and supply-side effects. To this end, and following the previous remarks on the labour input, we first make the simplifying assumption that total population equals the labour input; this in turn implies that the observed per-capita output ($y_t - f_t = \bar{y}_t$), can be described in terms of deviations from equation (2.2), i.e.

$$(6.1) \qquad \bar{y}_t = \beta_0 + \frac{1}{\alpha} \bar{\lambda}_t^* + v_t^y$$

where v_t^y is a stationary process.

On the basis of the restriction imposed by balanced growth, one can rewrite the previous relations for consumption (c) and investment (i):

$$(6.2) \qquad \bar{c}_t = \delta_c + \bar{y}_t^* + v_t^c$$

$$(6.3) \qquad \bar{i}_t = \delta_i + \bar{y}_t^* + v_t^i$$

where here also v_t^i are stationary processes. Since λ_t^* follows a non-stationary process (2.3), the system (6.1), (6.2), (6.3) and (2.3) is driven by a single long-run shock η_t^λ. The purpose of the empirical analysis is therefore to uncover such an innovation η_t^λ and to evaluate its relative importance in the explanation of output fluctuations.

Considering the historical per-capita time series of output, consumption and investment $\bar{y}, \bar{c}, \bar{\imath}$, defined in the previous sections, one can formulate the following model:

$$(6.4) \quad \begin{pmatrix} \Delta \bar{y}_t \\ \Delta \bar{c}_t \\ \Delta \bar{\imath}_t \end{pmatrix} = \sum_{i=1}^{k-1} \Gamma_{t-i} \begin{pmatrix} \Delta \bar{y}_{t-i} \\ \Delta \bar{c}_{t-i} \\ \Delta \bar{\imath}_{t-i} \end{pmatrix} + \alpha \beta' \begin{pmatrix} \bar{y}_{t-1} \\ \bar{c}_{t-1} \\ \bar{\imath}_{t-1} \end{pmatrix} + \begin{pmatrix} \varepsilon_t^y \\ \varepsilon_t^c \\ \varepsilon_t^i \end{pmatrix}$$

where the matrices α, β are the same as the ones defined in section 3, Γ_j are square $p \times p$ matrices and the vector ε_t includes the reduced form stochastic innovations.

With respect to the above system one can then:

— test for the rank of $\alpha\beta'$, that is test if and how many cointegration vectors exist; the existence of attractors for the variables in the system, identified by the linear combinations β, implies a number of driving forces in the growth of the system less than its dimension, and complementary with respect to the number of cointegration vectors. In such a case the variables share a number of common stochastic trends, as outlined in section 3;

— inquire the structure of β, i.e. test if the theoretical cointegrating vectors derived from the balanced growth assumption are statistically compatible with the observed data. If in fact the levels of $\bar{c}$ and of $\bar{\imath}$ are equal to the level of $\bar{y}$ plus a stationary noise, then:

$$\beta' = \begin{pmatrix} 1 & -1 & 0 \\ 1 & 0 & -1 \end{pmatrix} \quad \text{i.e.} \quad \beta' X_t = \begin{pmatrix} \bar{y}_t - \bar{c}_t \\ \bar{y}_t - \bar{\imath}_t \end{pmatrix}$$

are stationary processes;

— finally, test if the adjustment of the variables in the system to their long-run levels (determined by the matrix β and driven by the common trends) behaves in accordance to theory. Specifically in this system the variables $\bar{c}, \bar{\imath}$ are expected to adjust to $\bar{y}$; in such a case the process of output would convey the common stochastic permanent shock, which would then be identified with technology. This is tantamount to testing the hypothesis:

$$\alpha_\perp' = (1 \ 0 \ 0) \quad \text{i.e.} \quad \alpha_\perp' \varepsilon_t = \varepsilon_t^y$$

as can be seen from equation (3.6). Such an hypothesis coincides with the weak exogeneity of the corresponding variable (output) with respect to β, (Johansen [8]).

The above tests, calculated with respect to the system (6.4), are reported in Table 2. They are consistent with the existence of two cointegrating vectors, as expected, which indeed conform to the theoretical hypothesis that the logs of the consumption-output ($\bar{y} - \bar{c}$) and the investment-income ($\bar{y} - \bar{i}$) ratios are stationary. Besides, when testing about the adjustment coefficients, the hypothesis that $\bar{y}$ is weakly exogenous with respect to β can be rejected along with the one about $\bar{i}$, while $\bar{c}$ is the only variable in the system not to adjust to disequilibrium errors; in other words both $\bar{y}$ and $\bar{i}$ seem to adjust to $\bar{c}$, which would drive the only common trend in the system. The common trend would then be linked to the exogenous evolution in consumer preferences more than to technological progress; the innovations in consumer tastes (the modification of the standard of

TABLE 2

TEST ON THE RANK, THE COINTEGRATION SPACE AND THE ERROR CORRECTION ADJUSTMENT COEFFICIENTS: $X_t = (\bar{y}_t, \bar{c}_t, \bar{i}_t)'$, 1960.3-1989-4, $k = 2$

Cointegration test	$r \leq 2$	$r \leq 1$	$r = 0$
λ trace test (1)	7.745 (⁺)	24.294 (**)	51.751 (**)
Stationarity test of $\bar{i} - \bar{y}$ and $\bar{c} - \bar{y}$, $r = 2$	$-2 \ln (LR)$	degrees of freedom	$Pr(-2 \ln (LR) > \chi^2)$
	1.61 (*)	2	0.45
Weak exogeneity test	$-2 \ln (LR)$	degrees of freedom	$Pr(-2 \ln (LR) > \chi^2)$
$\bar{y}$	15.24 (**)	4	0.004
$\bar{c}$	2.12 (*)	4	0.713
$\bar{i}$	24.79 (**)	4	0.0001

(*) rejected hypothesis at the 5% significance level;
(**) 1%;
(⁺) non rejected hypothesis;
(1) see JOHANSEN [7].

On the Sources of Fluctuations of the Italian Economy etc. 53

living and life-style) would then precede the technological know-how. Such an interpretation is difficult to accept, at least at first sight; it is useful, anyway, to recall that Italy is indeed a small open economy, and, moreover, it is technologically dependent on the world economy.

The following tentative interpretation of this result could be put forward: the Italian economy has been catching up both foreign technological innovations and consumption patterns, with the latter more easily transmitted through the increase in imports. In order to substantiate such an interpretation it is important to gather more analytic evidence.

In the analysis of section 4 the hypothesis that world demand shocks could convey technological innovations to a small open economy has been put forward, thus suggesting to also include the variable d in the above-mentioned system. Specifically one could characterize the process for d as:

(6.5) $$d_t = \phi_0 + \phi_1 \lambda_t^* + v_t^d$$

In the previous system the international terms of trade have been included in order to capture international supply-side shocks. We therefore consider system (6.4) including among the left-hand-side variables d, and q as an exogenous regressor (14). The system then becomes:

(6.6) $$\begin{pmatrix} \Delta d_t \\ \Delta \bar{y}_t \\ \Delta \bar{c}_t \\ \Delta \bar{i}_t \end{pmatrix} = \sum_{i=0}^{k-1} \gamma_i \Delta q_{t-i} + \sum_{i=1}^{k-1} \Gamma_{t-i} \begin{pmatrix} \Delta d_{t-i} \\ \Delta \bar{y}_{t-i} \\ \Delta \bar{c}_{t-i} \\ \Delta \bar{i}_{t-i} \end{pmatrix} +$$

$$+ \alpha \beta' \begin{pmatrix} d_{t-1} \\ \bar{y}_{t-1} \\ \bar{c}_{t-1} \\ \bar{i}_{t-1} \end{pmatrix} + \begin{pmatrix} \varepsilon_t^d \\ \varepsilon_t^y \\ \varepsilon_t^c \\ \varepsilon_t^i \end{pmatrix}$$

---

(14) The sample behaviour af q suggests, in fact, to consider the system conditional on q.

The previous tests applied to system (6.6) do not lead to the rejection of two cointegrating vectors. Theoretical expectations suggest the presence of a unique common trend, that is the presence of three cointegrating vectors. Moreover, contrary to the case $r = 2$ and consistently with the previous model, in the case $r = 3$ one cannot reject the stationarity of $(\bar{y} - \bar{c})$ and $(\bar{y} - \bar{\imath})$. In this way the unique common stochastic trend could describe the «exogenous» evolution of the system. Regarding the adjustment coefficients, the likelihood ratio statistics indicate that world demand does not react to disequilibrium

TABLE 3

TEST ON THE RANK, THE COINTEGRATION SPACE
AND THE ERROR CORRECTION ADJUSTMENT COEFFICIENTS;
$X_t = (\bar{d}_t, \bar{y}_t, \bar{c}_t, \bar{\imath}_t)'$, CONDITIONALLY ON Δq_t, 1960.3-1989.4, $k = 2$

Cointegration rank	$r \leq 3$	$r \leq 2$	$r \leq 1$	$r = 0$
λ trace test (1)	0.905 (+)	10.94 (+)	27.683 (**)	73.637 (**)
Stationarity test of $\bar{\imath} - \bar{y}$ and $\bar{c} - \bar{y}$, $r = 3$	−2 ln (LR)	degrees of freedom		$Pr(-2 \ln (LR) > \chi^2)$
	2.146 (+)	2		0.34
Weak exogeneity test	−2 ln (LR)	degrees of freedom		$Pr(-2 \ln (LR) > \chi^2)$
$\bar{d}$	3.39 (+)	5		0.65
$\bar{y}$	33.64 (**)	5		0.00
$\bar{c}$	14.74 (*)	5		0.01
$\bar{\imath}$	37.61 (**)	5		0.01

(*) rejected hypothesis at the 5% significance level;
(**) 1%;
(+) non rejected hypothesis;
(1) see JOHANSEN [7].

errors in the relation with other variables in the system, thus implying that world demand innovations drive the common trend in the system. As for the remaining variables, consumption does not seem to be weakly exogenous any more, while showing a lower reactivity to disequilibrium errors than output and investment. On the whole, the present system seems to accord with the previous tentative interpretation.

The assumption that the labour force equals total population, underlying the previous analysis, seems at odds with the observed behaviour of the participation rate, see Graph 10. In a graphical analysis of such a variable both levels and first differences show an evolutionary pattern, that is the participation rate grows at an increasing growing rate. This fact contradicts the balanced growth hypothesis; its inclusion in the previous system, in order to isolate permanent labour shocks, would obviously dramatically alter the characteristics of the system.

On the whole, the metaphor of uniform growth through a

GRAPH 10

PARTICIPATION RATE:
LEVELS (LEFT SCALE),
FIRST DIFFERENCES (RIGHT SCALE)

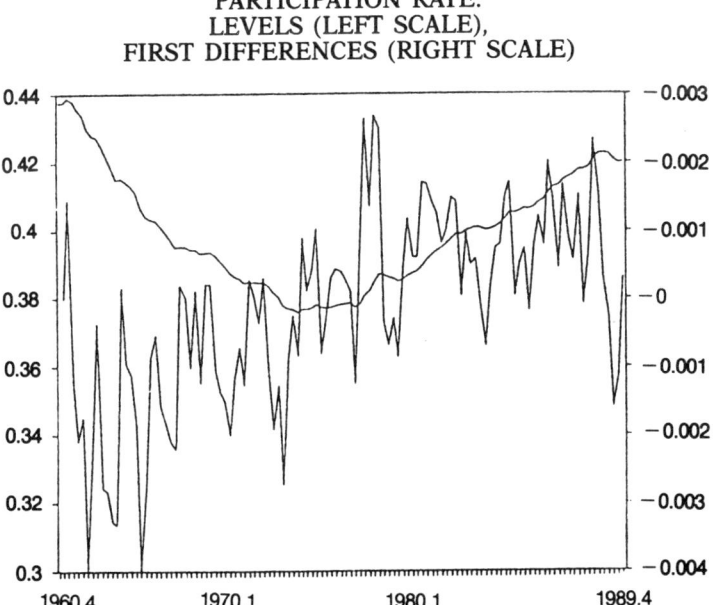

TABLE 4

PERCENTAGE OF VARIANCE OF $\bar{y}_t$ ACCOUNTED
FOR BY THE REAL PERMANENT SHOCK
(COMMON STOCHASTIC TREND),
IDENTIFIED AS PROPORTIONAL
TO REDUCED FORM INNOVATIONS IN d_t

1 quarter	8 quarters	16 quarters
23.8%	74.4%	87.6%

Cobb-Douglas production function including neutral technological change both à la Hicks and à la Harrod is not rejected by the data insofar as no attempt is made to assess specific contributions from the labour input. We will confine ourself, therefore, to that metaphor in order to further evaluate the explicatory power of the derived permanent innovations with respect to fluctuations in output. To this end we calculate the variance decomposition of $\bar{y}$ with respect to the permanent real shock and to the other transitory innovations.

The common stochastic trend explains one fourth of the variance of output after one quarter and already three fourths after 2 years. If the common trend innovations are interpreted as the supply contribution to output fluctuations, these results seem inconsistent with the ones reported in Table 1, where the residual supply (permanent) components explains 70% of the variance of output after 20 years, but already 60% after one quarter! The plots of the common trends and of the relative innovations are reported in graphs 11 and 12.

The time evolution of the innovation depicted in Graph 12 does not seem to be at odds with the common intuition regarding fluctuations in international trade. The easy conclusion that the same innovations indeed influence also the Italian economy may seem to be obvious. First of all it must be stressed that the above results give a much greater weight to international factors with respect to the analysis in section 4. Secondly from the present analysis it results that international trade shocks (wherever they come from) permanently affect the level of Italian output, thus transforming its internal production technology.

GRAPH 11

COMMON STOCHASTIC TREND

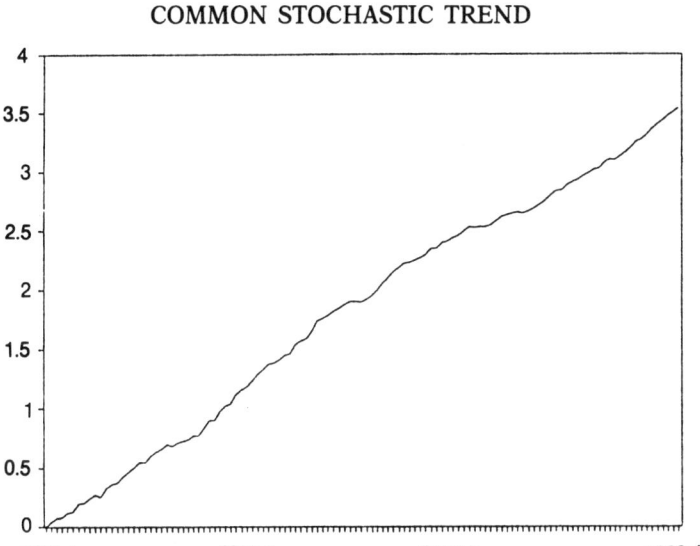

GRAPH 12

REAL PERMANENT SHOCK (4-TERMS MOVING AVERAGE)

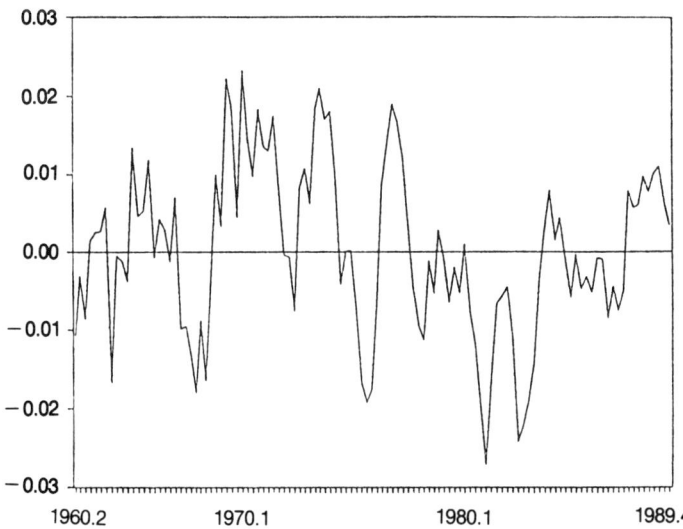

The incorporation of cointegration relations and of error-correction mechanisms in the empirical analysis of output fluctuations appears to attribute a greater weight to demand factors, even though only in the very first few periods, thus suggesting that the obtained non-permanent innovations are indeed more highly transitory than the ones obtained in section 4. The force of attraction of the common stochastic trend is linked to the error correction mechanisms, which

TABLE 5

TEST ON THE RANK, THE COINTEGRATION SPACE AND THE ERROR CORRECTION ADJUSTMENT COEFFICIENTS: $X_t = (d_t, \bar{y}_t, \bar{c}_t, \bar{i}_t)'$, CONDITIONAL ON $(\Delta q_t, \Delta \pi_t, \Delta u_t)$ 1960.3-1989-4, $k = 2$

Cointegration rank	$r \leq 3$	$r \leq 2$	$r \leq 1$	$r = 0$
λ trace test (1)	0.004 (+)	12.45 (+)	30.90 (**)	81.20 (**)
Stationarity test of $\bar{i} - \bar{y}$ and $\bar{c} - \bar{y}$, $r = 3$	$-2 \ln (LR)$	degrees of freedom	$Pr(-2 \ln (LR) > \chi^2)$	
	2.88 (+)	2	0.24	
Weak exogeneity test of	$-2 \ln (LR)$	degrees of freedom	$Pr(-2 \ln (LR) > \chi^2)$	
d	5.38 (+)	5	0.370	
$\bar{y}$	32.07 (**)	5	0.000	
$\bar{c}$	18.13 (**)	5	0.003	
$\bar{i}$	37.92 (**)	5	0.000	

(*) rejected hypothesis at the 5% significance level;
(**) 1%;
(+) non rejected hypothesis;
(1) see JOHANSEN [7].

express how quickly each variable readjusts to the other variables in the system, except, of course, for the world demand.

Contrary to the previous model (where the theoretical content is relatively low, as sums up to the identification, on the basis of some agnostic economic reasoning, of demand variables and long run constraints), the more theory-oriented approach of the present model and of the derived long run restrictions can account for the different, and somewhat more intuitive, present results.

Nevertheless the very rapid growth of the importance of supply factors in the explanation of output fluctuations cannot be denied. This result may also depend on the exclusion of variables possibly linked to demand shocks; in this respect it is interesting to note that King *et* Al. [9], in a very similar estimation strategy in a trivariate system with output consumption and investment, obtained very similar results in the variance decomposition exercise; their extension of the model to monetary variables allowed them to capture a greater weight for the demand shocks in the explanation of output fluctuations in the medium run.

A system with the above variables, conditional to the demand variables of section 4 (the male unemployment rate and the inflation rate), was therefore estimated; the corresponding tests are reported in Table 5. The temporal distribution of the percentage of output variance explained by the real permanent shock is hardly changed with respect to the previous one, being equal to 25.3% after 1 quarter, 64.9% after 8 quarters and 86.3% after 16.

7. - Conclusion

In a previous paper (Onofri - Paruolo - Salituro [11]) the authors reached the conclusion that innovations in labour input and total productivity growth represent the main engine of growth in the path of Italian GDP. In the short run (eight quarters), domestic and international supply shocks (labour, technical progress and manufactured goods/raw materials terms of trade) seem to explain 60% of the variance of output. In the longer run (eighty quarters) the weight of demand shocks declines to 14%. On this basis, two conclusions seemed plausible:

— in spite of the high and increasing degree of international integration of the Italian economy, international shocks provide an explanation for no more than a quarter of the variance of output;

— real business cycle propositions are not openly contradicted, but room seems to be left for short run effect of demand-side policies.

The aim of this work was twofold: to decompose the supply shocks into technical progress shocks and labour input shocks, and to explore the possibility that world demand shocks may be a vehicle of than technical progress, hence the role of international factors higher than that suggested by the previous estimates. The first step was to focus on the implications of balanced growth. To exploit such implications we redefined the output as private output, took into account total domestic consumption and gross fixed investment net of residential constructions; all these variables were expressed in per capita terms, thus eliminating the effects of population growth.

It must be said that the first goal (to isolate the labour input shocks) was not achieved. The non-stationarity of the participation rate and of its first difference, inconsistent with balanced growth assumptions, did not allow it.

The second goal (to explore the role of world demand as a vehicle of technical progress) was achieved. The variables investigated (world demand, output, consumption and investment) do not reject the assumption that they are driven by a unique engine, a common stochastic trend, and, moreover, the data reveal that such a stochastic process is the cumulated sum of the world demand shocks. If we agree to define demand shocks as a transitory component of output fluctuations, then we can consider the permanent shocks originating from abroad as a supply disturbance, hence as technical progress innovations.

Furthermore the weak exogeneity hypothesis is rejected for output, consumption and investment, even though the evidence is less strong for consumption. This is consistent with the results of the system excluding world demand. Under such conditions weak exogeneity cannot be rejected for consumption; in other words, in that case consumption plays the role of a driving force of the system.

As a whole, these empirical findings might suggest that for an open and catching-up economy (as was the Italian economy in the last thirty years) import of new consumption patterns might be a vehicle of stochastic growth. These new results give a different picture of the foreign impulses: for catching-up countries they do not seem to have transitory demand effects, but they work as a vehicle of diffusion of technical progress.

Our empirical investigation has found support for the implications of balanced growth, but within a reversed sequence. In the last thirty years of growth and fluctuation of the Italian economy, consumption does not seem to have conformed to the available technology, while, on the contrary, technology seems to have followed the changing consumption patterns resulting from international integration.

As a whole, both our papers, even though with different identifying assumptions, confirm the role played by permanent (=supply) components: after 16 quarters they explain from 60 to more than 80% of the variance of output, depending on the approach. Within both types of model, transitory shocks, possibly attributed to macro policies, do not seem to have exerted a negligible influence on the fluctuations of the Italian economy. The time distribution of these effects appears to be quite different in the two types of model. In the first case, the percentage of output variance explained by transitory effects declines very slowly from 40% after the first quarter to 30% after twenty years. In the second case, where the contribution of economic theory is stronger, such effects decline from 75% to 14% within four years.

* * *

Methodological Note

Consider the reduced form errors ε_t, and the structural innovations η_t in a «VAR» system cointegrated of order one [I(1)]. The innovations ε_t and η_t are assumed to be linked by the linear relation:

(A.1) $$\varepsilon_t = F\eta_t$$

and by the inverse transformation:

(A.2) $$\eta_t = G\varepsilon_t$$

where $G = F^{-1}$. The common trends rappresentation of the system is given by (3.6):

(3.6) $$X_t = C \sum_{i=1}^{t} \varepsilon_i + v_t = \beta_\perp \tau_t + v_t$$

where:

$$\tau = \xi\alpha_\perp' \sum_{i=1}^{t} \varepsilon_i, \quad \xi = (\alpha_\perp'\Psi\beta_\perp)^{-1}, \quad \Psi = \sum_{i=1}^{k} iA_i$$

Substituting equation (A.1) into equation (3.6) one obtains an analogous representation in terms of structural innovations:

(A.3) $$X_t = {}'CF \sum_{i=1}^{t} \eta_i + v_t$$

Given the structure of C,

$$C = \beta_\perp \xi \alpha_\perp'$$

if some columns of F are proportional to α, the corresponding components of η_t have null long run effect on the levels of X_t. Consider the partitions $G = (G_1, G_2)'$, $F = (F_1, F_2)$, where G_1, F_1 are $p \times (p - r)$ and F_2, G_2 are $p \times r$; adopting the specification:

$$G_1 = \alpha_\perp \kappa \qquad G_2 = \Omega^{-1}\alpha v \qquad F_1 = \Omega\alpha_\perp \kappa$$

$$F_2 = \alpha v \qquad \kappa = (\alpha_\perp'\Omega\alpha_\perp)^{-1/2} \qquad v = (\alpha'\Omega^{-1}\alpha)^{-1/2}$$

one obtains $Var(\eta_t) = I$ and $CF = (C_1, 0)$, that is a diagonal structure of the variance-covariance matrix of the structural innovations and a non-null impact matrix only with respect to the innovations η_t^p, where $\eta_t^p = G_1'\varepsilon_t$, and $\eta_t^{tr} = G_2'\varepsilon_t$. In order to prove such properties it is sufficient to substitute the definitions in $E(\eta_t\eta_t') = G\Omega G'$ and $\bar{C} = CF$, noting that the obtained structure is unique, i.e. identified, up to the choice of K and v.

BIBLIOGRAPHY

[1] ANSUINI A. - FORNASARI C. - PARUOLO P.: «Tassi di interesse monetari e bancari: un'analisi dei meccanismi di trasmissione», Proceedings *I mercati monetari e finanziari nel breve periodo: modelli per l'analisi e la previsione*, Roma 4-5 April 1991, 1992.

[2] ARDENI P.G. - PARUOLO P.: «Seasonality and persistence in Italian GDP: Relevance and Policy Implications», Procedings *XXXVI riunione scientifica Sis*, vol. II, Pescara 21-24 April 1992.

[3] BLANCHARD O. - WATSON M.: «Are Business Cycles All Alike?», in GORDON R.: *The American Business Cycles: Continuity and Change*, Chicago, University of Chicago Press, 1986, p. 126-56.

[4] BLANCHARD O. - QUAH D.: «The Dynamic Effects of Aggregate Demand and Supply Disturbances», *American Economic Review*, n. 79, 1989, pp. 655-73.

[5] ENGLE R. - GRANGER C.W.: «Cointegration and Error Correction: Representation Estimation and Testing», *Econometrica*, n. 55, 1987, pp. 251-76.

[6] GIANNINI C.: «Topics in Structural Var Econometrics», Università di Ancona, *Quaderni di ricerca*, n. 21, 1991.

[7] JOHANSEN S.: «Estimation and Hypothesis Testing of Cointegration Vectors in Gaussian Vector Autoregressive Models», *Econometrica*, n. 59, 1991, pp. 1551-80.

[8] —.—: «Testing for Weak Exogeneity and the Order of Cointegration in UK Money Demand Data», Institute of Mathematical Statistics, University of Copenhagen, *Preprint*, n. 4, 1991.

[9] KING R.G. - PLOSSER C.I. - STOCK J.H. - WATSON M.W.: «Stochastic Trends and Economic Fluctuations» *American Economic Review*, n. 81, 1991, pp. 819-40.

[10] LIPPI M. - REICHLIN L.: «Trend-Cycle Decompositions and Measures of Persistence: Does Time Aggregation Matter?», *Economic Journal*, n. 101, 1991.

[11] ONOFRI P. - PARUOLO P. - SALITURO B.: «Alla ricerca di fatti stilizzati dell'economia italiana: un sistema VAR strutturale», in BANCA D'ITALIA: *Ricerche applicate e modelli per la politica economica*, vol. I, 1992, pp. 267-94.

[12] PARUOLO P.: «Asymptotic Inference on the Moving Average Impact Matrix in Cointegrated I(1) VAR systems», Institute of Mathematical Statistics, University of Copenhagen, *Preprint*, n. 2, 1992.

[13] SHAPIRO M.D. - WATSON M.: «Sources of Business Cycle Fluctuations», NBER, *Annual Report*, 1988, p. 111-57.

[14] SIMS C.: «Macroeconomics and Reality», *Econometrica*, n. 48, 1980, pp. 1-48.

[15] SOLOW R.: «A Contribution to the Theory of Economic Growth», *Quarterly Journal of Economics*, vol. LXX, 1956, pp. 65-94.

[16] WARNE A.: *Vector Autoregressions and Common Trends in Macro and Financial Economics*, Stockholm School of Economics, 1990.

New Measures of the Permanent Component of Output: a Multi-Country Analysis

Stefano Fachin - **Andrea Gavosto** - **Guido Pellegrini**
Università «La Sapienza», Roma
Banca d'Italia, Roma

1. - Introduction (1)

It is a long time since economists and statisticians have started working on the identification of the trend in output. Only recently, have the developments in both time series and business cycle studies shown that there is a close relation between the concept of trend in economic theory and its empirical counterpart. In economics, the trend captures the movement of the long run equilibrium value. Therefore it is the "permanent" component of output, i.e. the value to which the series converges, after short run fluctuactions.

However, this definition gives little help toward a proper empirical specification of the trend, because long run equilibria cannot be found in nature. Statisticians have often assumed that the evolution of the long run equilibrium is "smoother" than the short run equilibrium dynamics, and that a straight line can be an adequate approximation

---

(1) A preliminary version of this paper was presented at the *Seminar on Time-Varying Parameter Models*, Società italiana di statistica, Roma, March 1992. Comments from M. Lippi and from the participants to the seminar are gratefully acknowledged. The paper is the result of a joint work; however, section 2 was drafted by G. Pellegrini, section 3 by A. Gavosto and S. Fachin. The views expressed in the paper are those of the authors and do not involve the responsibility of the Bank of Italy.

Advise: the numbers in square brackets refer to the Bibliography in the appendix.

of the permanent component (2). Therefore, regressions with a linear or a log linear specification of a time trend were commonly run, and the residuals were taken to be the short run fluctuations (or the "cycle") of the series. It was implicit, in this procedure, that the short run shocks to output could not affect its long run behaviour.

This approach prevailed in the sixties and the seventies: it was consistent with the economic theory at that time, which took growth and cyclical fluctuations as being independent from each other. The empirical performances were quite successful, because the cycle and persistency of the transitory component was as expected. Sometimes, a more flexible approach was used, trying to identify a "local" trend, by moving average filter techniques (3). On the other hand, this flexibility concerned only the estimation, as the deterministic nature of the method was preserved. In fact, filters are optimal only if the stochastic process, and in particular the frequency of cyclical waves, is known in advance (4).

The weaknesses of this procedure were highlighted during the eighties, when people became aware of the role played by the degree of integration on the long run behaviour of the series. The Real Business Cycle theory pointed out the close link between short run and long run dynamics, both due to the same (technological) innovations (5). Beveridge and Nelson [1] showed that if output is an integrated process, the series follows a stochastic trend. In this case, the value of the long run equilibrium changes after every shock, which has a permanent impact on output. The problem has been

---

(2) See, for instance, the path-breaking study by PERSONS [34].

(3) For instance, this approach is used in the X11-ARIMA seasonally adjusting procedure, where the trend is captured by a Henderson filter. Another deterministic filter is the HODRICK - PRESCOTT [21] filter, where the trend is a non linear, smooth function of time. For a detailed analysis of different detrending procedures and for references, see CANOVA [5].

(4) An example of this method is in KUZNETS [22], where a 5-terms moving average was applied in order to extract the business cycle fluctuations, the expected length of which was 5 years. The shortcomings of this procedure are well-known today. See, for instance, HARVEY [18].

(5) This idea was not new in economic thought, and the similarities with the work of SCHUMPETER [39] are quite evident. The main intent of RBC theory is to explain economic fluctuations in a perfectly competitive model, without introducing rigidities or market imperfections. From this point of view, these theories are alternative to the Keynesian and monetarist line of thinking.

emphasized by two papers: Nelson and Plosser [29], building from a previous contribution by Granger [17], showed that stochastic trends are very frequent in the economy (6); Nelson and Kang [27], [28], confirmed the danger of fitting a deterministic trend if the series has a stochastic one: the resulting cycle is spurious, and the autocorrelation functions of residuals only depend on the size of the sample.

The recent advances in time series analysis have explained why the deterministic trend is no longer adequate to describe the long run behaviour of output. As a consequence, a stream of applied economic studies has started introducing stochastic trends to represent the permanent component of the series (7). The new approach has given rise to a set of questions, not contemplated in the traditional approach to trend modelling: *a)* what is the role of the permanent component in explaining output variability?; *b)* is the decomposition between trend and cycle robust to different specifications?

This paper is concerned with both questions. Our purpose is to estimate stochastic trends in output for some European economies. In Section 2, a brief review of recent results on stochastic trends is presented. An application of a multivariate decomposition model, expanding the approach followed in Gavosto and Pellegrini [15], is shown in Section 3. Conclusions are drawn in the last Section.

2. - Permanent and Transitory Components: a Survey

The results of Beveridge and Nelson [1] and Nelson and Plosser [29] have stimulated a good deal of research on decomposition into permanent and transitory components. The main finding is that the role of permanent components in explaining output variability depends on the choice of the decomposition method. Actually, the specification of the shape of the permanent component greatly affects the decomposition results. The point we want to stress here is that we face a classical identification problem: the analysis of the series cannot

---

(6) See PERRON [33] for a critical analysis of these results.
(7) See, among others, HARVEY [20], WATSON [40], CAMPBELL - MANKIW [3], [4], CLARK [6], [7], COCHRANE [8], SHAPIRO - WATSON [38], BLANCHARD - QUAH [2], LIPPI - REICHLIN [23], QUAH [36].

give us enough information to decompose output into two components. The problem can be solved only imposing more structure on the decomposition.

Let us assume that output can be represented by the sum of a permanent component, that is an integrated process of order one, and of a cyclical component, which is stationary:

(1) $$Y(t) = T(t) + C(t)$$

where $Y(t)$ is output, $T(t)$ is the permanent component (trend) and C is the stationary component (cycle). The decomposition implies that output is an integrated variable of order one. If we take first differences of the process, the variable becomes stationary:

(2) $$\Delta Y(t) = \Delta T(t) + \Delta C(t)$$

The decomposition can be analyzed by looking at the special spectral density of a general process $\Delta Y(t)$, plotted in Graph 1, taken from Lippi and Reichlin [24].

The picture shows that the permanent component explains part of the variability at non zero frequencies. Two remarks are important here: 1) the spectral density of $\Delta Y(t)$ and the spectral density of $\Delta T(t)$ meet each other at frequency zero. This is not coincidental. The assumptions on the degree of integration of trend and cycle cause all output variability at frequency zero to be explained by the trend. Lippi and Reichlin [24] and Quah [36] show that this result does not depend on the correlation between trend and cycle innovations. The implication of this proposition is that we can measure the spectral density at frequency zero of a series, even if the impact of the trend on output variability depends on the shape of the permanent component, as proved in Lippi and Reichlin [24] and Quah [36]); 2) these results also indicate that our knowledge of stochastic trend is not sufficient. In fact, Quah [36] shows that there exists an infinite number of decompositions between trend and cycle that satisfy the conditions in Graph 1. Moreover, the variance of the permanent component can be reduced to be arbitrarily close to zero. In the case $\Delta Y(t)$ and $\Delta C(t)$ are not correlated, the intuition is simple: from Graph 1 we can note that

GRAPH 1

SPECTRAL DENSITY OF THE FIRST DIFFERENCES
OF A TIME SERIES (UPPER LINE) AND
OF ITS PERMANENT COMPONENT (LOWER LINE)

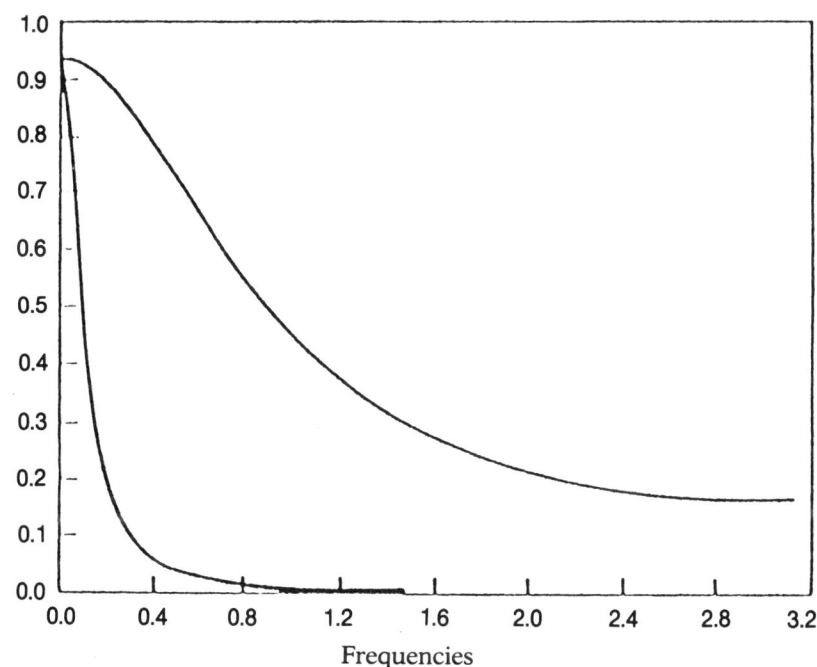

Source: LIPPI-REICHLIN [23].

they can be infinite curves, subtended to the spectral density of $\Delta Y(t)$, that meet at the ordinate at frequency zero. The variability of the permanent component can take different values even if the "size" (the spectral density at frequency zero) is the same.

The analysis of the general case shows that this approach cannot allow the identification of different components of one time series without imposing some restriction on the process: there is not enough information in order to disentangle trend and cycle.

The problem has been tackled in the following ways: *a*) a first approach, the oldest one, solves the identification problem by assuming a specific shape for the permanent component. The common assumption is that the trend is a random walk (Beveridge and Nelson

[1], Watson [40], Cochrane [8]); b) a second approach uses information coming from different sources, applying a multivariate decomposition model (Shapiro and Watson [38], Blanchard and Quah [2], Gavosto and Pellegrini [15]).

The assumption that the permanent component follows a random walk implies that the spectral density of its first differences is a straight horizontal line. In this case the decomposition can be pictured as in Graph 2, also taken from Lippi and Reichlin [24], under the hypothesis that trend and cycle are independent.

This restriction allows to compute the share of output variation that can be attributed to fluctuations of stochastic trend (8). This is not possible in the general case. On the other hand, the restriction does not place enough structure on the problem, because there exists an infinite number of different combinations of $\Delta T(t)$ and $\Delta C(t)$, depending on the covariance between the two processes, whose sum is equal to the spectral density of $\Delta Y(t)$, and therefore satisfy the decomposition. For instance, let us assume that $Y(t)$ follows a IMA(1,1) process, $T(t)$ is a random walk and $C(t)$ is a white noise as in the next formulation:

(3) $$Y(t) = Y(t-1) + \mu(t) + \theta\mu(t-1)$$

(4) $$T(t) = T(t-1) + \lambda\varepsilon(t)$$

(5) $$C(t) = \kappa\eta(t)$$

The process is fully described by the variance and the autocovariance at lag one. We obtain the following set of restrictions:

(6) $$\gamma(0) = \lambda^2\sigma_\varepsilon^2 + 2\kappa^2\sigma_\eta^2 + 2\lambda\kappa\sigma_{\varepsilon\eta}$$

(7) $$\gamma(1) = -\kappa\lambda\sigma_{\varepsilon\eta} - \kappa^2\sigma_\eta^2$$

The identification problem arises from the fact that we have 5 parameters (variance of $\varepsilon(t)$, variance of $\eta(t)$, covariance between the

---

(8) In this case have a parametric estimation of the spectral density at frequency zero of $\Delta Y(t)$. For a non parametric estimation, see COCHRANE [8].

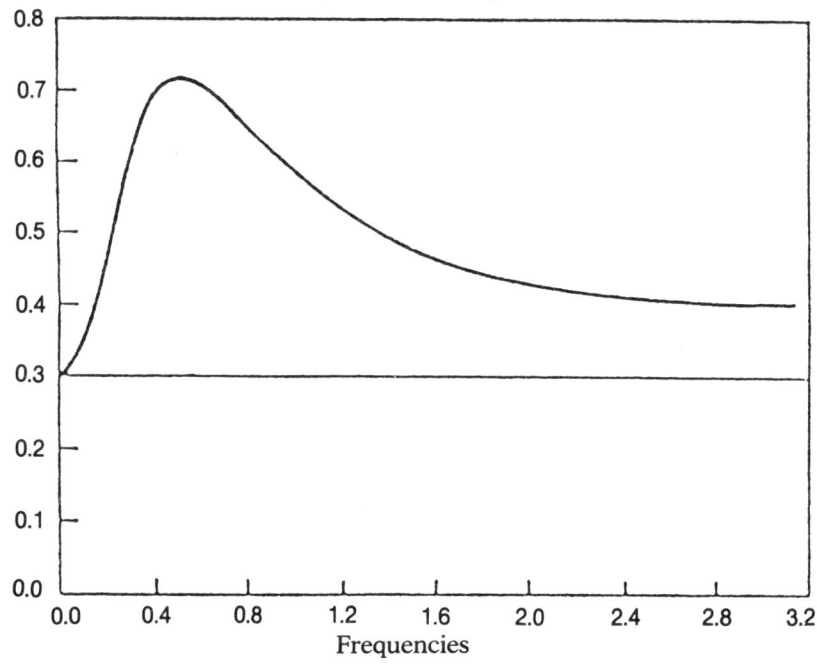

GRAPH 2

SPECTRAL DENSITY OF THE FIRST DIFFERENCES
OF A TIME SERIES (UPPER LINE) AND
OF ITS PERMANENT COMPONENT GIVEN BY A RANDOM WALK
(LOWER LINE)

Source: LIPPI-REICHLIN [23].

two and the parameters κ and λ), but only two constraints. Also in this case the solution has been twofold:

1) Beveridge and Nelson [1] have proposed to identify the two components by assuming that shocks to trend and cycle are perfectly correlated, and therefore equal to the innovations to the Wold representation of the process. In our example, the variance of $\varepsilon(t)$ is equal to the variance of $\eta(t)$ and therefore equal also to their covariance. The identification of λ is achieved assuming that it is equal to the sum of the parameters of the moving-average representation of the series. In our case, λ would be equal to $(1 + \theta)$, κ to $-\theta$;

2) Watson [40] has proposed that the shocks to trend and cycle

are perfectly uncorrelated. The identification is achieved normalizing λ and κ to one.

The Beveridge-Nelson decomposition has some nice properties: it is easy to apply, it can be used under fairly general conditions and it gives a parametric estimation of the spectral density of the process at frequency zero. If the process $Y(t)$ has a general Wold representation:

(8) $$\Delta Y(t) = B(L)\varepsilon(t)$$

the Beveridge-Nelson decomposition is as follows:

(9) $$\Delta Y(t) = B(1)\varepsilon(t) + [B(L) - B(1)]\Delta\varepsilon(t)$$

where $B(1)$ is the sum of the coefficients in the Wold representation. The stochastic trend is given by:

(10) $$\Delta Y(t) = B(1)\varepsilon(t)$$

and the spectral density of the process at frequency zero is:

(11) $$S_{\Delta Y}(0) = S_{\Delta T}(0) = |B(1)|^2 \sigma_\varepsilon^2$$

The main limit to the Beveridge-Nelson decomposition is that it delivers no new information on the long run behaviour of output in addition to the ones in the Wold representation. Moreover, the assumption that innovations to trend and cycle are perfectly correlated is of little help for an economist, who wants to investigate the different sources of shocks. This shortcoming was removed in the Watson decomposition, where the assumption is that the innovations are uncorrelated. In this case, forecasts of long run dynamics are different from what can be obtained by Wold representation. In our example, the Watson decomposition is obtained, under the assumption that the covariance between $\varepsilon(t)$ and $\eta(t)$ is equal to zero and the parameters are normalized to one, by solving:

(12) $$\sigma_\varepsilon^2 = -\theta\sigma_\mu^2; \quad \sigma_\eta^2 = (1 + \theta + \theta^2)\sigma_\mu^2$$

The Watson decomposition exists only under more strict conditions: from Graph 2 can be seen that the assumption of independence between shocks implies that the decomposition is feasible only if the shape of the spectral density of $\Delta Y(t)$ has a minimum at zero frequency.

The orthogonal decomposition stimulated the application of *Unidentified Component ARIMA models (UC-ARIMA)* to the decomposition problem. These are "structural" models, because they require a complete specification of model components. In the trend-cycle decomposition, the model identification is obtained by assuming a specific form not only for the trend but also for the cycle. These models impose specific constraints on the *ARIMA* structure of the series, and the decomposition can be inefficient if the constraints are not fulfilled by the data (Piccolo [35]). The Watson decomposition can therefore be considered as a special case of model analysis in the general *UC-ARIMA* framework. Moreover, the *UC-ARIMA* technique allows for decomposition models with time-varying parameters. Harvey ([19], p. 10) stresses that: «the principal time series models are... nothing more than regression models in which the explanatory variables are functions of time and the parameter are time-varying». Some time-varying parameter models can be considered just simple extensions of the Watson model. For instance, the so called "linear trend model", using the notation of equation *(1)*, is as follows:

(13) $$T(t) = T(t-1) + \beta(t-1) + \varepsilon(t)$$

(14) $$C(t) = \eta(t)$$

(15) $$\beta(t) = \beta(t-1) + \delta(t)$$

where the innovations to trend and cycle are uncorrelated and the parameter $\beta(t)$ also follows a random walk process. This model assumes that output is an integrated process of order two. Also model for series that are integrated of order one can be considered in *UC-ARIMA* framework. For instance, the previous model can be modified in a "damped trend" model, where $\beta(t)$ is a stationary autoregressive process. The cyclical component is often modelled, adopting Harvey's suggestion, by trigonometric waves generated by an autoregressive stationary process, the amplitude of which changes over time. Obviously, not all the decomposition in the *UC-ARIMA* framework assume time-varying parameters. In Clark's [6] paper, a decomposition is proposed where the drift component of the trend and the parameters of the second-order autoregressive process for the cycle are constant over time. On the other hand, even if the *UC-ARIMA* approach is very flexible, it suffers from the drawback of the trend specification (always assumed to be a random walk) that has been stressed for the Watson model.

A nice property of the *UC-ARIMA* framework is that the models are nested in a more general specification, and simple statistic tests on restrictions can be computed. Usually, these models are estimated by maximum likelihood methods, and tests based on likelihood ratio (*LR*) can be easily implemented. The algorithm is built on a two-stage recursive procedure: in the first stage, an estimation of residual variance is obtained by the Kalman filter, given the vector of parameters; in the second stage, the vector of parameters is estimated, maximizing the likelihood function, given the residuals. The application of *UC-ARIMA* models to trend-cycle decomposition is not yet common, also because a complete analysis of identification and estimation problems has been only recently concluded by Harvey [19] (9).

The assumption that the trend is a random walk implies that the total impact of a permanent shock is concentrated in the first period. This assumption is very stringent. Lippi and Reichlin [24] noted that, if the stochastic trend of output is originated by technological innovations, there are good reasons to believe that the process should be smoother, because: 1) the existence of learning processes at company level; 2) the different rate of diffusion of a technological innovation across heterogeneous firms. In this case, the modelling of the permanent component as a random walk can be inadequate, and a more general integrated process for trend is required. This step has been undertaken by a new approach to the decomposition, that has

---

(9) See HARVEY [20], for application to USA GNP, and PELLEGRINI [31] for a study of Italian industrial production index.

exploited the increased availability of information coming from a multivariate analysis. The most influential paper in this field was by Blanchard and Quah [2], and it was a development of the structural VAR approach (10). In the "structural" VAR analysis, the identification of orthogonal innovations from a Wold representation is achieved by imposing some constraints on the shape of impulse functions and on the variance-covariance matrix of shocks. In the bivariate case presented by Blachard and Quah [2], the decomposition requires the existence of a stationary variable $W(t)$ that Granger-causes $\Delta Y(t)$ and the assumption that the vector $(\Delta Y(t), W(t))$ is stationary. Under these hypotheses, there exists a decomposition, given by the equation (1), such that innovations are orthogonal (11):

$$(16) \qquad \begin{pmatrix} \Delta Y(t) \\ W(t) \end{pmatrix} = \sum_{j=0}^{\infty} C(j)\varepsilon(t\text{-}j) = \sum_{j=0}^{\infty} D(j)\eta(t\text{-}j)$$

where $\varepsilon(t)$ and $\eta(t)$ are two-components error vectors, $C(j)$ is the MVA representation and $D(j)$ is the "structural" one. The bridge between the two representations is given by the relation $D(1) = C(1)V$, where $VV' = P$ and P is the variance-covariance matrix of VAR residuals. $D(1)$ can be obtained by the Cholenski factorization of $C(1)PC(1)'$. This factorization is not unique, as equally legitimate solutions can be found by multiplying V by an orthonormal matrix. Therefore, more identifying assumptions are needed: we have to impose more structure on the problem.

Blanchard and Quah [2] derive the extra assumption from the hypothesis that transitory shocks do not affect, by definition, the long run behavior of output. The matrix of long run impact $D(1)$ is in fact triangular with a zero in the upper right element, and Blanchard and Quah show that, under this assumption, the decomposition is unique.

The trend component is given by:

$$(17) \qquad \Delta T(t) = \sum_{j=0}^{\infty} D_{11}(j)\eta(t-j)$$

---

(10) See GIANNINI [16] for a careful exposition of these models.
(11) A more formal treatment is in BLANCHARD - QUAH [2].

whereas the restriction implies:

$$(18) \quad \Delta C(t) = \sum_{j=0}^{\infty} D_{12}(j)\eta_2(t-j), \quad \sum_{j=0}^{\infty} D_{12}(j) = 0$$

The Granger-causality condition comes from the fact that if $C(1)$ is also triangular, the decomposition is meaningless. Many variables can Granger-cause $\Delta Y(t)$, and therefore the choice of the stationary series is crucial. This is one limit of multivariate decomposition. A further one is that the identification assumptions cannot be tested, and the model reliability can be verified only by the analysis of the plausibility of results. The main advantage, on the other hand, is that this approach does not force the permanent component to follow an established pattern, and therefore allows analyses of the impulse transmission of permanent shocks to output.

The results of a multivariate decomposition will be presented in the next Section of the paper. Here a brief review of some univariate decomposition techniques will be shown, using the result derived in Pellegrini [31] for the index of Italian industrial production in the period 1974-1988 (12). The series has been tested for stationarity: tests for different levels of temporal and sectorial aggregation have shown that the series is an integrated process of order one (Pellegrini [31]). The decomposition using a deterministic trend has been compared to the Beveridge-Nelson decomposition of an *ARIMA*(2,1,2) model and to a *UC-ARIMA* "cyclical model", whose reduced form is also a *ARIMA*(2,1,2). The cyclical variability of the deterministic trend model is greater than the variability of the cycle of both stochastic trends (the variance is equal to 0.0024 for the deterministic trend model, 0.0006 for the Beveridge-Nelson model and 0.0005 for the *UC-ARIMA* model). As expected, this result shows that errors in trend specification affect the pseudo-cyclical behavior of transitory components. If we consider the variance ratio (the R^2 of a regression of the differences of permanent component onto the differences of output), the variability of the trend explains 66% of variability in

---

(12) For a more complete analysis see PELLEGRINI [31].

output in the Beveridge-Nelson model, 82% in the *UC-ARIMA* model. Therefore, both models show that there exists a stochastic trend, the variability of which explains the major part of fluctuations in output.

3. - A Multivariate Estimation of the Permanent Component in Industrial Production Index for Germany, France, United Kingdom and Italy

3.1 *The Model*

In the previous Section, the theoretical basis for the estimation of the permanent component by structural *VAR*s was laid down. In what follows we will apply such methodology to the four largest European economies: Germany, France, United Kingdom and Italy. As for the latter, we will make use of the results of a previous work by two of us (Gavosto and Pellegrini [15]). Our primary concern is to investigate the effects of supply and demand shocks on industrial production in each of the four countries and to provide an estimate of their permanent components. However this is not the only purpose of the paper. As was stessed earlier, a coherent body of statistical tests for structural *VAR*s has not been developed yet: it is therefore very hard to gauge the validity and accuracy of the results. This is particularly true for final estimates of the impulse functions and of the permanent components which can only be assessed according to the (per force arbitrary) *a priori* judgement of the researcher. In order to overcome this limit, we have tried to extend the methodology, with respect to earlier works, in two directions. On the one hand, we computed the confidence intervals of the impulse responses, by using a bootstrap method. On the other hand, we applied the same procedure, and, especially, the same identifying assumptions, to a set of countries which are different in some respects, but are also sufficiently homogeneous and related among themselves. The underlying idea is that during the seventies and the eighties all four countries were affected by similar shocks (i.e. the oil shocks) or that, anyway, shocks which originated in any one country (i.e. deflationary policies) were rapidly transmitted to the others. By comparing the results, we hope to pass a preliminary judgement on the plausibility of the methodology we used.

The estimation procedure is quite straightforward (details can be found in Gavosto and Pellegrini [15]), being based on the work by Blanchard e Quah [2]. Initially we estimated a *VAR* in industrial output, employment (either total hours worked or number of employed) and an index of short-term orders, to proxy aggregate demand, for each country. We checked for the existence of Granger-causality among our variables. Then, we derived the Wold representation of the multivariate process. Finally we imposed identifying restrictions on the long-run behaviour of the variables of interest, in order to recover structural disturbances from the reduced-form residuals. This is the crucial step on which the plausibility of all our results impinges. Therefore a brief discussion of the identifying restrictions is needed. The pattern of industrial output, both in the short- and in the long-run, can be driven by several factors. However, it is our contention that three different categories of shocks lie at the heart of output fluctuations: *a) technology shocks*. Changes in output can be caused, *ceteris paribus*, by the diffusion of new ways of producing. These can follow true "inventions", often reflected in new techniques or equipment, or the upgrading of workers' knowledge or skills or, finally, improvements in the organisation of work; *b) labour supply shocks*. These can be due both to demographic factors, such as the entry of new cohorts in the labour market, and to individuals' decisions on whether to join the productive process and on the amount of work they are prepared to commit themselves to. Given the central role of trade unions in European manufacturing, such shocks can reflect collective decisions rather than the choice of optimising agents; *c) demand shocks*. Here we look at changes in the overall demand (both domestic and foreign) to the manufacturing sector. We will make no attempt to disentangle monetary and real shocks (see Gali [14], on this). The main object of our study is the impact these three shocks have on industrial production in the four countries. In other words, we want to assess how much of the change in output in every period can be attributed to tecnological, labour supply or demand factors. In order to provide an answer to this question, we have to distinguish, that is to "identify", the three disturbances. The road we follow is to assume that each shock has, in the long run, a different impact on the variables of interest (the ones included in the VARs). In addition, we posited that the disturbances are orthogonal. To sum up, our identifying restrictions, used to recover the structural disturbances $e(t)$ from the reduced form residuals $u(t)$, are: 1) the variance-covariance matrix of $e(t)$ is the identity matrix (after normalisation); 2) the matrix of long-run impacts, D, is triangular. This implies that *a*) the level of industrial output is finally affected both by technological and by labour supply shocks; *b*) long-run employment is affected only by labour supply shocks, and *c*) orders, being a stationary variable, are not affected by any shock in the long-run. These assumptions follow directly from economic theory, namely from the Solow-Swan growth model, where steady state output growth is uniquely determined by technical progress and labour supply, whereas demand is neutral in the long-run. The further restriction that technical progress does not affect labour supply in the long run follows from assuming that there are no wealth effects. This is a more debatable assumption, even though one which is widely used in the literature (see for instance Shapiro and Watson [38]). Although our identifying assumptions are well grounded in economic theory, they are inevitably somewhat ambiguous (and, as is well known, they cannot be directly tested). This is to say that if one believes that demand has a long-run impact on output, whereas labour supply does not, our interpretation of the origin of the shocks should be turned around: what we define as demand shocks would be in fact supply shocks and viceversa. Obviously, this is a problem not just with our procedure, but it is common to all estimation procedures, albeit it is perhaps more apparent in this case. A further caveat is that the three shocks we are considering do not cover all possible factors which influence output in the long run. Other sorts of disturbances, besides the ones we look at, are in fact likely to affect the path of industrial production: an obvious example are changes in the oil price. We have controlled for omitted factors in the most obvious cases, by way of *ad hoc* variables, as will be explained later. In general, however, the orthogonalisation of residuals makes sure that correlated effects are lumped together. As a consequence, the effect of an omitted explanatory factor, which is highly correlated with technology, say, will be attributed to the latter in our final results, leading to an "almost correct" decomposition, in the words of Blanchard and Quah [2].

3.2 VAR: *Specification, Estimates and Results*

The *VAR* specification is similar to the one used in the quoted paper by Pellegrini and Gavosto for Italy. Endogenous variables are: industrial production (Q); employment (N), measured by the total amount of hours worked for all countries except France where only the number of employed was available; and a demand variable (D), which captures the difference of orders from a "normal" level, except for UK where the index refers to the economic climate. Details on the data be found in the Appendix. Here we only note that the indeces of orders we used look more appropriate measures of the latent "demand" factor than some of the variables which have been employed in the past, like the unemployment rate (Blanchard e Quah [2]). Given the nature of our variables, we expected output and employment to be non stationary, whereas demand indices are $I(0)$. Tests of stationarity confirmed our *a priori*. Consequently, output and employment entered the regression in first differences, orders in levels.

As we mentioned earlier, dummies were introduced in order to capture such exogenous events as the oil shocks. In addition, we constructed a deterministic variable by regressing the (log) share of

TABLE 1

UNIT-ROOT TESTS (1)

Variable	France	Germany	Italy	UK
Q	2.66	2.42	3.17	2.56
N	3.07	2.46	2.46	3.47
D	3.49*	2.66*	3.17*	4.34*

(1) 1) *ADF* test in all cases except variable D in France, where a Perron-type test has been applied. Asterixed variables are stationary; 2) signs omitted; 3) on the basis of *LM* tests with 5% significance level the residuals are not autocorrelated; 4) the test statistic for manhours in UK is exactly equal to the 5% critical point. However some experimentation showed that estimates of the *VAR* coefficients obtained using first differences are not significantly different from those obtained using the residuals from a linear trend, and that the choice of rejecting or not rejecting the null is not critical.

TABLE 2

VAR STATISTICS

Country	Period	Lags	Dep. var.: Q	Dep. var.: N	Dep. var.: D
France	1971.1/1989.4	8	R^2 = 0.65 s = 0.01 Q = 26.74 [0.32]	R^2 = 0.89 s = 0.02 Q = 19.92 [0.70]	R^2 = 0.97 s = 7.17 Q = 17.21 [0.84]
Germany	1968.4/1991.2	10	R^2 = 0.71 s = 0.01 Q = 26.13 [0.51]	R^2 = 0.84 s = 0.01 Q = 28.13 [0.40]	R^2 = 0.97 s = 0.07 Q = 14.52 [0.98]
Italy	1967.1/1987.4	6	R^2 = 0.69 s = 0.02 Q = 25.11 [0.57]	R^2 = 0.72 s = 0.02 Q = 22.27 [0.72]	R^2 = 0.97 s = 4.60 Q = 28.17 [0.40]
UK	1973.3/1991.2	6	R^2 = 0.39 s = 0.02 Q = 24.83 [0.42]	R^2 = 0.40 s = 0.02 Q = 9.09 [0.99]	R^2 = 0.62 s = 0.25 Q = 12.38 [0.98]

industrial value added on GDP on a cubic trend. This variable (which is alike to the relative wage of manufacturing with respect to the rest of the economy, used in Gavosto e Pellegrini) was needed in order to capture the secular decline in importance of manufacturing *vis-à-vis* the service sector, common to all advanced economies. In general our equations fit the data well and show no serial correlation. Estimates of the coefficients are not reported for lack of space. Table 2 reports instead some diagnostics: s is the standard error of the estimates, Q the *portmanteau* test of Ljung-Box for autocorrelation of residuals with significance levels in brackets.

The most important impulse functions are in Graphs 3-8. For each function, 5% bootstrap bilateral confidence intervals based on the percentile method proposed by Efron [9] have been computed, Such method defines a bootstrap confidence interval for a parameter θ at the level 2α as the interval included within the percentiles 100α and $100(1 - \alpha)$ of the bootstrap (i.e. obtained by resampling the original data) distribution of the estimates θ^* of θ. For time series it is obviously not possible to resample directly, as the variables are not

GRAPH 3

RESPONSE OF EMPLOYMENT
TO A LABOUR SUPPLY SHOCK

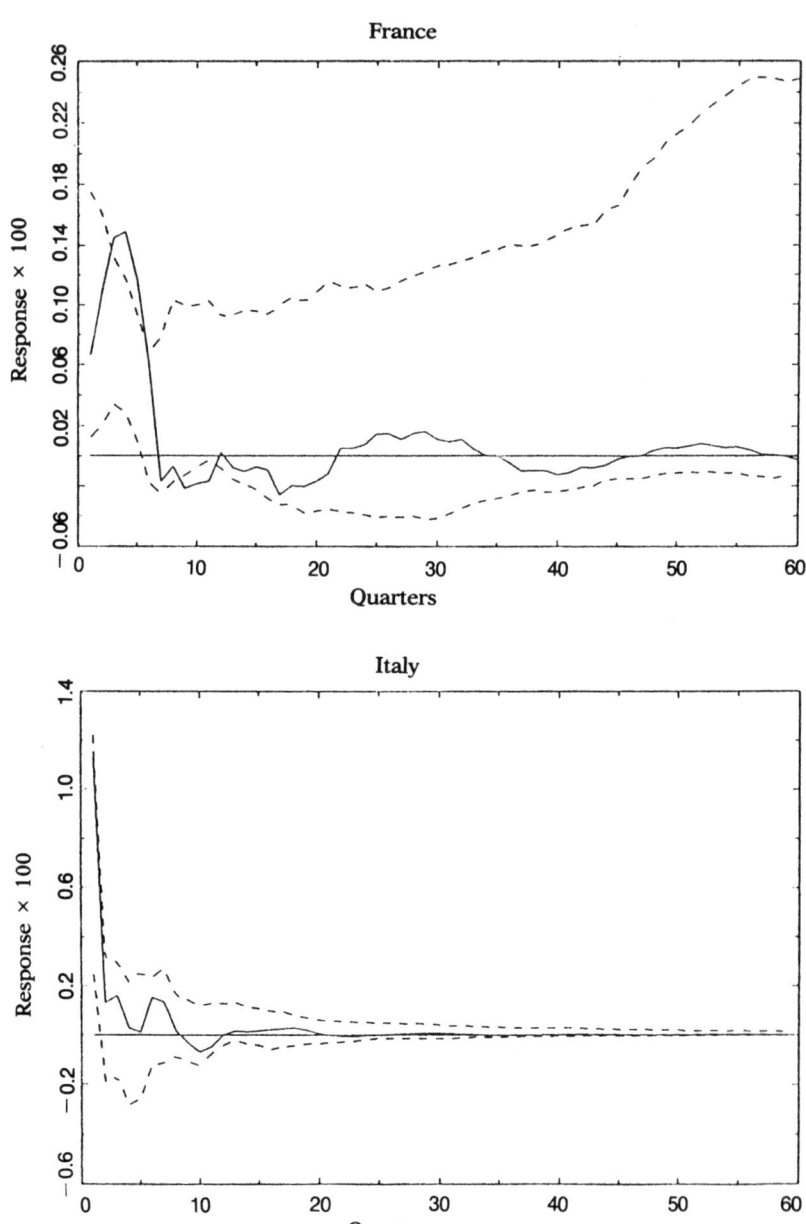

GRAPH 3 continued

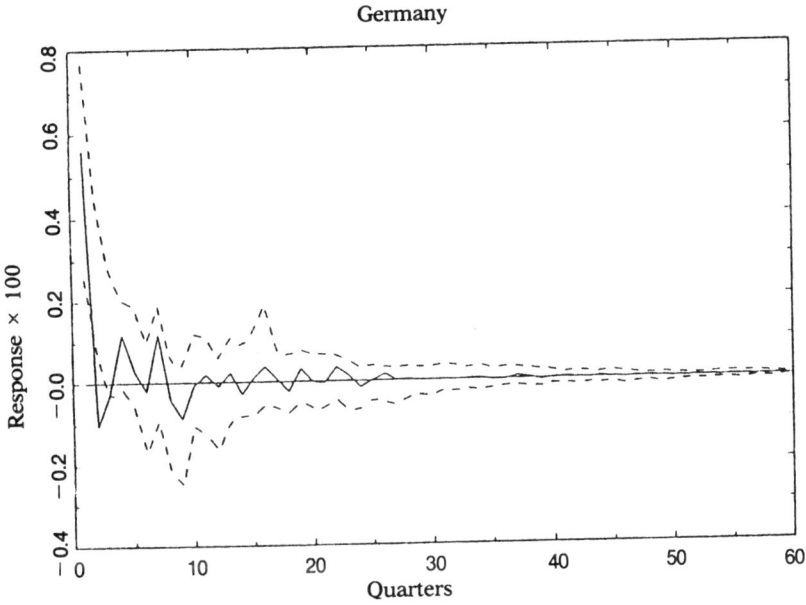

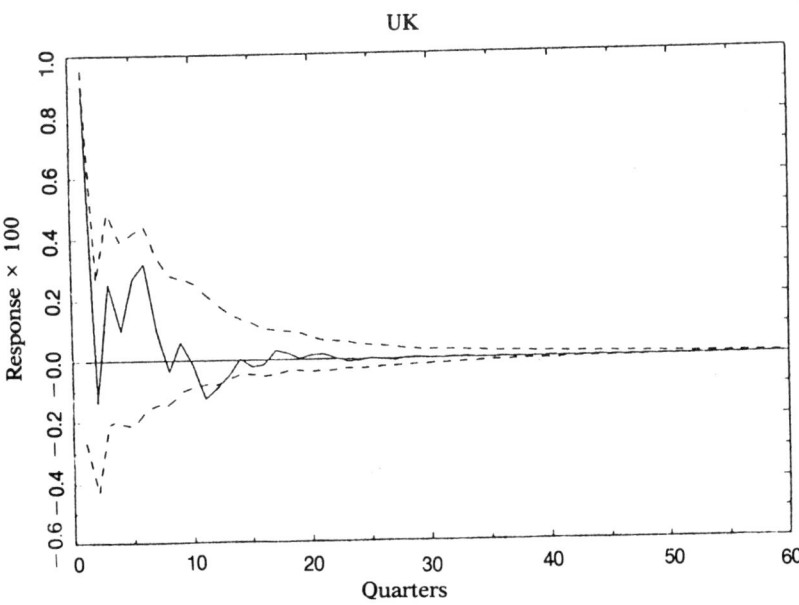

GRAPH 4

RESPONSE OF EMPLOYMENT
TO A TECHNOLOGY SHOCK

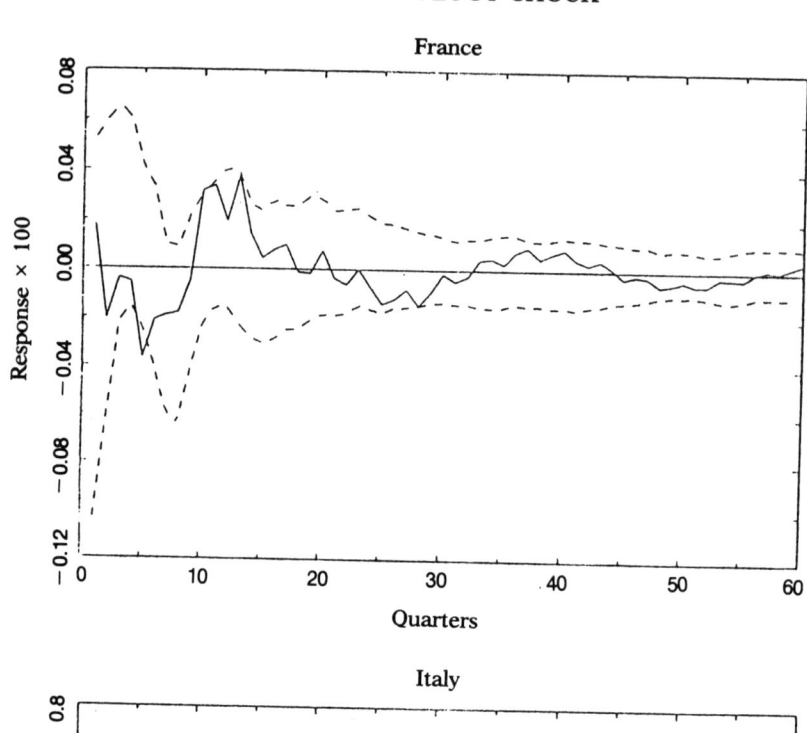

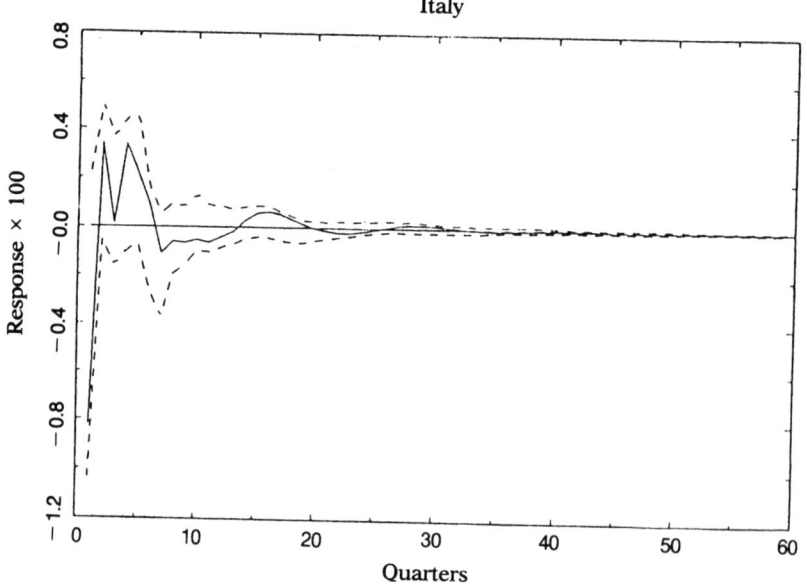

GRAPH 4 *continued*

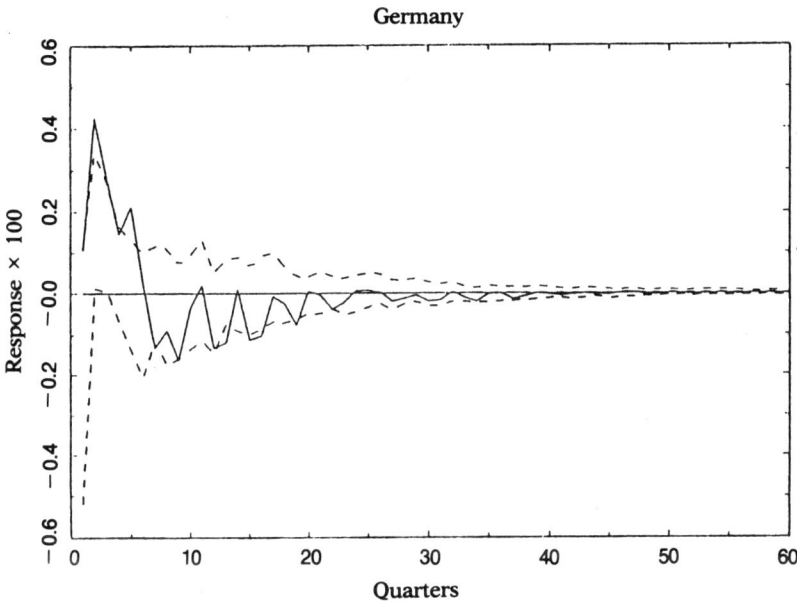

Germany

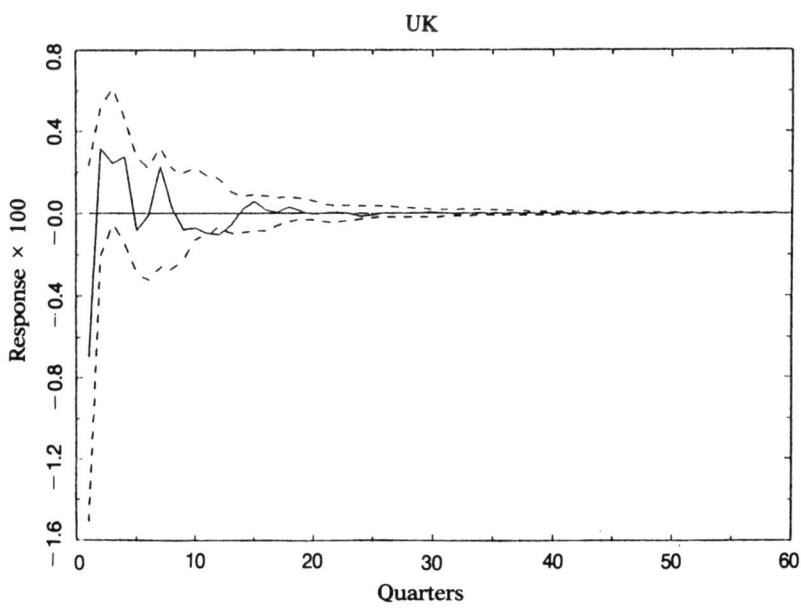

UK

GRAPH 5

RESPONSE OF EMPLOYMENT
TO A DEMAND SHOCK

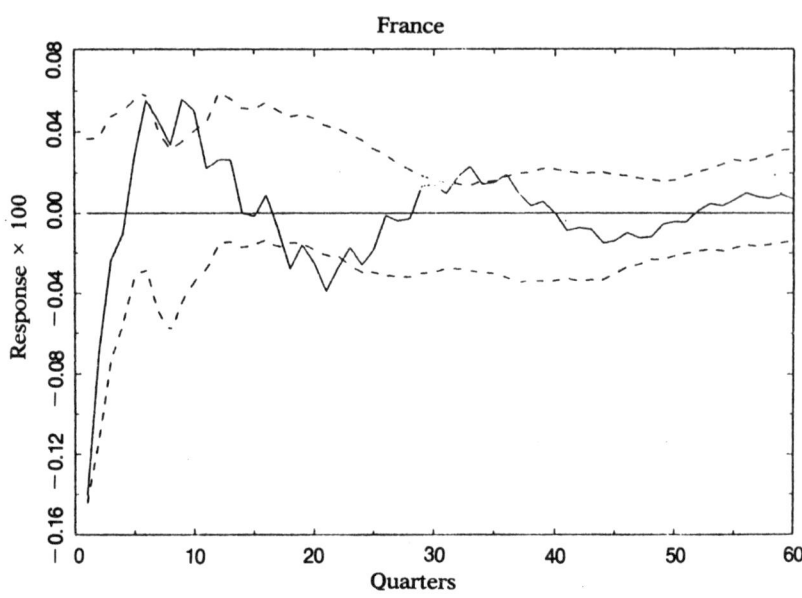

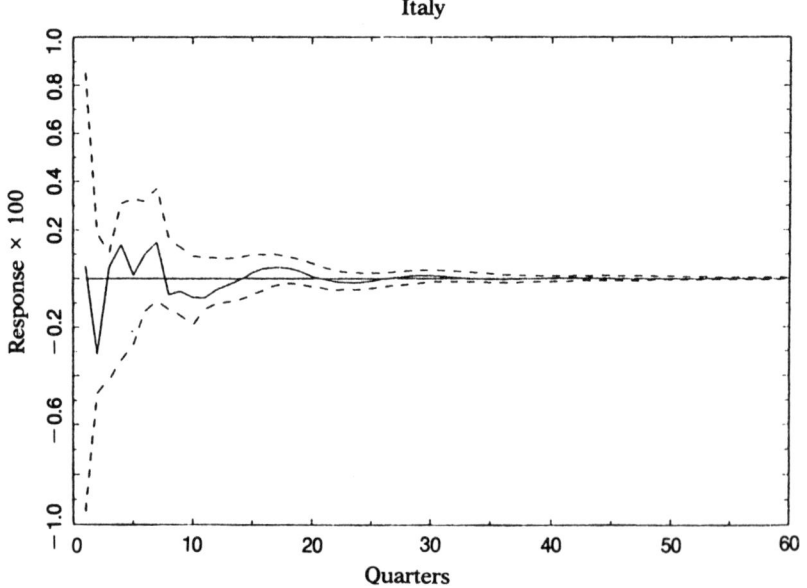

GRAPH 5 continued

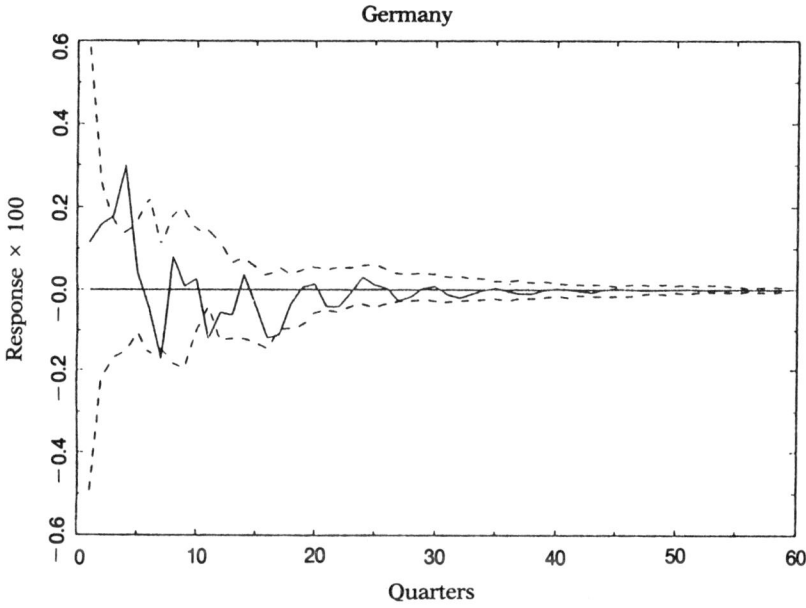

Germany

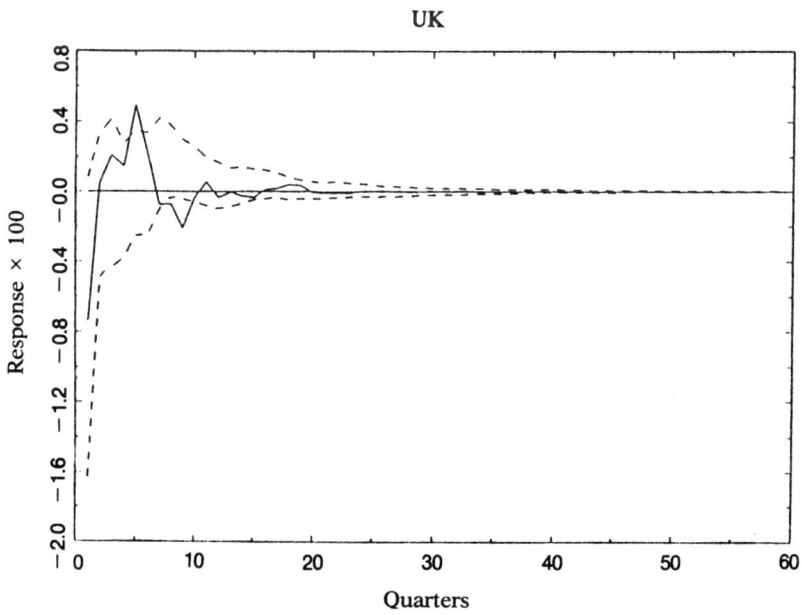

UK

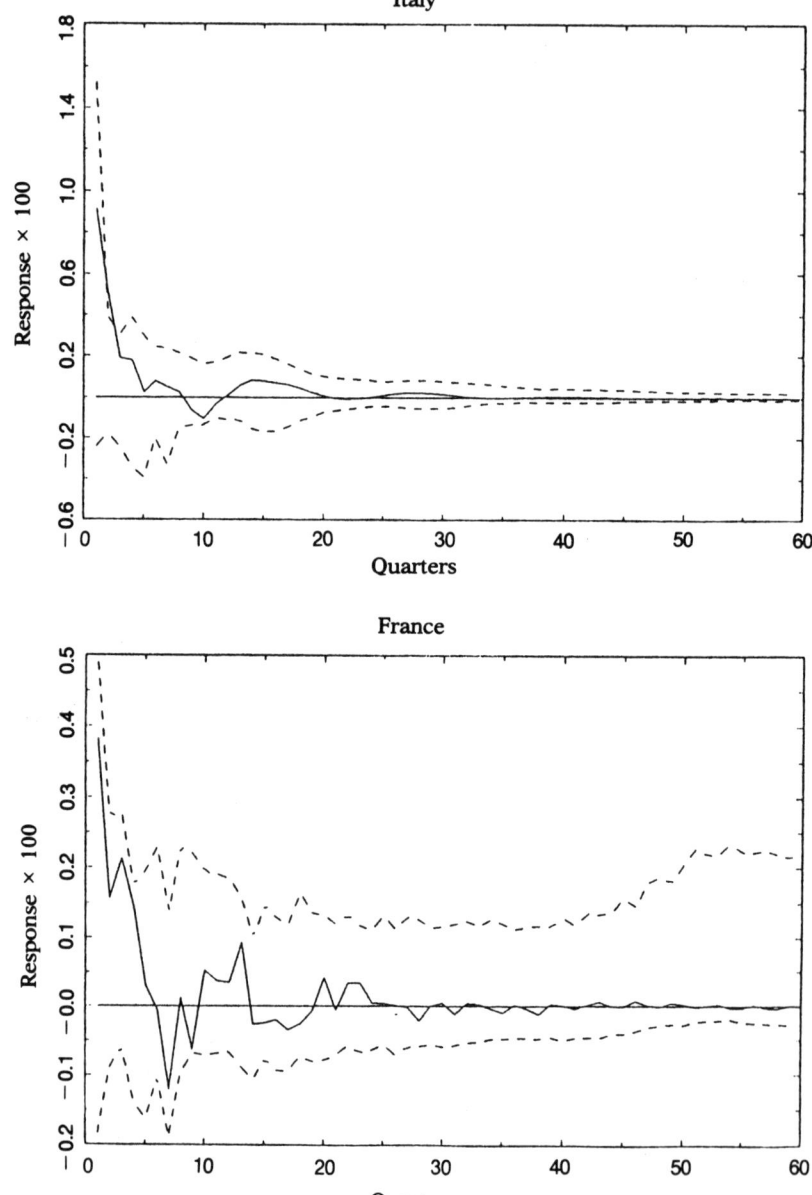

GRAPH 6

RESPONSE OF OUTPUT
TO A LABOUR SUPPLY SHOCK

GRAPH 6 continued

UK

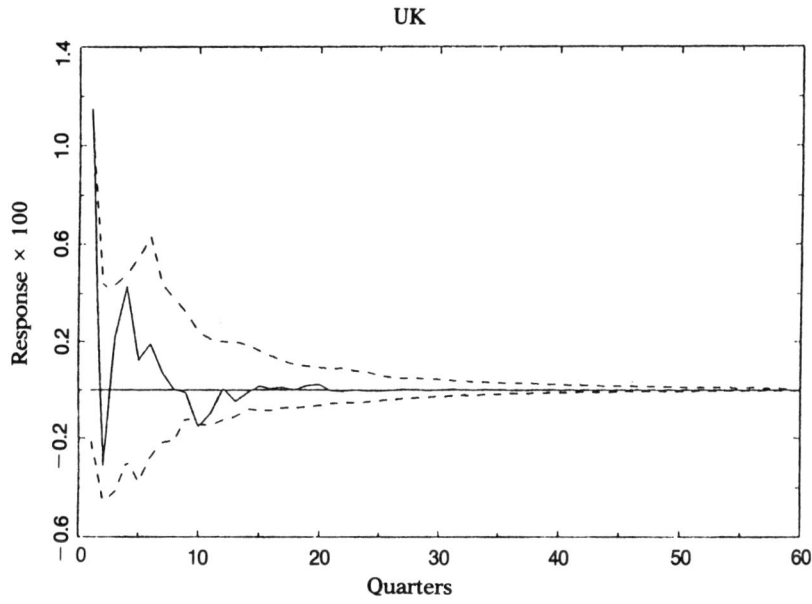

Germany

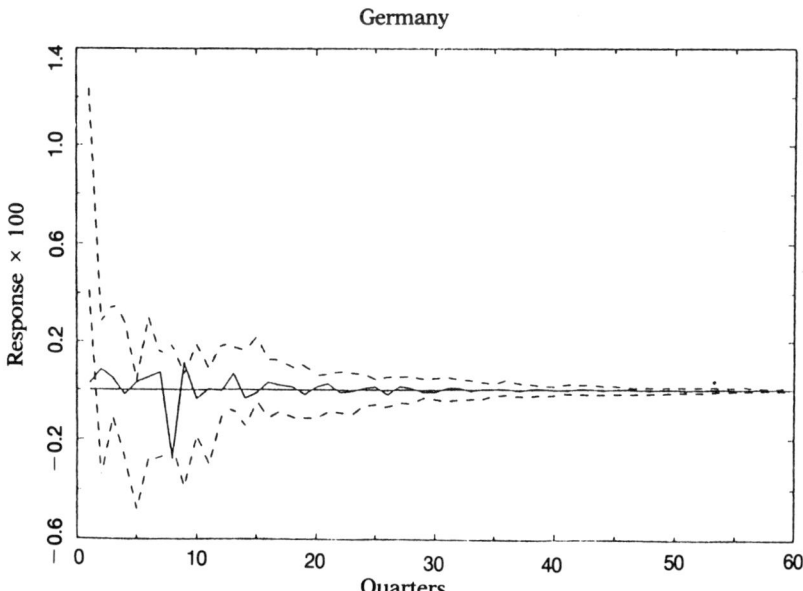

GRAPH 7

RESPONSE OF OUTPUT
TO A TECHNOLOGY SHOCK

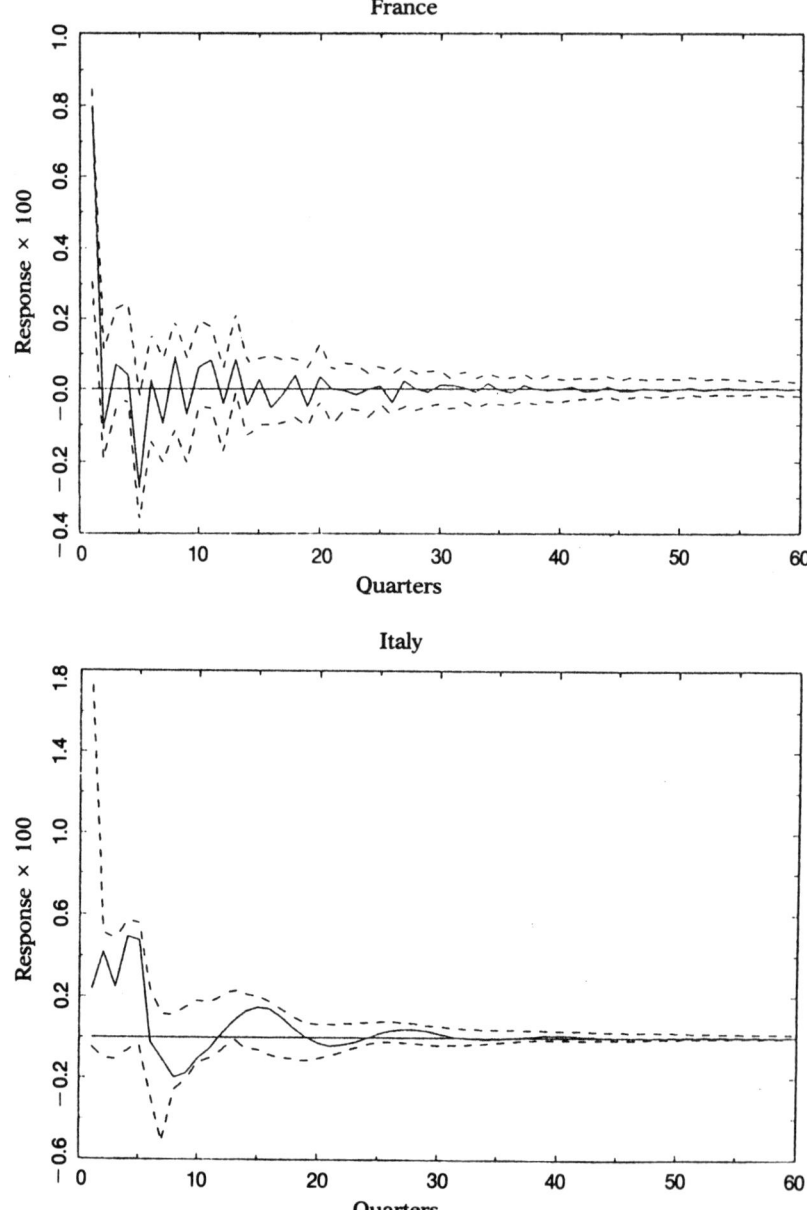

GRAPH 7 continued

Germany

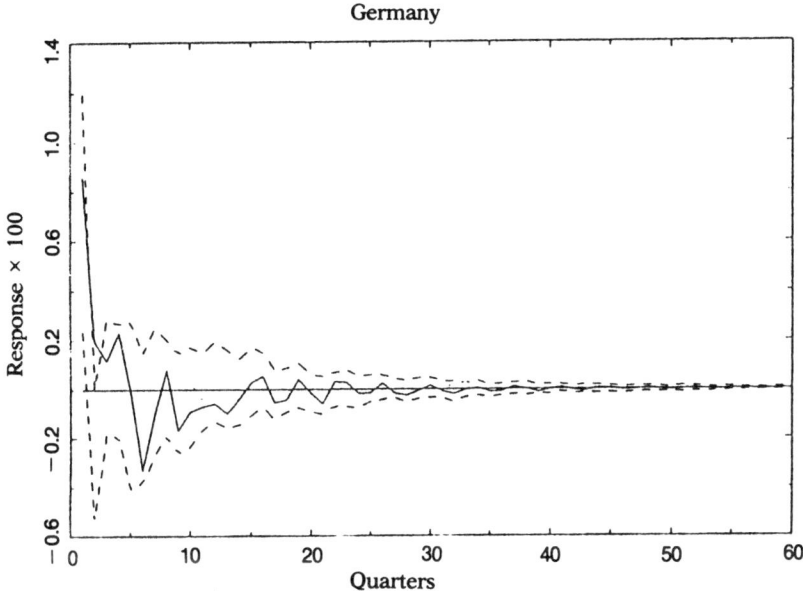

UK

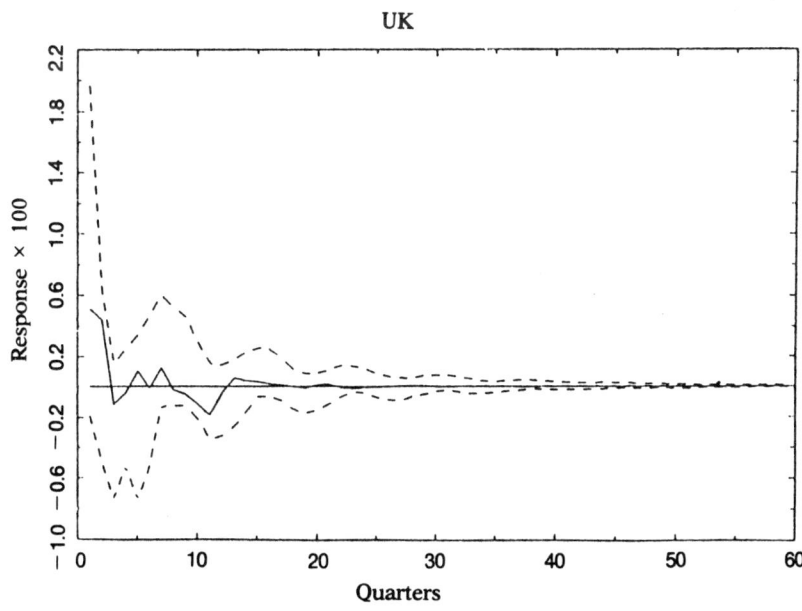

GRAPH 8

RESPONSE OF OUTPUT TO A DEMAND SHOCK

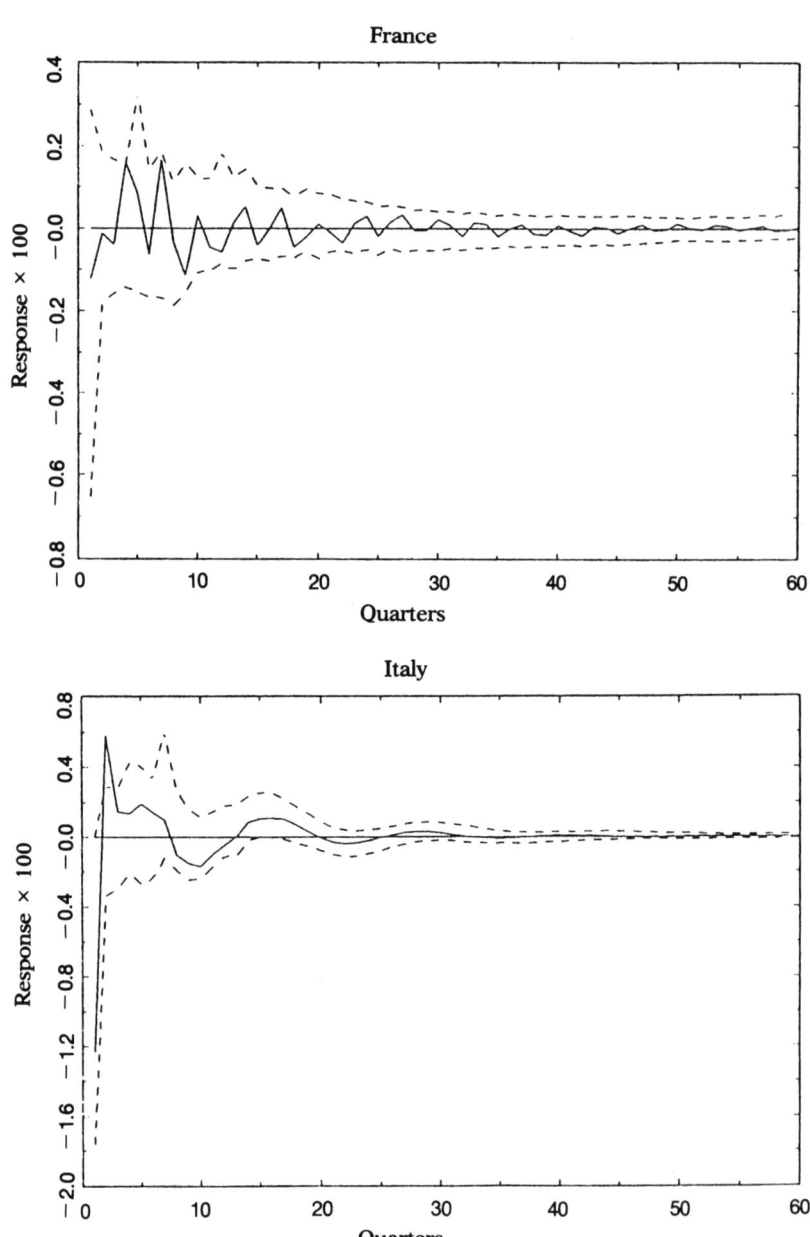

GRAPH 8 *continued*

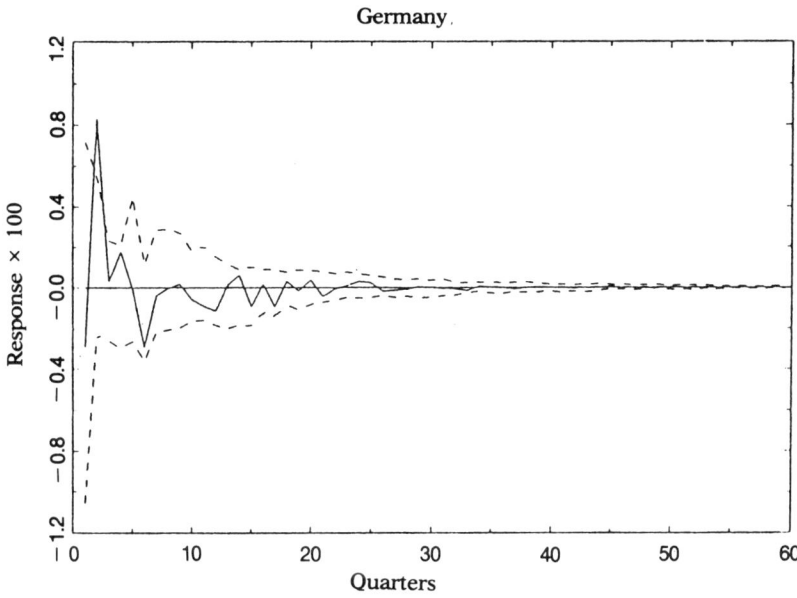

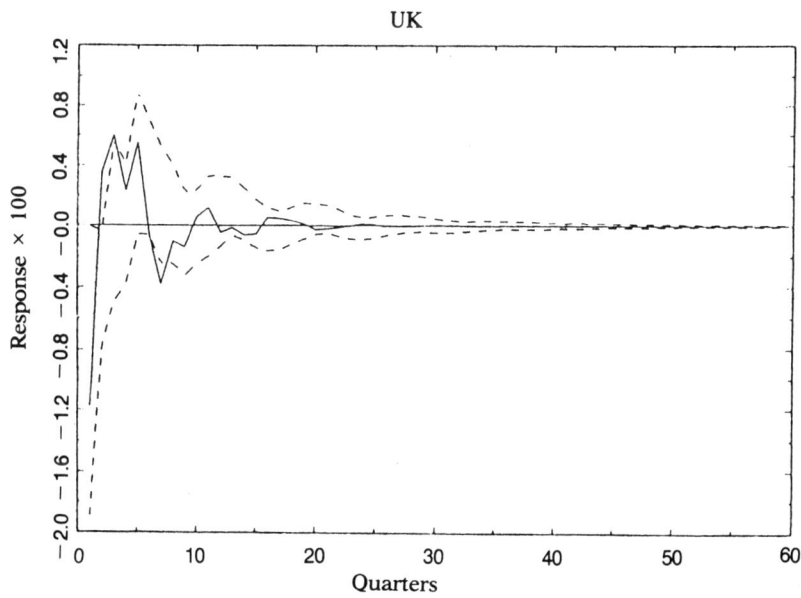

independently distributed, Our solution (Freedman [13], or Rayner [37]) was to follow a sequence of steps, starting from the estimated regression. For an autoregressive model, such as a *VAR*, the steps can be listed as follows: 1) estimate the equations; 2) center the residuals (this is a parametric correction, based on the hypothesis that shocks have zero mean); 3) resample with replacement the centered residuals (which are empirically independent and can thus be resampled). A series u_t^* of bootstrapped residuals is thus obtained; 4) construct the pseudo series on the basis of the initial conditions, the exogenous variables, the coefficient estimates for each equation and the bootstrap residuals. For instance, the bootstrap series of employment will be:

$$N_t^* = \hat{\alpha}_1 N_{t-1}^* + ... + \hat{\alpha}_p N_{t-p}^* + \hat{\beta}_1 Q_{t-1} + ... + \hat{\beta}_p Q_{t-p} + \hat{\gamma}_1 Q_{t-1} + \\ + ... + \hat{\gamma}_p Q_{t-p} + \hat{\phi}_1 D_{t-1} + ... + \hat{\phi}_p D_{t-p} + u_t^*$$

5) estimate the equations repeatedly on each of the *B* pseudo series constructed according to steps 1-4 (in our case, taking into account both the need to limit the computing time and the suggestions of Efron [10], we set $B = 1,000$); 6) construct the empirical distributions of the parameters of interest and compute the confidence intervals (in our case, the parameters are the *MA* coefficients of the *VARs* and the impulse functions).

From the figures, one can observe how the intervals do not always include the original estimates; Blanchard e Quah [2] adopting two standard errors bands (13) obtained also strongly asymmetrical intervals. This finding suggests that the estimates of the impulse functions may possess asymmetric bootstrap distributions. Efron and Tibshirani [11] discuss the case of the bootstrap distribution for the *OLS* regression coefficient in an *AR(1)* model: they show that it is asymmetrical, leading to non centered confidence intervals around the *OLS* estimate of the coefficient. Some preliminary investigations have indeed shown that the distributions of our impulse responses

---

(13) Note that this type of interval is optimal only if the estimators are normally distributed (EFRON - TIBSHIRANI [11]). Therefore, they imply a parametric assumption contradicting the non-parametric nature of the bootstrap.

have a similar shape (14). Such an asymmetry seems to be directly linked to the significance of the coefficients. In other words, the more distant from zero is the parameter, the more pronounced the asymmetry becomes and the thicker the tails of the distribution. This is potentially an important point. If proved, in fact, it would make the consequence of a bias in the estimates less serious, since the most critical parameters would also be the ones with more centered intervals. The results by Lütkephol [26] suggest that parametric corrections, such as the ones proposed by Efron e Tibshirani [11], could also be applied in this case. This is on our research agenda.

Looking at the results, the responses of industrial production to technology shocks (normalised by their standard deviations) are quite interesting. Strong analogies emerge. In all countries, the long-run impacts are positive and take similar values. Indeed, for France and UK, the elasticities in the long run are identical (0.6). It is slightly lower for Germany (0.4), whereas it more than doubles in the case of Italy (1.7). A visual exam of the confidence intervals show that these values are likely to be not significantly different (given that the VARs include constant terms, the elasticities have to be interpreted as deviations from trend). Differences among the countries emerge instead in the initial quarters. In Italy the diffusion of technical progress seems to occur more smoothly. After a strong initial impact, the level of output keeps rising, quite rapidly at the outset, more gently later on. It reaches its steady state target after about eight years. The response to a technological shock is faster in Germany. Here the peak is reached quite early, after five quarters. Immediately afterwards output declines rapidly, whereas the final convergence to its long-run value is achieved quite gradually. From these estimates, it would look as if the technological shock leads initially to an intense investment activity, overshooting the equilibrium level of production. Impulse functions for France and UK are quite similar. In both countries, initial gyrations are relatively modest and convergence to the long-run values occurs after a short time. However in the UK the initial overshooting persists for a longer period.

Labour supply shocks have similar effects on the industrial

---

(14) The hystograms are not reported for reasons of space.

outputs of all four countries. The initial responses are increasing everywhere, followed by a reversal of trend after a few quarters. Long-run targets are hit within three years. Deviations from trend are greater for Italy and the UK. In general, one can see how labour supply shocks take less time than technological shocks to exert their full impact. Wages need to adjust to the new labour market conditions in order for changes in the labour supply to have a permanent impact on output. Therefore, the time it takes to completely respond to a unit shock can be interpreted as an implicit measure of the degree of inertia in relative prices. As to the remaining impulse functions, it can be noted that the impact of a labour supply shock on employment is everywhere positive, albeit tiny in France (but the confidence interval lies in the positive quadrant predominantly). On the other hand, demand shocks have less predictable effects, displaying often negative elasticities. However the confidence bands are quite wide.

We can now examine our estimates of the permanent components of industrial output in the four countries. These are obtained by cumulating the effects of technological and labour supply shocks. The profiles of the permanent components are presented in Graph 9 together with the actual levels of output: the difference between the two is the cumulated sum of the demand shocks' effects. These are quite small. This result is quite typical in structural *VARs* decompositions (see for instance Shapiro and Watson [38]): the only exception is given by the paper by Blanchard and Quah [2]. In their work, however, demand effects can be overestimated, as they use the unemployment rate, which reflects both demand and supply factors, as a proxy for aggregate demand. In all countries, with the partial exception of France, the recession of the beginnings of the eighties is quite noticeable, with the actual level of output well below its permanent component. In Germany, the gap is more marked and prolonged, probably because of the policy enacted in 1982 to cut the public debt to size. Another common feature to all countries is the greater variability of the permanent component in the seventies *vis-à-vis* the eighties, which goes hand in hand with more pronounced fluctuations of actual production. Probably in that decade, the consequences of a worsening in the industrial relations' climate, which in our model are tantamount to a negative labour supply shock, were

GRAPH 9

OUTPUT (SOLID LINE)
AND PERMANENT COMPONENT

Italy

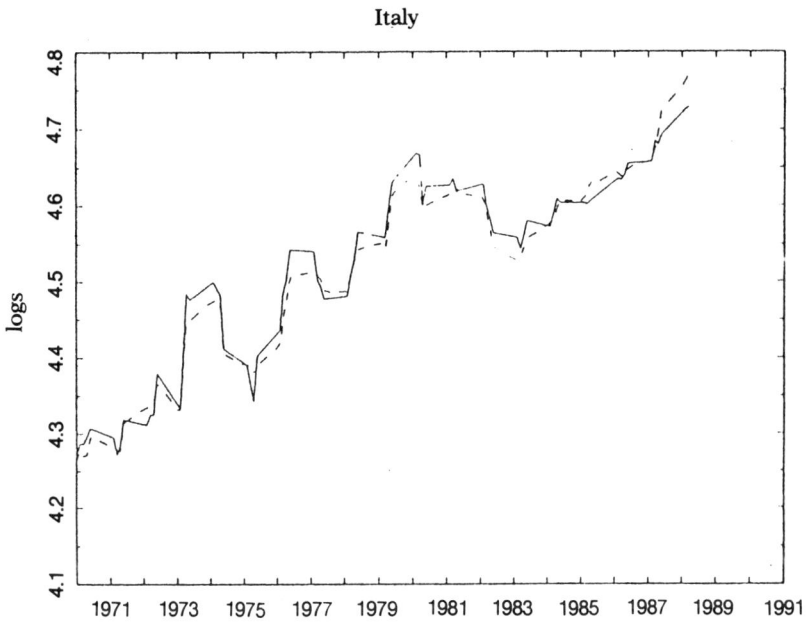

France

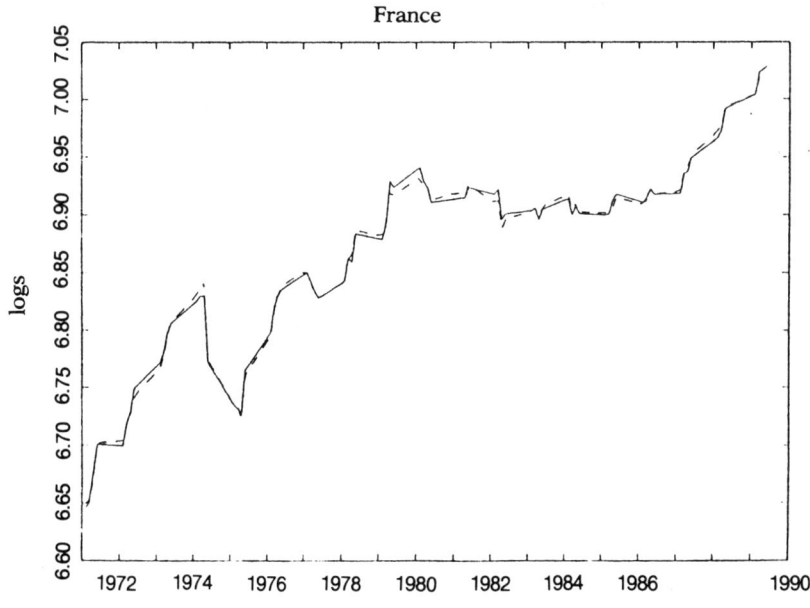

GRAPH 9 continued

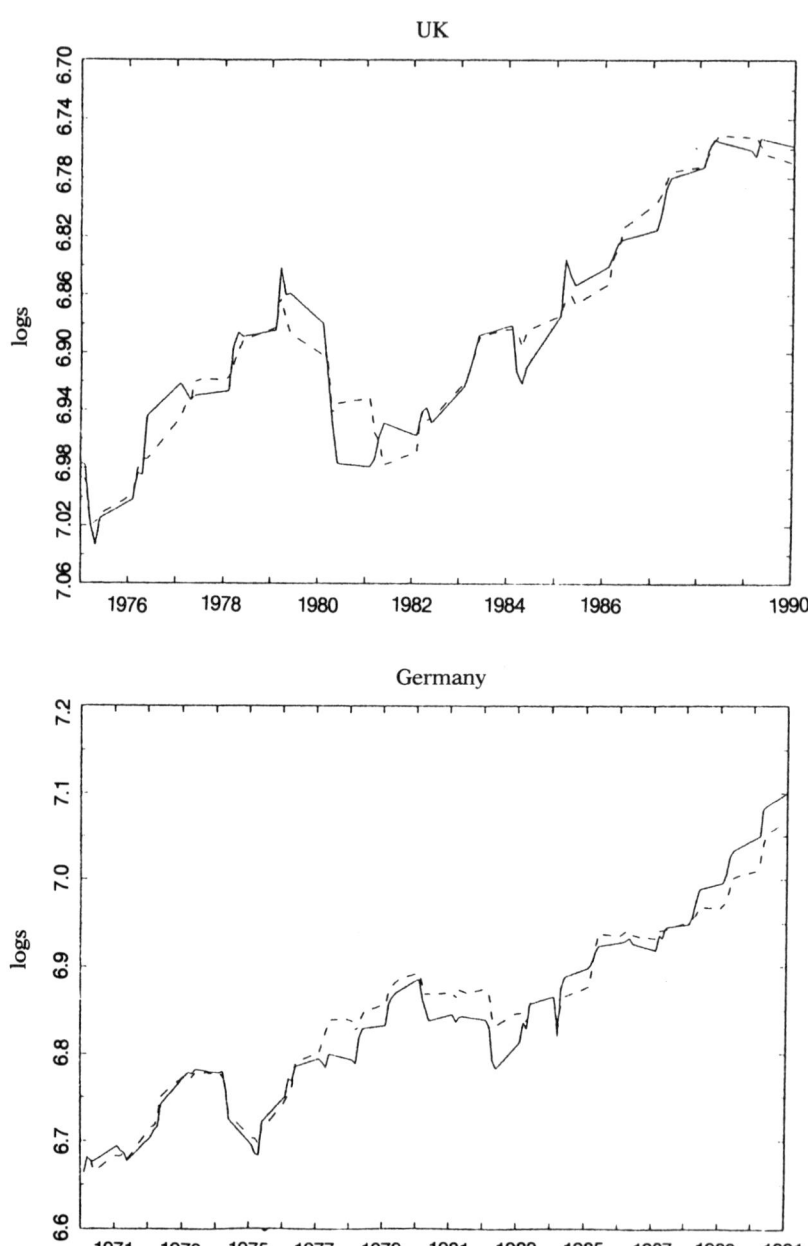

added to the two oil shocks. On the contrary, in the eighties both the actual output and its permanent component display a rapid growth, linked to positive technological developments.

In Italy and UK one can clearly observe both the contraction of the manufacturing sector at the beginning of the last decade and the following fast increase of production pushed by the introduction of new techniques and the abolition of some restrictive practices (in UK this was the so called Thatcher miracle). In the United Kingdom one can also see the overheating of the economy which took place around 1986, when the then Chancellor Nigel Lawson reduced tax rates, leading to a boom in consumption and a balance deficit. A more restrictive stance of economic policy followed as a consequence, as the picture clearly shows, reviving the "stop and go" policy of the earlier decades. Overall, output displays more variability than its permanent component (Table 3). In Germany too economists and authorities worried about a danger of overheating in the late eighties (Entorf et Al. [12] and the references therein). In fact our reconstruction shows how output was consistently above its permanent component. Its changes explain only about 60% of the variance of the output rate of change (a similar share was found for Italy). In France, on the other hand, there are no marked differences between the two profiles over the entire period, as is confirmed by the finding that first differences in the (log) permanent component explains up to the 95% of output variability. A possible interpretation is that French authorities managed to keep output in track with the underlying supply forces, at the cost however of a more subdue growth. On the other hand this explanation seems to contrast with the fact that

TABLE 3

VARIANCE DECOMPOSITION

	France	Germany	Italy	UK
(1)	1.04	0.64	0.78	0.50
(2)	0.95	0.64	0.76	0.38

Legend:
(1) $Var(\Delta Q^p)/Var(\Delta Q)$; Q^p: permanent component of output.
(2) R^2 of the regression of ΔQ^p on ΔQ.

serious mistakes in the conduct of economy policy were made, such as the reflation of 1981 which led to the franc devaluation. Our reconstruction is clearly unable to account for those events.

In conclusion, besides the interpretation of single events, always open to different interpretations, we feel that our results look quite reasonable. It is also of some confort that the same methodology, applied to different countries, produces outcomes which are directly comparable. This suggests that the method is sufficiently robust and can usefully complement more traditional means of investigation.

4. - Conclusions

The purpose of this work was in the first place to review some recent developments in the decomposition of time series into permanent and transitory components. Secondly, we wanted to assess the robustness of one of these methods, based on structural VARs, which has received a good deal of attention in recent times, by applying it to the industrial productions of four European countries: France, Germany, UK and Italy (for the latter we used results from a previous work by Gavosto and Pellegrini [15]). The yardstick we used in order to judge the goodness of the results was to check whether the final decomposition gave rise to plausible (and coherent) impulse responses to the primitive shocks. In that respect, our results appear to be satisfactory: responses have reasonable shapes and they look quite similar across different countries. Differently from Blanchard and Quah [2], our decompositions suggest that changes in the permanent component (which we assume to depend on supply factors) can explain a larger share of output variability than fluctuations in demand. Our future work will develop along two lines: on the one hand, we will try to investigate the optimality properties of inference for response functions based on resampling and asymptotic results; on the other hand, we will attempt to model the process of transmission of shocks across different countries, building on a recent work by Pellegrini [32].

* * *

Data Appendix

For Italy, see Gavosto and Pellegrini [15]. All the remaining data used in this paper come from OECD, *Main Economic Indicators*, various issues. Definitions are as follows:

Output: index of industrial production excluding buildings. Seasonally adjusted, 1985 = 100.

Employment: for Germany and UK, total number of employed workers times the average weekly hours worked, in manufacturing (excluding energy and building). Seasonally adjusted, 1985 = 100; France, number of employed in manufacturing.

Demand: for Germany and France, difference between the number of firms who say that the level of orders is above normal and those who say that is below; for UK, difference between the number of firms who say that the economic climate is positive and those who say it is negative.

BIBLIOGRAPHY

[1] BEVERIDGE S. - NELSON C.R.: «A New Approach to the Decomposizion of Economic Time Series Into Permanent and Transitory Component with Particular Attention to the Measurement of the Business Cycle», *Journal of Monetary Economics*, n. 7, 1981, pp. 151-74.

[2] BLANCHARD O. - QUAH D.: «The Dynamic Effects of Aggregate Demand and Supply Disturbances», *The American Economic Review*, n. 79, 1989, pp. 655-73.

[3] CAMPBELL J.Y. - MANKIW N.G.: «Are Output Fluctuations Transitory?», *Quarterly Journal of Economics*, n. 102, 1987, pp. 857-80.

[4] —— ——: «International Evidence on the Persistence of Economic Fluctuations», *Journal of Monetary Economics*, n. 16, 1989, pp. 331-4.

[5] CANOVA F.: *Detrending and Business Cycles Facts*, Mimeo, Firenze, Eui, 1991.

[6] CLARK P.K.: «The Cyclical Component of US Activity», *Quarterly Journal of Economics*, n. 102, 1987, pp. 797-814.

[7] CLARK P.: «Trend Reversion in Real Output and Unemployment», *Journal of Econometrics*, n. 45, 1989, pp. 15-32.

[8] COCHRANE J.H.: «How Big is the Random Walk in GDP», *Quarterly Journal of Economics*, n. 103, 1988, pp. 893-920.

[9] EFRON B.: *The Jacknife, the Bootstrap and other Resampling Plans*, Philadelphia, Siam-NSF, 1982.

[10] ——: «Better Bootstrap Confidence Intervals», *Technical Report*, Stanford, Stanford University, 1984.

[11] EFRON B. - TIBSHIRANI R.: «Bootstrap Methods for Standard Errors, Confidence Intervals, and Other Measures of Statistical Accuracy», *Statistical Science*, n. 1, 1986, pp. 54-76.

[12] ENTORF H. - FRANZ W. - KOENIG H. - SMOLNY W.: «The Development of German Employment and Unemployment», in DREZE J. - BEAN C. (eds.): *Europe's Unemployment Problem*, Cambridge (Mass.), MIT Press, 1990.

[13] FREEDMAN D.A.: «On Bootstrapping Two-Stage Least Squares Estimates in Stationary Linear Models», *The Annals of Statistics*, n. 3, 1984, pp. 827-42.

[14] GALI J.: *How Well Does the AD/AS Model Fit Postwar US Data?* Mimeo, Cambridge, MIT, 1988.

[15] GAVOSTO A. - PELLEGRINI G.: «Demand and Supply Shocks in Industrial Output», Roma, Banca d'Italia, *Temi di discussione*, n. 158, 1991.

[16] GIANNINI C.: «Topics in Structural VAR Econometrics», *Lectures Notes on Economics and Mathematical System*, Hedelberg, Springer-Verlag, 1991.

[17] GRANGER C.W.J.: «The Typical Spectral Shape of an Economic Variable», *Econometrica*, n. 1, 1966, pp. 150-61.

[18] HARVEY A.C.: *Time Series Models*, Oxford, Philip Allan, 1981.

[19] ——: *Forecasting, Structural Time Series Models and the Kalman Filter*, Cambridge, Cambridge University Press, 1989.

[20] ——: «Trends and Cycles in Macroeconomic Time Series», *Journal of Business and Economic Statistics*, n. 3, 1985, pp. 216-27.

[21] HODRICK R. - PRESCOTT E.C.: *Post-War US. Business Cycles: an Empirical Investigation*, Mimeo, Carnegie-Mellon University, 1980.

[22] KUZNETS S.S.: *Capital and the American Economy: its Formation and Financing*, New York, NBER, 1961.
[23] LIPPI M. - REICHLIN L.: «Permanent and Transitory Components in Macroeconomics» in THYGESEN W. - VELLUPILLAI K. - ZAMBELLI S. (eds.): *Business Cycles: Theories, Evidence and Analysis*, New York, New York University Press, 1989.
[24] —— ——: *Diffusion of Technical Change and the Identification of Trend*, Mimeo, Roma, Università La Sapienza, 1991.
[25] LONG J.B. - PLOSSER C.I.: «Real Business Cycles», *Journal of Political Economy*, n. 91 (2), 1983, pp. 39-69.
[26] LÜTKEPHOL H.: «Asymptotic Distributions of Impulse Response Functions and Forecast Error Variance Decompositions of Vector Autoregressive Models», *Review of Economics and Statistics*, n. 1, 1990, pp. 116-25.
[27] NELSON C.R. - KANG H.: «Spurious Periodicity in Inappropriately Detrended Time Series», *Econometrica*, n. 49, 1981, pp. 741-51.
[28] ——————: «Pitfalls in the Use of Time as an Explanatory Variable in Regression», *Journal of Business and Economic Statistics*, n. 2, 1984, pp. 73-82.
[29] NELSON C.R. - PLOSSER C.I.: «Trends and Random Walks in Macroeconomic Time Series: Some Evidence and Implication», *Journal of Monetary Economics*, n. 10, 1982, pp. 139-62.
[30] PAGAN A. - WICKENS M. (1989): «A Survey of Some Recent Econometric Methods», *Economic Journal*, n. 398, 1989, n. 962-1025.
[31] PELLEGRINI G.: *Trend stocastico e ciclo economico nella produzione industriale*, Doctor's thesis, Roma, Università «La Sapienza», 1990.
[32] ——: «Sharing Stochastic Trends», Mimeo, University College, London, *Department of Economics Working Paper*, forthcoming 1992.
[33] PERRON P.: «The Great Crash, The Oil Price Shock and the Unit Root Hypothesis», *Econometrica*, n. 57, 1989, pp. 1361-401.
[34] PERSONS W.: «Indices of Business Conditions», *The Review of Economics and Statistics*, n. 1, 1919, pp. 5-107.
[35] PICCOLO D.: *Introduzione all'analisi delle serie storiche*, Roma, NIS, 1990.
[36] QUAH D.: «The Relative Importance of Permanent and Transitory Components: Identification and Some Theoretical Bounds», *Econometrica*, n. 60(1), 1992, pp. 107-29.
[37] RAYNER R.K.: «Bootstrapping p-Values and Power in First Order Autoregression: A Monte Carlo Investigation», *Journal of Business and Economic Statistics*, n. 8, 1990, pp. 251-73.
[38] SHAPIRO M. - WATSON M.: «Sources of Business Cycle Fluctuation», in NBER: *Macroeconomics Annual*, MIT Press, Cambridge (Mass.), n. 3, 1988, pp. 111-56.
[39] SCHUMPETER J.A.: *Capitalism, Socialism, Democracy*, London, Unwin, 1943.
[40] WATSON M.W.: «Univariate Detrending Methods with Stochastic Trends», *Journal of Monetary Economics*, n. 18, 1986, pp. 1-27.

The Real Business Cycle Theory

Giuseppe Schlitzer
Banca d'Italia, Roma

1. - Introduction (1)

After a long hibernation, the business cycle theory began to take a new and vigorous interest in macroeconomic analysis starting from the 1970s (2). It is no coincidence that it was during this same period that the major market economies were experiencing a greater variability in the real income growth rates thus ending the period of sustained and almost uninterrupted growth which most of the industrialised economies had enjoyed after the second world war.

This renewed interest in the business-cycle theory, which coincided with the crisis of "Keynesian" economics, became increasingly identified with the profound rethinking of the macroeconomics which has taken place over the past twenty years. As we all know, this rethinking derived from the absence of solid "microeconomic foundations" in the prevailing model, i.e., from the fact that it was not at all clear how the aggregated relations derived from the precise rules of individual behaviour. The static character of the Keynesian model was

---

(1) The author would like to thank Paolo Annunziato, Alberto Bisin and Andrea Brandolini for their useful comments on a first draft of the article. The Banca d'Italia is in no way responsible for the statements and opinions contained in this article for which the author bears sole responsability.
Advise: the numbers in square brackets refer to the Bibliography in the appendix.
(2) In April 1967, a numerous group of economists from all parts of the world met, on the initiative of Lawrence Klein, to discuss the state and evolution of cyclical fluctuation phenomena. The proceedings of the conference are collected in a volume edited by BRONFENBRENNER [14] with the eloquent title *Is the Business Cycle Obsolete?*

a further cause of vexation (3); the subsequent addition of the accelerator mechanism and some dynamic price-wages adjustment relations were considered as lacking any justification in terms of the first principles of microeconomics.

The need to reconsider the neo-classical models of individual choice, extending them to dynamic situations, was directly associated to the role of expectations. In effect, the manner in which the latter's formation mechanism was conceived could have profound consequences for the foundations of Keynesian political economy (4).

For these reasons, analysis of the business-cycle based on intertemporal choice models in Walrasian equilibrium, hence called "equilibrium analysis", is centre-stage of any planned research in *New Classical Macroeconomics (NCM)*. Starting from the original asymmetric information models developed by Lucas and Barro in the 1970s (5), equilibrium business cycle analysis has gradually evolved into the so called *Real Business Cycle (RBC)* theory. Drawing on the tradition of the linear stochastic models first developed by Ragnar Frisch and Eugene Slutsky in the 1930s, the *RBC* approach, in the pioneer version presented in the early 1980s, furnishes an exclusively "real" interpretation of the business cycle. Within a general equilibrium model with no imperfections, the business cycle is generated by random impulses to technology and by the intertemporal optimisation of the players. The Pareto-optimality characteristics of the equilibrium here repropose the result of economic-policy inefficiency as had already happened with the asymmetric information models mentioned above.

The author is of the opinion that the use of an extreme version of the general equilibrium model and the Pareto-efficiency characteristic of the equilibrium achieved have ended up overshadowing the most important contribution of the "real" approach which essentially regards "methodology". Spurred by *RBC* theory, business-cycle analysis has in fact been enriched with extremely innovative elements.

---

(3) «A primary consequence of the Keynesian revolution was the redirection of research effort away from this question [Why is it that, in capitalist economies, aggregate variables undergo repeated fluctuations about trend, all of essentially the same character] toward the apparently simpler question of the determination of output at a point in time, taking history as given» Lucas [63], pp. 8-9).

(4) See Lucas [62] and Lucas-Sargent [66].

(5) The reference is to Lucas [59] and [60] and Barro [5].

On the theoretical plane, some interrelations between the growth and business cycle theory have been clarified while, on the empirical plane, the approach has not only led to a reconsideration of the utility of detrending the time series of a deterministic trend, thanks to the closer link between cycles and growth, but it has revised the very definition of econometrics, drawing it closer to that of one of its founding fathers, Ragnar Frisch. Moreover, as has been subsequently shown, neither the assumption that the business cycle is generated exclusively by technological impulses nor the Pareto-optimality of the equilibrium are essential characteristics of equilibrium analysis.

This paper attempts to illustrate and critically evaluate the contribution of the *RBC* theory to the business cycle analysis.

The paper is organised as follows. After having reviewed business-cycle models based on the misperception assumption and illustrated the reasons for their subsequent fall from favour (Section 2), the *RBC* approach is introduced (Section 3) and its effects as regards both economic analysis and econometric analysis and techniques is assessed (Sections 4 and 5). Some recent extensions of the original *RBC* model are then analysed (Section 6) and the conclusions drawn in the final section.

2. - Equilibrium and Cyclical Fluctuations

As explicitly pointed out by Lucas [63], *NCM* typically move within a general economic equilibrium model. Drawing on the thought of F. von Hayek, Lucas moves to oppose the Keynesian disequilibrium theory (6). The Arrow-Debreu model suitably adjusted to take account of market imperfections or incompleteness, would appear an ideal model for this purpose (7).

---

(6) «...Keynes chose to begin the *General Theory* with the declaration (for Chapter II is no more than this) that an equilibrium theory was unattainable: that unemployment was not explainable as a consequence of individual choices and that the failure of wages to move as predicted by the classical theory was to be treated as due to forces beyond the power of economic theory to illuminate» (LUCAS [63]).

(7) «Indeed, the Arrow-Debreu model is often said to be operational only under some unrealistic assumptions as full information, complete markets, and no diversity. Here, however, an alternative view is argued. The Arrow-Debreu model can ac-

The first effective application of the general equilibrium model to the business cycle was Lucas's "islands' model" [59], a variant of the standard overlapping generations model which utilised a device previously proposed by Phelps [75]. Lucas wanted to show that it was possible, in a Walrasian equilibrium model, to reproduce the relationship between price and production levels which is typical to business cycles and known as the "Philipps' curve". In this model the business players are dispersed in two completely separate markets and do not have complete information concerning the money supply and how the young generation agents will be allocated between the two markets. Since the agents are unable to distinguish between absolute and relative variations in the demand for the goods they supply, the result is that changes in the general price level due to variations in the supply of money stock are confused with changes in relative prices. The supposed changes in relative prices obviously lead the optimising agents with rational expectations to review the quantities supplied and demanded in the markets. The result is that unanticipated variations in the money supply cause "real" effects on the system and an inverse relationship between price and wage levels — one of the many versions of the Phillips' curve — while remaining within a framework of general economic equilibrium.

Lucas' model, later reproposed in an equally famous article (Lucas [60]), and by Barro [5] is nonetheless unable to generate any persistence in the effects of random impulses in money supply. These effects last only for the duration of the shock and are destined to exhaust themselves once the information is complete. Lucas [61] wished to remedy this shortcoming: the islands' model was reproposed with producer-agents which lived for ever and which consumed or invested in accordance with the classical model of capital accumulation. It was this mechanism of capital accumulation that enabled Lucas to establish a link between present and future which allowed him to obtain the desired result: non-systematic monetary and/or

---

comodate not only diversity in preferences and endowments but also private information, indivisibilities, spatial separation, limited communication, and limited commitment» TOWNSEND [97], p. 379. On the general economic equilibrium model according to «modern» lines, classical references are ARROW [3] and DEBREU [22] and [23].

fiscal shocks can generate cyclical fluctuations in output and procyclical movements in prices (8).

After having remained centre-stage of the economic debate for the rest of the 1970s, the popularity of Lucas and Barro's imperfect information models fell sharply (9). On the theoretical ground, the hypothesis of the players' lack of information regarding the general level of prices and the money stock began to appear, even to *NCM* theoreticians, unconvincing, given the speed with which information on such variables is available in reality. On the empirical ground, the evidence furnished by Sims ([88], [89] and [90]) and by Nelson and Plosser [72] was a major cause of perplexity (10). Using "vector autoregression" techniques on US economic data, Sims concluded that unanticipated disturbances in the money supply had practically no influence on the level of variability of output. Nelson and Plosser reached equally destructive results for the Lucas-Barro model (11).

The vexation with Lucas-Barro "monetary" models has led *NCM* business cycle analysis to turn to models which tend to favour "real" factors as the ultimate determinants of cyclical fluctuations, without obviously modifying the formulation in terms of the general equilibrium. One of the main contributions in this new direction is that of Grossman and Weiss [38]. The two authors propose a model in which the general level of prices and money supply are publically known but the agents have private information regarding the productivity of their

---

(8) The essential result of the Lucas-Barro model, that unanticipated monetary disturbances can affect real variables, appeared to be borne out at an empirical level by, amongst others, BARRO [6], ATTFIELD-DUCK [4] and KORMENDI-MEGUIRE [51].

(9) It is impossible to furnish a complete bibliography here of the numerous authors who have expressed reservations of varying nature concerning the validity or conformity to reality of these models. As regards *NCM*, BARRO [6] and the discussion by the author in the Introduction to BARRO [7] are useful references.

(10) But see also LITTERMAN-WEISS [7].

(11) In their 1982 work, the two authors test on numerous aggregate series for the postwar US economy the «unit root» hypothesis. The hypothesis holds that the series in question contain a stochastic trend together with a stationary component. The authors conclude that the hypothesis cannot be rejected and that monetary factors alone are responsible for bringing about the variance of the latter component whose contribution to the series variability is much less than that of the non-stationary component. The methodology used and the results obtained by Nelson-Plosser and Sims have been frequently criticised, see amongst all MCCALLUM [69]. See also the paper by LIPPI-REICHLIN [56].

investments. Nevertheless, information on the value of the real productivity of the investment at the level of the economy as a whole, which is an opportunity cost for the individual investor, is not perfectly channeled by the level of the stock market interest rate and prices. In conclusion the typical agent's investment function will depend on the difference between his own productivity and the rational expectation of aggregate productivity. The model shows that technology shocks at the level of the aggregate economy are propagated and amplified giving rise to fluctuations in the level of investment, and hence of income. The mechanism is therefore substantially similar to that of the Lucas-Barro "monetary" models, but the attention is now completely shifted in favour of "real" shocks.

Like the Lucas-Barro "monetary" models, the Grossman-Weiss "real" model appears to contrast with the fact that in reality data on aggregate variables is almost always abundant and immediately forthcoming. Indeed, the interest rates and prices on the money markets should reflect information regarding events which affect the economic system as a whole, even when the information on these events is dispersed at the single-player level (12).

The importance of the random impulses as the primary cause of cyclical fluctuations, which is central to the equilibrium models examined up to now, is therefore a characteristic element of *NCM* business-cycle analysis. The possibility of reproducing the typical shape of the economic variables, that is to say the series which show persistent fluctuations around a trend which does not however take on a periodic character using completely independent random variables was pointed out for the first time by Slutsky and Frisch around the 1930s. In a pioneering article in 1927, Slutsky showed that by simply using the moving averages of random "white noise" variables, one could obtain correlated series which produced the trend of macroeconomic variables. To the linear solution with

---

(12) It was GROSSMAN [33], [34], [35] and [36] who provided the theoretical assumptions, using a rational expectation equilibrium concept as an extension of the Walrasian notion of equilibrium, for the capacity of securities' prices and interest rates in the financial markets to aggregate the information dispersed between the various players and hence concluded that these markets are therefore "efficient". GROSSMAN-STIGLITZ [37], however, obtained results showing that no equilibrium existed.

damped fluctuations derived from a precise economic model, Frisch [31] added random disturbances which permitted the renewal of the wave motion. Frisch first attributed Wicksell with the idea that the business cycle can be kept alive via simple independent random impulses (13) and directly referred to Schumpeter's theory of innovations (14).

However interesting this debate on the nature of the final causes of the business cycle (the impulse problem in Frisch's terminology), macroeconomic analysis in the early 1980s nonetheless concentrated its attention on the manner in which the shocks were interpreted by the economic players and then propagated within the system (propagation problem).

3. - The Real Business Cycle Theory

As a consequence of the dissatisfaction with the imperfect information general equilibrium models, in the early 1980s the *NCM* analysis of the business cycle theory evolved within a model which favoured the role of "real" shocks but excluded imperfections of any type (15). The basis of this approach to *RBC*, as this line of *NCM* research is called, consists in showing how cyclical fluctuations can generate themselves in an Arrow-Debreu world with complete markets, lacking both monetary means and a state sector. In the model originally presented by Kydland and Prescott [52] and Long and Plosser [58], presented here in a simple and general version, the cyclical impulses are derived from stochastic disturbances in technology and the fluctuations are solely the natural consequence of the agents' intertemporal optimisation process (16). In addition, the

---

(13) See FRISCH [31] p. 198.
(14) See FRISCH [31] p. 203-5.
(15) For a discussion on the evolution of business cycle analysis in the last decade and other closely related topics see in particular LUCAS [64].
(16) Strictly speaking, random changes in preferences can be assumed (see PLOSSER [76]) but in fact the technology shock hypothesis has decisively prevailed. Recently, real equilibrium models have been proposed in which the business cycle is the result of movements in productivity generated not by a shock to the production function but by increasing returns to scale (see MURPHY-SHLEIFER-VISHNY [71]. We will not dwell on this class of models here since they belong to a very minor line of study.

equilibria triggered by the models are Pareto-optimal, which excludes any opening for stabilisation policy.

The base model can be described as follows: The economy is populated by a large number of identical consumers or optimising households with infinite lives.

The utility function of the typical household (consumer) is given by $U(c, l)$, where:

$$c = \{c_t\}_t \qquad (t = 1,...)$$

is the consumption sequence of the sole good present in the economy and:

$$l = \{l_t\}_t \qquad (t = 1,...)$$

is the leisure time sequence. The economy also comprises m identical firms. The typical firm has access to a neoclassical production function:

$$y_t = F(n_t, k_t; z_t),$$

where y_t denotes the output at time t, k_t and n_t respectively the available capital input at the start of period t (the good in the economy can in fact be "saved") and the labour input. Finally, z_t is a stationary stochastic process which summarises all the possible shocks which can alter the level of the production function for a given combination of inputs (17).

Both the consumers and the firms form "rational expectations" in the sense that they know the density function of the stochastic process z_t.

In the model, the households own the firms' capital; the firms hence rent capital and employ labour from the households at the start of every period, paying them at the market prices r_t and w_t respectively. In the same period they sell the goods produced at the market

---

(17) It should be noted that since only one good is present in the economy, the company's output here includes the part of the capital used in production but not depreciated.

price p_t (with w_t, expressed in an abstract unit of account) (18). The profits achieved at the end of the production process are therefore allocated to the households.

All the economic transactions can be imagined as being carried out at time zero in a single market.

At time zero the "representative household" plans its consumption, labour and investment activities for its entire life horizon, that is to say for each period t ($t = 1...$) and for each possible disturbance realisation sequence or "state of the world". This latter will be denoted by $z^t = (z_1, ..., z_t)$, where z_s indicates a shock realisation at time s.

Using capital letters to denote the quantities for the representative consumer, Π for profits, K^s for the capital rented to the firms, the consumer's optimum problem is therefore

(1) $\quad max \; V(C, L) = \Sigma_z \; Prob \, (z^t \mid \Omega_0) \; U(\{C_t(z^t)\}_t, \{L_t(z^t)\}_t)$

where Σ_z indicates the summation on all the possible states of the world and $Prob\,(z^t \mid \Omega_0)$ denotes the probability that state of the world z^t may be realised, conditioned by the set of information available in the planning period zero, Ω_0 — with respect

$$\{(C_t(z^t), I_t(z^t), K^s_{t+1}(z^t), N^s_t(z^t), L_t(z^t)) \mid \forall \, z^t\}_t$$

and subject to the constraints:

(2) $\quad \Sigma_t \, p_t \, [C_t(z^t) + I_t(z^t)] = \Sigma_t \, [r_t \, p_t \, K^s_t + w_t \, N^s_t(z^t)] + \Pi_t(z_t), \; \forall \, t, z^t$

(3) $\quad K^s_{t+1}(z^t) = (1 - \delta) \, K^s_t + I_t(z^t), \; \forall \, t, z^t \, ; \, K_1 \; \text{given}$

(4) $\quad C_t(z^t), K^s_{t+1}(z^t), N^s_t(z^t), L_t(z^t) \geq 0, \; \forall \, t, z^t$

(5) $\quad N^s_t(z^t) + L_t(z^t) = 1, \; \forall \, t, z^t$

(6) $\quad \lim_{t \to \infty} \lambda_t(z^t) \, K^s_{t+1}(z^t) = 0, \; \forall \, t, z^t$

---

(18) The model could be easily modified by assuming that the families sell rather than rent their available capital or that they cannot hold the capital directly but via shares. Other modifications can also be easily accomodated.

In model *(1)-(6)*, C_t, I_t, K^s_{t+1}, N^s_t and L_t are "indexed" to the state of nature z^t to indicate that the representative consumer chooses consumption, savings and leisure time *contingency plans*.

In particular, *(1)* generically specifies the consumer's preferences as regards the consumption and leisure time sequences; *(2)* is nothing more than a budget constraint (to be observed for every possible state of nature); *(3)* is the law of capital accumulation (19), with δ the depreciation coefficient; *(4)* imposes obvious conditions of non-negativity; *(5)* ensures that the sum of labour and leisure time is always equal to the overall availability of time, made equal to one for the sake of convenience; finally *(6)* is the so-called "transversality condition" (λ_t the Lagrangean multiplier on constraint *(3)*), necessary to ensure that the capital stock equals zero at the end of the consumer's life (20).

We will now consider the "representative firm". Having assumed for the sake of convenience that the firms rent capital, employ labour and sell their products to the families every period, the optimum problem is in this case single-period, namely:

(7) $\qquad \max \Pi_t(z^t) = [p_t Y_t(z^t) - r_t p_t K^d_t(z^t) - w_t N^d_t(z^t)]$

with respect to

$$\{(Y_t(z^t), K^d_t(z^t), N^d_t(z^t)) \mid \forall\ z^t\}_t$$

and under the constraint:

(8) $\qquad\qquad Y_t(z^t) = F(K^d_t(z^t), N^d_t(z^t)\ ;\ z^t)$

where the decisional values, in this case the demand for capital and labour, K^d_t and N^d_t, and output Y_t, are once again indexed at the state of the world z^t.

---

(19) We have avoided distinguishing between capital actually owned and that loaned out since it is obvious that in equilibrium these two quantities will always be equal (for $r > 0$).

(20) On the significance of this condition within the context of the Kuhn-Tucker method, see ROMER [81].

The Real Business Cycle Theory

The model's solution, which constitutes a "competitive equilibrium" is given by: a price sequence,

$$\{(p_t(z^t), w_t(z^t), r_t(z^t)) \mid \forall\ z^t\}_t$$

a contingency allocation plan:

$$\{(C_t(z^t), I_t(z^t), K^s_{t+1}(z^t), N^s_t(z^t), L_t(z^t)) \mid \forall\ z^t\}_t$$

for the representative consumer and a plan:

$$\{(Y_t(z^t), K^d_t(z^t), N^d_t(z^t)) \mid \forall\ z^t\}_t$$

for the representative firm such that:

(i) the contingency plan for the representative consumer solves the problem *(1)-(6)* for the given price vector;
(ii) the contingency plan for the representative firm solves the problem *(7)-(8)* for the given price vector;
(iii) all the markets are in equilibrium, i.e.

$$K^s_t(z^t) = K^d_t(z^t), \quad N^s_t(z^t) = N^d_t(z^t),$$
$$C_t(z^t) + I_t(z^t) = Y_t(z^t) - (1-\delta) K^s_t, \quad \forall\ t, z^t$$

Applying the first theorem of welfare economics allows one to establish an equivalence between allocations deriving from the competition mechanism, synthesised in the definition of equilibrium given above, and those obtained by using a fictitious social planner (SP). In this second case the problem becomes:

(9) $$\max V(C, L)$$

against:

$$\{(C_t(z^t), L_t(z^t), K_t(z^t)) \mid \forall\ z^t\}_t$$

under constraints *(3)-(7)* and the market clearing condition:

(10) $\quad C_t(z^t) + I_t(z^t) = Y_t(z^t) - (1 - \delta) K_{t}^{s}, \; \forall \, t \, , z^t$

where V is (generically) defined as in the representative consumer problem and obviously there is no further differentiation between the quantities demanded and the capital and labour supplies. The idea is that *SP* maximises the collective's preferences over the time horizon having the representative firm's technology at his disposal. The definition of equilibrium can at this point be consequently modified. Obviously the solution to the *SP* problem will be Pareto-efficient.

The similarity between the competitive equilibrium and that of the planned economy considerably simplifies a description of the model's mechanisms, permitting one to directly consider the optimum and contingency sequences of the aggregate variables referring to the *SP* or, if preferred, to a hypothetical Robinson Crusoe *(RC)* (21).

Once the preferences, the available technology (with the initial condition K_1) and the nature of the stochastic process of the technological disturbance z_t, have been specified, one may proceed to resolve the maximisation problem and obtain the decision rules for all the variables controlled by *SP*. In general, it will be seen that these decision rules can be expressed simply as functions of the "state variables" of the problem, i.e., of those variables which characterise the economy in every period t and over which *SP* has no control. For example, for the capital stock, consumption and labour supply it is seen that these rules take the form:

(11) $\quad\quad\quad\quad\quad\quad C_t = C(K_t \, , z_t)$

$$K_{t+1} = K(K_t \, , z_t)$$

$$N_t = N(K_t \, , z_t)$$

---

(21) On the interrelation between the *RC* and decentralised economy, in addition to the previously cited and well-known contributions by Arrow-Debreu, see LUCAS-PRESCOTT [65].

where K_t and z_t represent the "state variables", (it should be recalled that K_t is the capital stock at the *start* of the period) (22). It is demonstrated, in practice, that the equilibrium values directly depend on the realisations of technological shocks and hence the aggregate variables will fluctuate in concurrence with the latter.

Without investigating the model's results on the analytical plane, we will proceed to discuss how the *RBC* model is able to generate cyclical fluctuations purely as a consequence of the *SP*'s optimising behaviour in response to the realisations of technological shock.

It is assumed that *SP,s* preferences are of the additive-separable type, namely:

$$U(\{C_t(z^t)\}_t, \{L_t(z^t)\}_t) = \Sigma_t \beta^t u(C_t, L_t), \qquad 0 < \beta < 1$$

and the production function is $Y_t = z_t F(K_t, N_t)$, with $z_t > 0$. In this case any change in z_t is Hicks-neutral since it does not alter the optimum relationship which governs how capital and labour are employed in the production process. The higher z_t, the higher the marginal productivity of the two production factors. We will now assume that an unspecified period t, has a relatively high (above the average) value of z_t and we also assume that this value is completely "transient" as is the case when z_t is a "white noise" (that is to say z_t is identically and independently distributed with $E(z_t) = z > 0$ and Var $(z_t) = \sigma^2 \; \forall \; t)$. Since *SP* has rational expectations he is aware of the fact that this particular value of z_t is actually transient.

The above now opens various possibilities to *SP*. He can limit himself, for example, to leaving his labour supply unchanged and consuming all the additional product in a single period. In this case

---

(22) There are basically two methods for resolving *RC*'s intertemporal stochastic problem, however a formal description lies outside the scope of this note. The first is the Kuhn-Tucker method as described for example in ROMER [81] which uses the Lagrangean function. The other is the "dynamic planning" method which uses the Bellman equation (for a description of which see STOKEY-LUCAS [94] and SARGENT [86], Chapter 1). In most cases even after having selected preferences and technology so as to guarantee a "stable" solution the first order conditions provide non-linear difference equations which make it impossible to solve the problem analytically. Some useful approximation techniques have been identified however, for a brief description of which see PLOSSER ([76], p. 74), KING-PLOSSER-REBELO ([46], p. 204-6) and DANTHINE-DONALDSON-MEHRA [21].

the effects of a high (low) z_t will be felt solely within this single period. On the other hand, it is more logical to expect that *SP* does not wish to consume all the additional product in one period, but rather to distribute it over the entire time horizon, investing a part of it. In this case a specific value of z_t will also have an effect on future periods.

Nonetheless, it is more plausible that a high value of z_t will induce *SP* to intertemporally substitute his labour (leisure time), that is to say increase the current labour supply and eventually reduce the future supply (substitution effect). On the other hand, the greater production capacity will increase *SP*'s wealth and this will engender a tendency to reduce the amount of labour and increase leisure time for the current period and also future periods. The net effect on these two variables, labour and leisure time, cannot obviously be determined *a priori* since they depend on the relative strength of the income and substitution effects.

Hence the model demonstrates that even a merely transitory disturbance to productivity has generally "wide-ranging" effects, that is to say on all the decisional variables under consideration. If the disturbance to technology is not independent but serially correlated, the effects will be not only wide-ranging but also "persistent". If for example z_t follows a random walk process, i.e., $z_t = z_{t-1} + \varepsilon_t$ (with ε_t a white noise) a high z_t value (due to a high ε_t value) will increase expectations (conditioned by current information) of z_t for all future periods (23). In this case therefore, a favourable value of productivity *today* would directly increase the productivity expected in the future. And since the increase in wealth will be greater than in the case in which z_t is white noise, given that the *SP* also expects *Y* to remain high for the future, it is possible he plans lower investments, increased current consumption and a lower current labour supply.

Since the disturbances to the production function repeat themselves with different intensity in each period, the process described above will tend to repeat itself and the aggregate variables, which follow the *SP's* decisional rules *(11)*, will terminate as the cyclical tendency develops.

---

(23) It can be easily verified that in this case $E_t(z_{t+j}) = z_t$, $j = 1,...$

To summarise, in the *RBC* model, cyclical fluctuations are generated as the optimising agents' response to productivity shocks, while remaining within a perfect market framework. As Prescott puts it «...given the people's ability and willingness to intertemporally and intratemporally substitute consumption and leisure, it would be puzzling if the economy did not display these large fluctuations in output and employment...» (Prescott [78], p. 11).

4. - The Main Innovatory Features of the "Real" Approach

The *RBC* approach has two main innovatory features.

The first is that the roots of the model now being examined directly derive from the traditional capital accumulation models inaugurated by Ramsey [79] and followed mainly in the works of Cass [18] and Koopmans [50]. As we know, these contributions examine the problem of the optimum level of savings for a centralised economy in a deterministic intertemporal context (a subject known as the *Ramsey problem*). It is precisely as a consequence of its close interconnection with capital accumulation models that the *RBC* approach has ended up by proposing integration between the business cycle theory and growth theory. This is in clear juxtaposition to the previous tradition, which dealt with these two topics as separate branches of macroeconomics.

The integration of the business cycle theory with the growth theory has obviously also led to pervasive effects as regards statistics and econometrics. It is well-known that the most traditional practice, close to the idea that cycles and growth are separate phenomena, models time series of macroeconomic variables as given by the sum of a deterministic component representing the long-term component, normally the linear trend, plus a stochastic component of the *ARMA* type representing the cycle. If one accepts the idea that business cycle and growth are inseparably linked, as can be seen when even transient disturbances to technology influence the capital accumulation process, this type of representation is not necessarily adequate. And in effect we have seen how in the

RBC model the realisations of technological shock influence all the decisional variables under consideration, including capital stock (24).

The problem of possible interactions between business cycle and growth and the implications for processing data is by no means new to business cycle analysts. Burns and Mitchell, for example, in the introduction to Chapter 7 of their famous *Measuring Business Cycles* [15] state: «... business cycles are a development of late modern times. They emerged with the intensification of technical changes, the vast expansion of commercial life and industrial activity and the widening organization of economic life on the basis of making and spending money incomes. Cyclical fluctuations are so closely interwoven with these secular changes in economic life that important clues to the understanding of the former may be lost by mechanically eliminating the latter».

Thus, the *RBC* theory for the first time formalises this interaction between business cycle and growth within a general economic equilibrium model.

The approach's second important innovation is directly related to its empirical verification. Once the stochastic process for z_t has been specified, the appropriate functional forms for technology and preferences chosen and the values of the parameters and the initial conditions fixed, it is possible to obtain the *SP*'s decisional rules, simulate the trend of the significant aggregate variables and compare these trends with those encountered in reality. This is precisely the procedure followed in the contributions of Long-Plosser and Kydland-Prescott cited above which utilise models not very dissimilar to the *RBC* presented here but which we cannot comment further on here due to lack of space. To determine the model's parameters and various functional forms, it is possible and desirable to resort to data deriving from the observations available at both microeconomic and aggregate

---

(24) The topic has stimulated a theoretical debate which ended up also involving analysts of time series. At the moment the opinion that the stochastic trend should be modelled using a random walk would appear to prevail, on this matter see NELSON-PLOSSER [72], CAMPBELL-MANKIW [17], KING-PLOSSER-STOCK-WATSON [48], WATSON-STOCK [98]. In the italian literature we would mention the paper by PELLEGRINI [73]. For a more general critique of the traditional approach see PRESCOTT [78]. See also the criticism by LIPPI-REICHLIN to the random-walk hypothesis [55].

level as do Kydland-Prescott. The authors term this procedure "calibration" (25).

Within this calibration process, the determination of the stochastic process of technological disturbance is of particular interest. For this purpose Prescott [78] follows the methodology proposed by Solow [92] for the case of a production function with constant returns to scale. Solow demonstrates that for a function of the type $Y_t = F(K_t, N_t; z_t)$, assuming that the payments to the capital and labour factors are equal to their respective marginal productivity, the following relation holds:

$$g_t = q_t - r_t (K_t/Y_t) k_t,$$

where g_t is the rate of variation to the technological shock z_t, best known as *Solow's residual*, q_t is the growth rate of per-capita product and r_t is the price of capital, equal to its marginal productivity. If the time series for Y, K, N and r are available one can calculate the time series of *Solow's residual*, g, and from this easily obtain the time series of z. The latter is used to infer the stochastic process of z_t (26).

Once calibrated, the model can represent the time series of the significant variables as derived from the equilibrium solution and compare their moments with those of the real series. The *RBC* models therefore for the first time provide an example of how intertemporal stochastic models can be empirically tested through simulation exercises.

---

(25) KYDLAND-PRESCOTT [52], who use a single-sector model, assume that more than one period is necessary for the investment project to become a fundamental cause in explaining the cycle. They also assume a particular specification of preferences according to which utility depends on not only current but also past leisure time (a "habit formation" hypothesis). All this together with a suitable calibration of the model's parameters allow the authors to obtain time series for the main aggregates whose moments and level of correlation with output are very close to those which can be calculated for the US economy. LONG-PLOSSER [58], on the other hand, use a model with n sectors the output of which acts not only as final consumption but also as input for the other productions. The model, which uses simpler specifications for technology and preferences, is particularly adapted to "mimic" the co-movements among the various sectors of the economy.

(26) Applying its methodology to the US economy, Solow calculated that for the period 1909-1949 the production function had undergone a "shift", attributable to the "technology" shock, avering 1,5% per year. (see SOLOW ([92], p. 316).

The calibration of the model and comparison with the real series in terms of the moments is, to use Kydland-Prescott's terminology, *The Econometrics of the General Equilibrium Approach*, which counters the system equation approach typical of the Keynesian tradition (27). Kydland and Prescott refer directly to Frisch to justify the philosophy which subtends the equilibrium approach to econometrics. Frisch, who in 1939 together with other neoclassical authors including Irving Fisher and Joseph Schumpeter, founded the *Econometric Society* and was one of the leading promoters and editors of the journal *Econometrics*, which was the *Society* organ, held that «... (the) mutual penetration of quantitative economic theory and statistical observation is the essence of econometrics» (28). Under this new definition, econometrics would not be always and exclusively identified with the applications of the regression methods in their various forms or, more precisely, should not necessarily entail an "estimate" process. The methodology proposed by the *RBC* approach, which involves simulating the tendency of aggregate economic variables derived from a precise theoretical model to compare their moments with those of the corresponding series of the real economy is a full-blooded econometric application.

5. - The Weaknesses and Most Recent Developments of the Real Approach

An overall assessment of Kydland-Prescott's and Long-Plosser's contributions from an exclusively empirical viewpoint would conclude that the intertemporal stochastic model used manages to successfully repeat some "stylised" aspect of the business cycle, namely: 1) the persistent character of the fluctuations (in the sense that a variable remains below or above its own trend for more than one period); 2) the "co-movements" between the various aggregates (with a greater variability of investments *vis-à-vis* output and of the latter *vis-à-vis*

---

(27) See KYDLAND-PRESCOTT [53]. Some limits to the use of the calibration technique, in particular in those situations where there was a role for policy measures, were shown by INGRAM-LEEPER [42].

(28) Cited in KYDLAND-PRESCOTT [53], p. 162.

consumption); 3) the "co-movements" between the various production sectors. The result is certainly surprising if one considers that, as seen in Section 4, the model is based on extreme assumptions, i.e., on the total absence of money, government and frictions of any type; on perfect information concerning the current variables and rational expectations regarding future variables; on the absolute homogeneity of families and firms; on the exogeneity of technological progress and on a population which does not vary over time.

Despite its good capacity to reproduce the time series of the main macroeconomic variables of the US economy, the *RBC* model became subject to a series of criticisms. These targeted, on the one hand, on the model's extreme assumption and, on the other, on the nature and centrality of the technological shocks in explaining the business cycle.

As regards this latter aspect, there would now appear to be considerable empirical evidence that the business cycle cannot be explained in terms of a single exogenous cause on the supply side. Blanchard and Watson [13], for example demonstrated not only that the evidence shows that the business cycle should rather be explained by a plurality of causes, but also that there is no evidence to support the hypothesis that the cycle is generated exclusively by small and frequent shocks and not also by large and infrequent impulses.

The interpretation itself to attribute to the disturbance to the production function appears uncertain. To the extent that the model remains limited to representing a closed economy, z_t is destined to also represent the impulses which may derive from a change in the terms of trade, as for example in the case of an "oil shock" (29). Furthermore, as long as a monetary-credit sector is not specified in the model, z_t will also represent the effects which a change in the regulation of the financial and credit markets may engender; for example, a change in the reserve requirements imposed on the banking system by the monetary authorities. These changes alter the cost of financial services for the industrial sector and should be correctly classified among shocks of a real and not monetary nature (30). On the other hand, even if we limit ourselves to interpreting z_t in

---

(29) See the recent contribution of KIM-LOUNGANI [43], where the effects of energy factor shock is made explicit on an *RBC* model.
(30) See PLOSSER [77].

terms of purely technological changes, doubts still linger concerning its correct interpretation. If we wish to venture beyond an explanation which remains within the simplistic framework of "changeable weather", and z_t is therefore taken as indicative of the level of "technological knowledge", then reductions in z_t which entail a fall in the production function, would be seen as representative of a full-blooded "technological regression" situation.

Numerous doubts have also been raised concerning the Solow-Prescott procedure of "quantifying" the technological disturbances. Hall ([39] and [40]), for example, has reinterpreted the variations in *Solow's residual* in terms of variations in the mark-up of prices on marginal costs which is typical of those markets which have more or less monopolistic firms. Other authors have at the same time pointed out that in conditions of price rigidity, the procyclical tendency of *Solow's residual* could be attributed to the presence of "labour hoarding" phenomena resulting from the deferment of aggregate demand and not at all from technological changes (31). Finally, it is by no means certain that productivity shocks, as measured by *Solow's residual*, are actually exogenous as theory would have them. Evans [30] has very recently shown, using US economic data, that Solow's measure is not independent of the influence exercised by monetary and fiscal policy variables (32).

Numerous attempts have been made in recent years to modify or extend the original *RBC* model to reduce the number of restrictive hypotheses and hence improve the degree to which it matches data from the real economy. As has been pointed out in many of these subsequent attemps, the assumption that the shocks considered are real in nature and the outcome is that the equilibria are Pareto-optimal, as is the case in the pioneer contributions by Long-Plosser and Kydland-Prescott, is not a necessary condition for the *RBC* approach (33). At least in theory, the model can be gradually made more complex through the introduction of the public sector, money, va-

---

(31) See BURNSIDE-EICHENBAUM-REBELO [16] and ROTEMBERG-SUMMERS [82].
(32) In addition to the contributions now cited in the text, see SUMMERS [95], MANKIW [67], MCCALLUM [69] and [70], EICHENBAUM [27], BERNANKE-PARKINSON [12] and ENTORF [29].
(33) on this point see for example PLOSSER [76].

rious types of external factors and information or any other types of differences among the economic agents, all of which can alter the results to the point of justifyng an economic-policy intervention. As will be seen below, some of these extensions are suited to an interpretation of the cycle which is not exclusively based on a productivity shock. However, most of these extensions remain at a preliminary stage of analysis and still appear unsatisfactory (34).

Three of the possible extensions of the intertemporal stochastic model merit particular mention, not so much for the manner of their realisation but rather because they represent a first, necessary evolution of the original model.

The first extension regards the treatment of the labour market. In effect, one of the major problems of the *RBC* model, more precisely of its Kydland-Prescott version, is that it is unable to take into account some important characteristics of this market, in particular the fact that the level of variability in hours worked is actually much higher than that simulated by the model. The particular form of the utility function employed by the two authors (35) only partially succeeds in avoiding this inconvenience. Hansen [41] attempted to right the problem by introducing an "indivisibility" in a single person's labour supply. The latter, in practice, is destined to work a predetermined number of hours or, alternatively, not work at all. The Hansen model as it stands is capable of generating much wider values for the variability of the hours worked input. However, the attempt does not develop beyond a mere exercise aimed at highlighting the utility of the "indivisibility" hypothesis. The model in fact leaves the decision regarding the person's destiny with regard to working or not to a lottery and the person is remunerated regardless of the lottery's outcome. It turns out that the welfare of those who "lost" the lottery and are thus destined to remain unproductive is greater that those active in the labour market.

A second extension of the original *RBC* model involves the introduction of monetary means. Among the main contributions in

---

(34) It is impossible to deal with the numerous extensions (modifications) of the *RBC* model here. An extensive bibliography and a description of the model's possible extensions can be found in KING-PLOSSER-REBELO [47].

(35) See note (26).

this field are those by Eichenbaum and Singleton [28] and Cooley and Hansen [19] who use a "cash in advance" constraint. Since such models assign no role either to price and/or wages inelasticities or to imperfections in information, the cycle's characteristics are not in the least altered by the inclusion of money (36). King and Plosser [45] made a more general attempt, assuming the presence of banks within the "monetary" sector. Here again though the model remained based on the assumption of perfect markets, which would appear to run against the recent evolution of the theory of financial institutions, which remains solidly based on the assumption of asymmetric information (37). In short, these attempts appear more aimed at justifying the use of purely real cycle models rather than making the models more realistic. As a matter of fact, on a more general ground, this strand of thought would appear to be dominated by the opinion that «... the role of money in an equilibrium theory of growth and fluctuations remains an open area for research». (King-Plosser-Rebelo [46], p. 196) (38).

The third, most recent, evolution of the *RBC* model, which unlike the other two is much more promising, involves consideration of the market forms with imperfect competition and price and wage inelasticity. The extensions in this direction in fact provide a link to some topics which are specific to *New Keynesian Economics (NKE)* thus throwing a totally new light on possible developments of the cyclical fluctuations theory.

It is known how this latter strand of thought has been concentrat-

---

(36) «We conclude that if money does have a major effect on the cyclical properties of the real economy it must be through channels that we have not explored here» (see COOLEY-HAUSEN [19], p. 735).

(37) This is in both DIAMOND-DYBVIG's [25] approach based on "liquidity risk" and in DIAMOND's [24] "monitoring" approach.

(38) There have recently been proposed some attempts (see among others TOWNSEND [96], KIYOTAKY-WRIGHT [49] and GINTIS [32]) to modify the Walrasian general equilibrium model and allow a role for money as an exchange medium. Nonetheless, at the moment, it is impossible to foresee, also in view of the analytical complexity of these contributions, how they can be efficiently integrated in the cyclical and growth intertemporal models. Leaving aside the theoretical problems, the empirical debate continues between those who consider monetary disturbances the main cause of cyclical fluctuations, of these see in particular the paper by ROMER-ROMER [80], and those, for the most partisans of the *RBC* approach, who emphasise real disturbances, whose position is summarised in PLOSSER [77].

ing on analysis of non-Walrasian markets in its attempt to produce a microfounded Keynesian theory (39). However, this has taken place mainly within single-period and deterministic contexts. On the other hand, the assumption of perfectly competitive markets would not appear to be indispensable for equilibrium analysis. Kydland and Prescott, for example, state, without any reference to perfectly competitive markets: «By general equilibrium we mean a framework in which there is an explicity and consistent account of the household sector and of the business sector. To answer some research question, one must also include a sector for the government, which is subject to its own budget constraints. A model within this framework is specified in terms of the parameters that characterize preferences, technology, information structure, and institutional arrangements». Kydland and Prescott ([53], p. 168) (40).

In this sense, the attempts to integrate cycle analysis according to the intertemporal stochastic approach and some topics dear to *NKE* would appear to be a completely natural development for business-cycle study. Furthermore, it is precisely in these cases that the equilibria finish by being Pareto-efficient and there emerges a role for political interventions.

With regard in particular to the possibility of incorporating imperfectly competitive market forms, it has already been noted that this could have important effects on the *RBC* model, if nothing else at the empirical level. On the other hand, numerous authors have recently demanded that these forms of market be used within business

---

(39) See on this subject the collection of papers edited by MANKIW-ROMER [68].

(40) Strictly speaking, the subject of uncertainty in economic analysis and the related mechanism of the formation of expectations are another field in which the Keynesians and Neo-classicists have clashed. The subject does not lie within the scope of this *excursus* and hence will not be discussed here. With reference to the business cycle, the use of the hypothesis of rational expectations would be justified on the base of the consideration that «Insofar as business cycles can be viewed as repeated instances of essentially similar events, it will be reasonable to treat agents as reacting to cyclical changes as "risk" or to assume their expectations are rational, that they have fairly stable arrangements for collecting and processing information, and that they utilize this information in forecasting the future in a stable way, free of systematic and easily correctable biases». (LUCAS [63] p. 224). Apart from the doubts regarding the capacity of individuals to acquire all the information available to draw up rational expectations, it should be pointed out that some recent contributions have highlighted that this hypothesis can be inconsistent with the first principles of microeconomics. On this subject, in addition to the often-cited PESARAN [74], see also BENASSY [10].

cycle models — and in macroeconomic analysis in general — as a result of considerations of both a theoretical and empirical nature (41).

One of the most interesting attempts to incorporate the non-competitive market forms in an intertemporal stochastic model is that by Rotemberg and Woodford [83], who analyse in an oligopolitic market framework the effects on the business cycle of demand shocks, the latter represented by variations in military spending. In addition to the specific contribution by these two authors, it should be noted that the inclusion of imperfect market forms enables one to modify a fundamental aspect of the intertemporal stochastic model. In a perfectly competitive market, the labour demand curve is determined by the condition of equality between the marginal productivity of labour and real wages and is altered according to the technological shock realisations. In this situation, the effects of a aggregate demand shock on the level of employment and hence output can only derive from falls in the labour supply curve which, conversely, is dependent on other variables and not just productivity shock. Since empirical evidence would appear to favour the assumption that cyclical fluctuations follow oscillations in the labour demand curve and, hence, real wages are procyclical (42), the RBC model ends up by not recognising any role for aggregate demand shocks in business-cycle analysis. Conversely, when there are firms with market power, the labour demand curve becomes dependent on the level of mark-up on marginal costs. In this case a change in aggregate demand can have an effect on the level of economic activity through labour demand if it acts on the mark-up itself. Moreover the empirical evidence would appear to favour the hypothesis of a controcyclical rather than a procyclical mark-up (43).

---

(41) Among the empirical contributions see in particular HALL [39], [40] and LEBOW [54].

(42) See in particular AKERLOF-ROSE-YELLEN [2].

(43) The reasoning can be illustrated considering a neo-classical production function of the type $Y = F(K, L; z)$, where z is the technology shock. In the case of perfectly competitive markets, the first order condition for L, $F_L(K, L; z) = w$, where w is real wage, implicitly defines a labour demand function of the type $L = L(w; K, z)$. In this case the labour demand curve shifts in tandem with changes in z as well as K and the aggregate demand shocks can influence the labour market equilibrium solely by acting

The role of demand shocks, in particular those of monetary origin, is further increased if one considers price and/or wage inelasticities. It is widely recognised, even by neo-classical authors, that there is considerable empirical evidence that monetary shocks can influence short-term economic activity and that this influence is normally due to nominal inelasticities (44). *NMC*'s attitude to price and wage inelasticities does not appear, on the other hand, aprioristic and prejudicial but would appear justified given the convincing interpretation of said inelasticities in terms of the traditional decision theory. And in fact, despite the contributions to this furnished by *NKE*, the theoretical aspects of this topic remain open. In this regard, we would mention a recent attempt by King [44] to examine the consequences on cyclical fluctuations of nominal price and wages inelasticities introduced in accordance with some *ad hoc* relations in an intertemporal stochastic model with a "cash in advance" constraint. While unsatisfactory analytically, King's contribution should be mentioned for having highlighted how the introduction of nominal inelasticities allows a further increase in the degree of matching between the cycle generated by the capital accumulation model and that observed in real life. In particular, it is possible to repeat the temporary impact money supply variations produce on real variables, generally known as *"triangular response"* (45).

Another interesting attempt to provide a link to *NKE* topics is that by Danthine and Donaldson [20] who include a wage formation mechanism of the type analysed by the *Efficiency Wage Theory* in an *RBC* model. In this case, the firm may not find it convenient, even in the presence of an excess labour supply, to reduce the nominal wage since a direct link between the latter and the productivity or "effi-

---

on the labour supply curve. Conversely, in the case of imperfectly competitive markets, it is easy to show that the optimum condition becomes $F_L(K, L; z) = mw$ where m is the mark-up of prices over marginal costs. In this case the labour demand curve is implicity defined as $L = L(w; K, z, m)$, with $F_{LL} < 0$, $L_m < 0$. The demand shocks can therefore induce slips of the same sign in the labour demand curve when they are such as to induce changes in the opposite sense of m, which implies a countercyclical mark-up (on the countercyclical character of the mark-up see, amongst others, ROTEMBERG-WOODFORD [84]).

(44) Amongst others and in addition to the contributions of BARRO [5] and [6] see also BARRO-RUSH [8].

(45) On this subject, in addition to KING [44] cited above, see also BARRO-RUSH [8].

ciency" of the workers is hypothesised (46). The move away from the Walrasian model is here due to the introduction of an assumtion of wage setting by the companies and also the possible nominal wage inelasticities, generated by the assumed wage setting. Danthine and Donaldson show how, in the case where the individual worker's commitment also depends on the wages which can be potentially obtained from companies other than the one where he is presently employed, the competitive equilibrium can be characterised by an excess or shortfall in investment levels *vis-à-vis* the equilibrium which would be obtained in the centralised version of the model, since the companies end up by neglecting the external effects of their own investment decisions on the efficiency of the workforce employed.

6. - Concluding Considerations

The *RBC* theory which we have attempted to illustrate in this paper has furnished a substantial contribution to developing the "equilibrium" approach to business cycle analysis. It has allowed clarification of interesting aspects of the propagation problem, namely the manner in which unexpected disturbances can propagate themselves within the economic system giving rise to cyclical phemonema. The explanation given is not that of a mysterious malfunctioning of the economy, but rather of the optimising behaviour of the economic players. Some possible interrelations between the business-cycle and growth theories have thus been brought to light with decisive consequences not only on the strictly theoretical ground, but also as regards statistical-economic practice.

Nonetheless, the new approach leaves various problems unresolved. Considerable theoretical and empirical perplexities have arisen from the attribution of the role of driving forces of cyclical fluctuations to technological disturbances alone. Neither has it been proven that it is possible to interpret *Solow's residual* in terms of changes in the level of technology.

---

(46) The development of this theory is due to contributions from various authors, but see in particular SOLOW [93], SALOP [85], AKERLOF [1] and SHAPIRO-STIGLITZ [87].

The paper has examined some recent developments in the new approach. Of these, of particular promise are those which provide a link to *NKE*, modifying the intertemporal stochastic model with non-Walrasian market forms, thus allowing the demand factors a role in explaining the cyclical fluctuations and possibly also economic policy interventions. Some other of these developments appear unsatisfactory, in particular those which attempt to introduce money and credit.

Setting aside one's judgement of the "real" approach as "cycle theory", one should emphasise its methodological contribution. The Kydland-Prescott models demonstrated that intertemporal stochastic general equilibrium models could be used to draw quantitative conclusions. This new approach has enabled a new and broader definition of "econometrics" to emerge, a definition which appears closer to the conception of its founding fathers. In its new version, empirical verification of economic models is no longer limited to estimating equations or systems of equations but also tends to include simple simulation analysis as it is carried out by *RBC* theoreticians.

BIBLIOGRAPHY

[1] AKERLOF G.A.: «Labor Contracts as Particular Gift Exchanges», *Quarterly Journal of Economics*, n. 4, 1982.
[2] AKERLOF G.A. - ROSE A.K. - YELLEN J.L.: «Job Switching and Job Satisfaction in the US Labor Market», *Brookings Papers on Economic Activity*, n. 2, 1988.
[3] ARROW K.J.: «An Extension of the Basic Theorem of Classical Welfare Economics», in NEYMAN J. (ed.): *Proceedings of the Second Berkeley Symposium on Mathematical Statistics and Probability*, Berkeley, University of California Press, 1951.
[4] ATTFIELD C.L.F. - DUCK N.W.: «The Influence of Unanticipated Money Growth on Real Output: Some Cross-Country Estimates», *Journal of Money, Credit and Banking*, n. 15, 1983.
[5] BARRO R.J.: «Rational Expectations and the Role of Monetary Policy», *Journal of Monetary Economics*, n. 2, 1976.
[6] ——: «Unanticipated Money and the Economic Activity in the United States», *Money, Expectations and Business Cycles*, New York, New York Academic Press, 1981.
[7] —— (ed.): *Modern Business Cycle Theory*, Harvard, Harvard University Press, 1989.
[8] BARRO R.J. - RUSH M.: «Unanticipated Money and Economic Activity», in FISHER S. (ed.): *Rational Expectations and Economic Activity*, NBER, Chicago, University of Chicago Press, 1980.
[9] BAXTER M. - KING R.G.: «Productive Externalities and Cyclical Volatility», Center for Economic Research, University of Rochester, *Working Paper*, n. 245, 1990.
[10] BENASSY J.P.: «Incomplete Markets and the Suboptimality of Rational Expectations», *Economic Letters*, n. 36, 1991.
[11] BERNANKE B.S.: «Bankruptcy, Liquidity and Recession», *American Economic Review Proceedings*, n. 71, 1981.
[12] BERNANKE B.S. - PARKINSON M.L.: «Procyclical Labor Productivity and Competing Theories of the Business Cycle: Some Evidence from Interwar US Manufacturing Industry», *Journal of Political Economy*, n. 3, 1991.
[13] BLANCHARD O.J. - WATSON M.: «Are Business Cycles All Alike?», NBER, *Working Paper*, n. 1392, 1984.
[14] BRONFENBRENNER M.: *Is The Business Cycle Obsolete?*, New York, Wiley & Sons, 1969.
[15] BURNS A. - MITCHELL W.: *Measuring Business Cycles*, New York, NBER, 1947.
[16] BURNSIDE C. - EICHENBAUM M. - REBELO S.: «Labor Hoarding and the Business Cycle», NBER, *Working Paper*, n. 3556, 1990.
[17] CAMPBELL J.M. - MANKIW N.G.: «Are Output Fluctuations Transitory?», *Quarterly Journal of Economics*, n. 102, 1987.
[18] CASS D.: «Optimum Growth in an Aggregate Model of Capital Accumulation», *Review of Economic Studies*, n. 32, 1965.
[19] COOLEY T.F. - HANSEN G.: «The Inflation Tax in a Real Business Cycle Model», *American Economic Review*, n. 79, 1988.
[20] DANTHINE J. - DONALDSON J.B.: «Efficiency Wages and the Business Cycle Puzzle», *European Economic Review*, n. 34, 1990.

[21] DANTHINE J. - DONALDSON J.B. - MEHRA R.: «On Some Computational Aspects of Equilibrium Business Cycle Theory», *Journal of Economic Dynamics and Control*, n. 13, 1989.

[22] DEBREU G.: *Valuation Equilibrium and Pareto Optimum*, in Proceedings of the National Academy of Sciences, Cambridge, Cambridge University Press, 1954.

[23] — —: *The Theory of Value*, New Haven, Yale University Press, 1959.

[24] DIAMOND D.W.: «Financial Intermediation and Delegated Monitoring», *Review of Economic Studies*, n. 51, 1984.

[25] DIAMOND D.W. - DYBVIG P.H.: «Bank Runs, Deposit Insurance, and Liquidity», *Journal of Political Economy*, n. 91, 1983.

[26] DOMOWITZ I. - HUBBARD R.G. - PETERSEN B.C.: »Market Structure and Cyclical Fluctuations in US Manufacturing», *The Review of Economics and Statistics*, n. 1, 1988.

[27] EICHENBAUM M.: «Real Business Cycles Theory: Wisdom or Whimsy?», NBER, *Working Paper*, n. 3432, 1990.

[28] EICHENBAUM M. - SINGLETON K.J.: «Do Equilibrium Real Business Cycle Theories Explain Post-War US Business Cycles?», NBER, *Working Paper*, n. 1932, 1986.

[29] ENTORF H.: «Real Business Cycles Under Test. A Multi-Country, Multi-Sector Exercise», *European Economic Review*, n. 35, 1991.

[30] EVANS C.L.: «Productivity Shocks and Real Business Cycles», *Journal of Monetary Economics*, n. 2, 1992.

[31] FRISH R.: «Propagation Problems and Impulse Problems in Dynamic Economics», *Essays in Honour of Gustav Cassel*, London, Allen & Unwin, 1933.

[32] GINTIS H.: *Money in General Equilibrium*, Amherst, University of Massachussets, Dept. of Economics, Mimeo 1991.

[33] GROSSMAN S.J.: «On the Efficiency of Competitive Stock Markets Where Traders Have Diverse Information», *Journal of Finance*, n. 31, 1976.

[34] — —: «Further Results on the Informational Efficiency of Competitive Stock Markets», *Journal of Economic Theory*, n. 18, 1978.

[35] — —: «An Introduction to the Theory of Rational Expectations under Asymmetric Information», *Review of Economic Studies*, n. 68, 1981.

[36] — —: *Rational Expectations and Prices*, in BARRO [7].

[37] GROSSMAN S.J. - STIGLITZ J.E.: «On the Impossibility of Informationally Efficient Markets», *American Economic Review*, n. 70, 1980.

[38] GROSSMAN S.J. - WEISS L.: «Heterogeneous Information and the Theory of the Business Cycle», *Journal of Political Economy*, n. 93, 1982.

[39] HALL R.E.: «Market Structure and Macroeconomic Fluctuations», *Brookings Papers on Economic Activity*, n. 2, 1986.

[40] — —.: «The Relation Between Price and Marginal Cost in the US Industry», *Journal of Political Economy*, n. 96, 1988.

[41] HANSEN G.D..: «Indivisible Labor and the Business Cycle», *Journal of Monetary Economics*, n. 16, 1985.

[42] INGRAM B. - LEEPER E.M.: «Post Econometric Policy Evaluation: A Critique», Board of Governor of the Federal Reserve System, International Finance, *Discussion Paper*, n. 393, 1990.

[43] KIM I - LOUNGANI P.: «The Role of Energy in Real Business Cycle Models», *Journal of Monetary Economics*, n. 2, 1992.

[44] KING R.G.: *Money and Business Cycles*, NBER, Economic Fluctuations Research Meeting, 1991.
[45] KING R.G. - PLOSSER C.I.: «Money, Credit and Prices and a Real Business Cycle», *American Economic Review*, n. 74, 1984.
[46] KING R.G. - PLOSSER C.I. - REBELO S.T.: «Production, Growth and the Business Cycles: the Basic Neoclassical Model», *Journal of Monetary Economics*, n. 21, 1988.
[47] —— —— ——: «Production Growth and Business Cycles: New Directions», *Journal of Monetary Economics*, n. 21, 1988.
[48] KING R.G. - PLOSSER C.I. - STOCK J. - WATSON M.: «Stochastic Trends and Economic Fluctuations», American Economic Review n. 4, 1991.
[49] KIYOTAKI N. - WRIGHT R.: «On Money as a Medium of Exchange», *Journal of Political Economy*, n. 97, 1989.
[50] KOOPMANS T.: «On the Concept of Optimal Growth», *The Econometric Approach to Development Planning*, Chicago Rand McNally, 1965.
[51] KORMENDI R.C. - MEGUIRE P.G.: «Cross-Regime Evidence of Macroeconomic Rationality», *Journal of Political Economy*, n. 92, 1984.
[52] KYDLAND F.E. - PRESCOTT E.C.: «Time to Build and Aggregate Fluctuations», *Econometrica*, n. 50, 1982.
[53] —— —— ——: «The Econometrics of the General Equilibrium Approach to Business Cycles», *Scandinavian Journal of Economics*, n. 93, 1991.
[54] LEBOW D.E.: «Imperfect Competition and Business Cycles: An Empirical Investigation», *Economic Inquiry*, January 1992.
[55] LIPPI M. - REICHLIN L.: «Permanent and Transitory Components in Macroeconomics», in THYGESEN N. - VELUPPILLAI K. - ZAMBELLI S. (eds.): *Business Cycles: Theories, Evidence and Analysis*», New York, New York University Press, 1991.
[56] —— —— ——: «On Persistence of Shocks to Economic Variables», *Journal of Monetary Economics*, n. 29, 1992.
[57] LITTERMAN R.B.. - WEISS L.: «Money, Real Interest Rates and Output: A Reinterpretation of Postwar US Data», *Econometrica*, n. 53, 1985.
[58] LONG J.B. - PLOSSER C.I.: «Real Business Cycle», *Journal of Political Economy*, n. 91, 1983.
[59] LUCAS R.E. JR.: «Expectation and the Neutrality of Money», *Journal of Economic Theory*, n. 4, 1972.
[60] ——: «Some International Evidence on Output-Inflation Tradeoffs», *American Economic Review*, n. 63, 1973.
[61] ——: «An Equilibrium Model of the Business Cycle», *Journal of Political Economy*, n. 83, 1975.
[62] ——: «Econometric Policy Evaluation: A Critique, in The Phillips Curve and the Labor Market», in BRUNNER-MELTZER (eds.): *Carnagie-Rochester Conference Series on Public Policy*, vol. 1, Amsterdam, North Holland, 1976.
[63] ——: «Understanding Business Cycles», in BRUNNER K. - MELTZER A.H. (eds.): *Stabilization of the Domestic and International Economy*, vol. 5, Amsterdam, North-Holland, 1977.
[64] ——: *Models of Business Cycles*, Oxford, Basil Blackwell, 1987.
[65] LUCAS R.E. JR. - PRESCOTT E.: «A Note on Price Systems in Infinite Dimensional Space», *International Economic Review*, n. 13, 1972.

[66] LUCAS R.E. JR. - SARGENT T.J.: «After Keynesian Macroeconomics», *After the Phillips Curve: Persistence of High Inflation and High Unemployment*, Boston, Federal Reserve Bank of Boston, 1978.
[67] MANKIW N.G.: «Real Business Cycles: A New Keynesian Perspective», *Journal of Economic Perspective*, n. 3, 1989.
[68] MANKIW N.G. - ROMER D.: *New Keynesian Economics*, vol. 1 and 2, London, MIT Press, 1991.
[69] MCCALLUM B.T.: «On "Real" and "Sticky-Price" Theories of the Business Cycle», NBER, *Working Paper*, n. 1933, 1986.
[70] — —: *Real Business Cycle Models*, in BARRO [7].
[71] MURPHY M.K. - SHLEIFER A. - VISHNY R.W.: «Building Blocks of Market Clearing Business Cycle Models», NBER, *Macroeconomic Annual*, 1989.
[72] NELSON C.R. - PLOSSER C.R.: «Trends and Random Walks in Macroeconomic Time Series: Some Evidence and Implications», *Journal of Monetary Economics*, n. 10, 1982.
[73] PELLEGRINI G.: *Trend stocastico e ciclo economico nella produzione industriale*, mimeo, Roma, Banca d'Italia, 1990.
[74] PESARAN M.H.: *The Limits to Rational Expectations*, Oxford, Basil Blackwell 1987.
[75] PHELPS E.S. et AL.: *Microeconomic Foundations of Employment and Inflation Theory*, New York, Norton, 1969.
[76] PLOSSER C.J.: «Understanding Real Business Cycles», *Journal of Economic Perspective*, vol. 3, n. 3, 1989.
[77] — —: «Money and Business Cycles: A Real Business Cycle Interpretation», NBER, *Working Paper*, n. 3221, 1990.
[78] PRESCOTT E.: «Theory Ahead of Business Cycle Measurement», Federal Reserve Bank of Minneapolis, *Quarterly Review*, n. 10, 1986.
[79] RAMSEY F.: «A Mathematical Theory of Saving», *Economic Journal*, n. 38, 1928.
[80] ROMER C. - ROMER D.: «Does Monetary Policy Matter: A Test in the Spirit of Friedman & Schwartz», NBER, *Macroeconomic Annual*, 1989.
[81] ROMER P.M.: *Capital Accumulation in the Theory of Long Run Growth*, in BARRO [7].
[82] ROTEMBERG J.J. - SUMMERS L.H.: «Inflexible Prices and Procyclical Productivity», *Quarterly Journal of Economics*, n. 105, 1990.
[83] ROTEMBERG J.J. - WOODFORD M.: «Oligopolistic Pricing and the Effects of Aggregate Demand on Economic Activity», NBER, *Working Paper*, n. 3206, 1989.
[84] — — — —.: «Markups and the Business Cycle», NBER, *Macroeconomics Annual*, 1991.
[85] SALOP S.C.: «A Model of the Natural Rate of Unemployment», *American Economic Review*, n. 69, 1979.
[86] SARGENT T.J.: *Dynamic Macroeconomic Theory*, Harvard, Harvard University Press, 1987.
[87] SHAPIRO C. - STIGLITZ J.: «Equilibrium Unemployment as a Worker Discipline Device», *American Economic Review*, n. 74, 1984.
[88] SIMS C.A.: «Macroeconomics and Reality», *Econometrica*, n. 48, 1980.
[89] — —: «Comparison of Interwar and Postwar Business Cycles: Monetarism Reconsidered», *American Economic Review*, n. 73, 1980.

[90] SIMS C.A.: «Policy Analysis with Econometric Models», *Brookings Papers on Economic Activity*, n. 1, 1982.
[91] SLUTSKY E.: «The Summation of Random Causes as the Source of Cyclical Processes», *Econometrica*, n. 5, 1937.
[92] SOLOW R.M.: «Technical Change and the Aggregate Production Function», *Review of Economics and Statistics*, n. 39, May 1957.
[93] ——: «Another Possible Source of Wage Stickiness», *Journal of Macroeconomics*, n. 1, 1979.
[94] STOKEY N.L. - LUCAS R.E. JR.: *Recursive Methods in Economic Dynamics* Harvard, Harvard University Press 1989.
[95] SUMMERS L.H.: «Some Sceptical Observations on Real Business Cycle Theory», Harvard Institute of Economic Research», *Discussion Paper*, n. 1278, 1986.
[96] TOWNSEND R.M.: «Models of Money with Spatially Separated Agents», in KAREKEN J.H. - WALLACE N.: (eds.): *Models of Monetary Economics*, Minneapolis, Federal Reserve Bank, 1980.
[97] ——: «Arrow-Debreu Programs as Microfoundations of Macroeconomics», in TRUMAN F. - BEWLEY (eds.): *Advances in Economic Theory. Fifth World Congress*, Cambridge, Cambridge University Press, 1987.
[98] VICARELLI F.: «Leggi di natura e politica economica: considerazioni sui fondamenti teorici della nuova macroeconomia classica», *Politica economica*, n. 1, 1985.
[99] WATSON M.W. - STOCK J.H.: «Variable Trends in Economic Time Series», *Journal of Economic Perspective*, n. 3, 1988.

II - CYCLE INDICATORS AND ANALYSIS

The Use of Cyclical Indicators in Business Cycle Analysis

Paolo Annunziato
Confindustria, Roma

1. - Introduction

The cyclical indicator approach, which is extensively used as a business cycle analysis tool, employs a series of variables which tend to anticipate, coincide with or lag behind the movements of economic activity to indicate the phases of the business cycle.

The proof that cyclical indicators are useful and deserve further investigation is shown by their international diffusion, and also by their resistence to advances in both business cycle theory and statistical methods for analysing time series (1).

It is unarguable, as Moore [53] emphasises, that the low level of precision of macroeconometric models has kept this methodology alive despite the heavy criticism received, primarily the claim that it is a "measurement without theory" (Koopmans [38]). Nonetheless, it would be limiting and to a certain extent erroneous to use cyclical indicators as an alternative to macroeconometric models. Rather they complement these models for at least two reasons. The first is that cyclical indicators make more direct use of the information contained in the available data, most of which is not generally used in macroeconometric models (or in models for analysing time series). The

---

(1) For a survey of the diffusion of these indicators, see KLEIN - MOORE [34] MOORE [54] and the proceedings of the conferences on this subject organised by CIRET (Center for International Research on Economic Tendency Surveys).

Advise: the numbers in square brackets refer to the Bibliography in the appendix.

second is that they can be used to obtain monthly forecasts of economic trends, while most models generally use quarterly or annual data (2).

A further difference between this approach and other alternative forecasting and analysis methods lies in the definition of "cyclicity". Cyclicity does not refer to the cyclical pattern which characterises the reference series (in which case any forecasting method would be "cyclical"), but rather the capability to detect and predict the various phases of the business cycle and in particular its turning points.

These characteristics of cyclical indicators furnish a basis on which to read and interpret this methodology but at the same time they highlight the limits to the indicators' use. This paper proposes to analyse these mechanisms in order to identify and define their fields of application and evaluate their potential contribution to business cycle analysis.

This paper pays particular attention to comprehending their correct use, and its analysis is therefore mainly methodological and constitutes the preliminary phase of a project for developing other indicators as an alternative to those available (3).

The second Section of this paper illustrates the origin and evolution of cyclical indicators from their birth to the formulation used at present, pointing out the principal problems implicit in their construction and some of the solutions adopted. The application of statistical analysis of time series has given rise in the last decade to important developments in this field, often proposing alternative configurations to the traditional ones. In the third Section some of the principal proposals are analysed, while the fourth Section takes a more detailed look at the relation between cyclical indicators and theories of economic fluctuation. The concluding Section summarises considerations regarding the correct use of cyclical indicators.

---

(2) E. Giovannini's monthly model for business cycle fluctuations presented in this volume is an exception.

(3) The literature in this field is very extensive and differentiated. Nonetheless, for an accurate description of the methodology and problems regarding cyclical indicators, reference should be made to the works of MOORE [51], [52] and [54] and STOCK - WATSON [70].

2. - Classical Methods of Constructing Cyclical Indicators

2.1 *Classical Cycles*

In 1937, during the recession which followed the recovery of 1933-1937, the US Treasury Secretary Henry Morgentau, requested the National Bureau of Economic Research (NBER), to identify a group of time series capable of predicting the end of the recession in progress (4). Within six weeks NBER's research director, Wesley Mitchell, with the help of Arthur F. Burns, prepared a classification of an extensive group of time series and divided them into "leading", "coincident" and "lagging" indicators. This classification of the time series was published for the first time in 1938 (5).

Mitchell and Burn's leading indicators did in fact forecast the recovery which took place in June 1938. Since then, cyclical indicators have been studied in greater detail by NBER and subsequently by the Department of Commerce (DOC) of the Bureau of Economic Analysis and are nowadays commonly used in all the major industrialised countries (6). Furthermore, the OECD has published on a monthly basis for some years a series of composite leading indicators for the main western economies and for groups of countries. In Italy, ISCO, in close collaboration with NBER, has been developing cyclical indicators since the 1960s. At present, a coincident indicator (constructed on the basis of 26 series) is published monthly in the journal *Congiuntura italiana*.

Most of these indicators are constructed on the basis of the same methods developed by NBER, and hence can generally be compared with each other. Before this paper defers analyses of alternative methodologies in the following Section, it investigates the philosophy behind the construction of the "classical" indicators, so as to bring their weaknesses and strengths to the fore.

---

(4) The formal origin of the cyclical indicators as given in the text is described in MOORE [53], pp. 350-1.
(5) See MITCHELL - BURNS [50].
(6) In the US in addition to the DOC, cyclical indicators are studied and developed by the Center of International Business Cycle Research directed by G.H. Moore. The DOC publishes two principal composite indicators: a coincident indicator (constructed on the base of four national accounting series) and a leading indicator (constructed on the base of 11 series in real and financial sectors).

W. Mitchell [49] gave the definition of the business cycle most often referred to in the subsequent literature on cyclical indicators. Burns and Mitchell [8] later reformulated Mitchell's: «Business cycles are a type of fluctuation encountered in the aggregate economic activity of nations in which labour is principally organised in industrial firms: a cycle is composed of expansions, which take place almost at the same time in many economic activities, followed by equally general recessions, contractions and recoveries which merge with the expansionary phase of the following cycle; this sequence of changes is recurrent but not periodic...».

On the basis of the definition given by Burns and Mitchell, the main characteristics of the business cycle can be identified: generality (in the sense of the representative nature of economic activity), extent and diffusion. With regard to generality, there is a certain amount of discretion in the choice of the series which comprise the reference cycle. It is generally recognised that a single measurement of the total activity, for example GDP, is not sufficiently reliable to describe the business cycles as defined above, due to problems in measuring the GDP's single components and imperfect correlation with other variables considered important such as the level of employment or profits.

The main problem regarding the extent of cyclical fluctuation is detecting the cycle's turning points. The traditional methodology requires first detecting whether the phase in question is expansionary or recessionary. Once the hypothesis that an expansionary phase has ended and a contraction has commenced is confirmed, one can then determine the cycle's peaks and troughs. These are obtained using a complex procedure based on repeated applications of moving averages (which filter the irregularities of the series considered). Peaks and troughs are also obtained using comparisons with fluctuations detected in the past (7).

---

(7) In 1971, two researchers at NBER, G. Bry and C. Boschan, developed a computer program which automatically calculated the turning points of a time series with cyclical fluctuations. The methodology used became a reference standard for detecting turning points. After having deseasonalised the series and reduced the irregularity by means of a Spencer curve, the identification of the cycles is obtained on a moving average of 12 terms. The provisional peaks and troughs are then obtained by placing these phases on a 15-term Spencer curve. The procedure is then repeated to determine the definitive turning points.

The measurement of the comovements between different economic activities, or between different industrial sectors or regions, plays an important role in the process of detecting a cycle's turning points.

In fact, at the start of a cycle the inversion signals are generally limited to a subset of the reference aggregate and become more clearly defined and generalised when the phase is under full steam. The diffusion index is a simple statistical instrument which synthesises this type of information. It represents the percentage of the time series in the expansionary phase against the total of the series considered. This index varies between 0 and 100, and the economic significance is generated by the fiftieth percentile, which indicates the passing from a majority of series in expansion to a majority of series in contraction and vice versa. However, the diffusion index contains some drawbacks when used to determine the cycle's chronology; one drawback derives from the index high level of irregularity calculated on monthly or quarterly data. As a result, this index is generally used in a moving average or cumulative form for a determined period (8). A further drawback is that the diffusion index attributes an equal weight to all the series examined, and thus overlooks important information about how the variables considered are correlated to the reference aggregate. Finally, the diffusion index only provides indications concerning the direction of the variables, but not the extent of their movement.

Nevertheless, the diffusion indicators can be applied to the separate components of a specific composite indicator; these components may be the regions of the national aggregate, the sectors of the industry aggregate or even the individual companies. In this case, the diffusion index can be used to obtain information on the homogeneity of the variations per single region, on sectors or companies, as well as to ascertain whether their movements are representative.

The behaviour of the coincident indicators further assists in detecting turning points in a cycle. Their "coincidence" is no mere accident since many of them are components of the reference aggregate; however their peaks and troughs do not coincide with

---

(8) See the treatment of diffusion indexes by MICONI - DE NICOLA [46].

TABLE 1

CHRONOLOGICAL ORDER
OF ITALIAN ECONOMIC CYCLES

Isco (26 series composite index)					Oecd (industrial production index)				
maximum levels	minimum levels	length of time (months)			maximum levels	minimum levels	length of time (months)		
		(*)	(**)	(***)			(*)	(**)	(***)
Sept. 1947	March 1948	28	6	34	June 1960	Dec. 1960	—	6	—
Apr. 1951	March 1952	37	13	50	Jan. 1962	Sept. 1962	13	8	21
Sept. 1957	Aug. 1958	64	11	75	Sept. 1963	March 1965	12	18	40
Oct. 1963	Jan. 1965	62	15	77	Febr. 1967	March 1968	23	13	36
Oct. 1970	Oct. 1971	69	12	81	Jan. 1969	Apr. 1972	10	39	49
June 1974	Sept. 1975	32	15	47	Jan. 1975	Maj 1975	21	16	37
Febr. 1977	Dec. 1977	17	10	27	Dec. 1976	Dec. 1977	19	12	31
March 1980	June 1983	27	39	66	Apr. 1980	June 1983	28	38	66
Nov. 1989									

Legend:
(*) expansion; (**) slope; (***) complete cycle.
Source: Isco, Oecd.

GRAPH 1

COMPOSITE CYCLICAL INDICATORS (*)

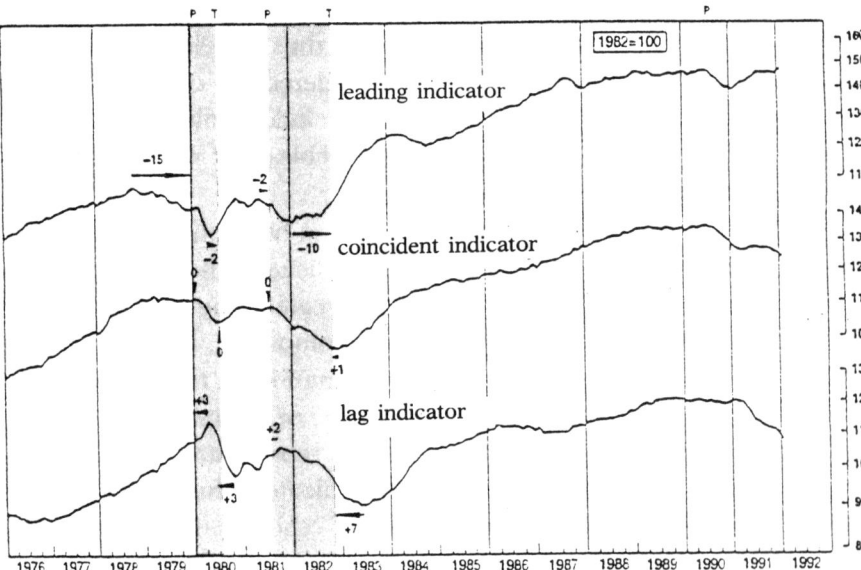

(*) P (*peak*) indicates the maximum level (the end of an expansive phase and the start to a slope phase) and T (*through*) indicates the minimum level: the shaded areas thus indicate the slope phases. The NBER identified a maximum level in July 1990, but has not yet identified a minimum level. The arrows indicate leads (−) or lags (+) in months with respect to the date of the turning point.
Source: USA, Department of Commerce, 1992.

those observed for the reference aggregate, and hence they may suggest possible alternative timings. Leading and lagging indicators are also used to confirm the validity of the choices made.

As an example, Table 1 shows business cycles in Italy calculated by ISCO and OECD using the method described; those on the left refer to a composite indicator comprising 26 series, while those on the right refer to the industrial production index. Graph 1 on the other hand shows the leading, coincident and lagging indicators calculated by the US Department of Commerce; the component series and their grouping according to economic processes are shown in Table 2.

2.2 Growth Cycles

During the 1960s, the relatively regular expansion of the major economies gave rise to a discussion on the possible abandonment of the classical concept of the business cycle as defined by Burns and Mitchell. In fact, real declines in economic activity were being replaced by slowdowns in the rhythm of expansion, giving rise increasingly frequently to alternating periods of acceleration and slowdown in growth rates.

The need for a concept of the business cycle more in line with reality led to the development of the concept of the growth cycle (9); this concept was used to detect and measure the phases of accelerated growth, differentiating them from the phases of slow growth. The first difficulty implicit in this alternative approach to business cycles is to define the "normal" variation rates of the series being studied, since this definition of normality is used to measure difference between the cyclical phases and the "normal" growth rate. One way of representing this reference rate is to identify it with a specifically calculated trend; the percentage distance between the historic realisation and the trend therefore constitutes the deviation cycle which, like a classical cycle, is characterised by alternating maxima-minima-maxima.

A further problem derives from the disturbance exercised by the extreme rates; these are particularly erratic values which can reflect

---

(9) See MINTZ [47], [48].

TABLE 2

DOC CLASSIFICATION OF THE COMPONENTS OF CYCLICAL INDICATORS BY ECONOMIC PROCESS

Index	Economic process	Employment and unemployment	Production and income	Consumption, trade, orders and deliveries	Capital and investments	Stocks	Prices, costs and profits	Money and credit
leading indicator		hours worked in manufacturing (average per week) unemployment benefit requests (average per week)		new orders: consumer and intermediate goods in the manufacturing industry (constant prices) index of the speed of product deliveries (percentage values) household climate of confidence	contracts and orders for plant and machinery (constant prices) index of building licences variation in manufacturing's outstanding orders: Durables		variations in the prices of raw materials index of stock market trends	money supply: M2

TABLE 2 continued

Index	Economic process	Employment and unemployment	Production and income	Consumption, trade, orders and deliveries	Capital and investments	Stocks	Prices, costs and profits	Money and credit
coincident Indicator		workforce (excluding agriculture)	available income (constant prices) industrial production index (constant prices)	turnover of the manufacturing and retail sectors (constant prices)				
lagging Indicator		average duration of unemployment				ratio of stocks to the manufacturing and retail sectors' turnover	variation in labour cost per unit produced: manufacturing	bank prime rate loans to the industrial and retail sectors (constant prices) consumer credit/income ratio

Source: USA, DEPARTMENT OF COMMERCE, 1992.

exceptional political, economic or climatic events, or even just measurement errors. Extreme rates should be distinguished from the normal irregularity with respect to which they represent anomalous events or events with a high degree of irregularity. Nonetheless, even normal levels of irregularity can cause problems in detecting cyclical turning points; for this reason, normal irregularity must be filtered before commencing examination of the cyclical phases. This is done by substituting the particularly erratic values with those obtained from a symmetric acceptance band around an equalised function which is considered as representative of the phenomena. The function generally used is a Spencer curve (10), which comprises a 15-term moving average. The levels of the original series, whose relations vis-à-vis the corresponding levels on the Spencer curve are higher than the threshold decided by the analyst, are replaced with the curve values. To eliminate normal irregularity, the equalising function is instead substituted by a 3-6 months moving average, which has the advantage of systematically correcting the original series with a lower loss of observations at the end of the series. On the other hand, such short-period series would not be able to adequately remove the extreme rates of irregularity (11).

---

(10) The Henderson curve is also widely used. It is more flexible than Spencer's and particularly suited to highlighting the cycle's components and trends. See MARRUCO - DE NICOLA [42].

(11) In the 1960s, NBER introduced a method for optimising the length of the moving average necessary to eliminate the erratic component of the series analysed. This method, called *Months for cyclical dominance* (MCD) is applicable to a series of seasonally adjusted monthly data which can be broken down into a cycle-trend component and an erratic component:

$$Y_t = CT_t + u_t \qquad t = 1, \ldots n$$

Considering the difference of order k for the two components $D_k CT_t$ and $D_k u_t$ one can see that an increase in k should be followed by an increase in $D_k CT_t$ while $D_k u_t$ should remain constant. Using the averages of these differences, one can define an MCD index as the minimum value of k such that:

$$\frac{\sum_{t=1}^{n} (D_k CT_t)}{k} > \frac{\sum_{t=1}^{n} (D_k u_t)}{k}$$

For any value of k, the erratic component u_t is calculated as the difference between the series observed and the cycle-trend component CT_t calculated as a moving average of the order k.

According to the terminology used in time series analysis (De Nicola [18]), each series can be broken down into four main components: seasonal, cycle, trend and casual or irregular movement. Using symbols, with Y defining the variable being studied:

(1) $$Y_t = S_t + C_t + T_t + u_t$$

Classical or Mitchellian business cycle analysis removes seasonal components and sometimes also irregular components, leaving $C_t + T_t$, which is then called the cycle-trend. Growth cycles on the other hand also remove the time series from the trend component, and hence analyse the behaviour of the C_t component alone.

The validity of growth cycles largely depends on the choice of trends which, when there is no underlying theoretical model, is subject to a certain amount of arbitrariness. NBER initially used a 75-term moving average on monthly observations which was considered capable of eliminating the cyclical component from the series. When using a moving average a technical problem generally arises, that is, the need to extrapolate the long-term values for the initial and final months of the series used. This shortening of the moving average in the two extreme periods is the most widely used solution, but implies rather arbitrary assumptions concerning series behaviour. In any case, the trend obtained for the initial and final years is subject to error.

To alleviate these problems, at the end of the 1970s W. Ebanks and C. Boschan of NBER developed the *Phase average trend* method (*PAT*), which is still used by OECD and the EEC. PAT uses variable-length moving averages (from 60 to 75 terms) which take into account the various lengths of the business cycle's phases. However, this method has two important drawbacks: first, that it reduces the possibility of a variation in the trend itself in the short or medium-term, and second, that at least thirty monthly values at the two extremes of the series have to be extrapolated through other methods which are more or less arbitrary.

Graph 2 (taken from Schlitzer [66]), breaks the classical cycle (cycle-trend) of industrial production down into its cyclical and trend components calculated using the method described.

GRAPH 2

INDUSTRIAL PRODUCTION CYCLE
(1970-1991) (*)

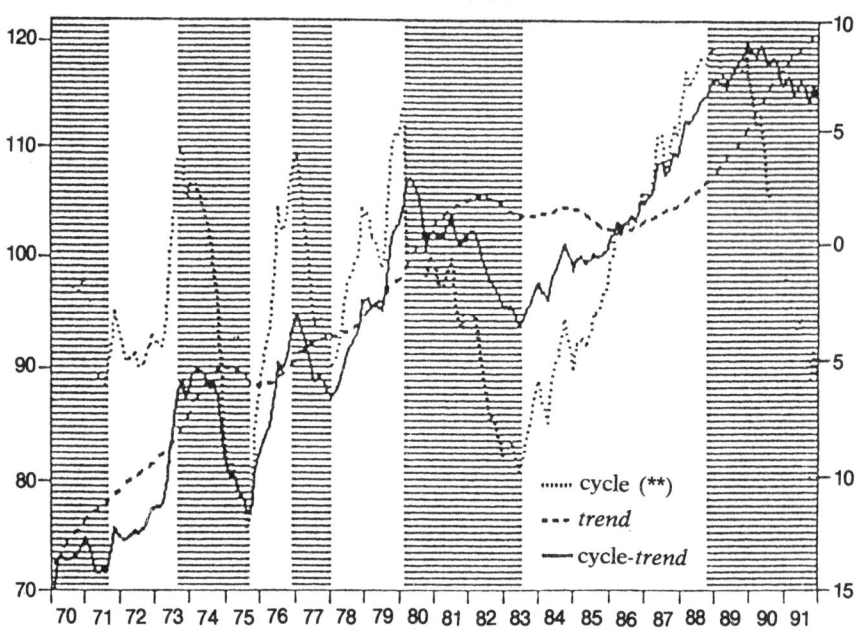

(*) The shaded areas indicate slope-phases according to growth cycle criterion;
(**) right scale.
Source: SCHLITZER [66].

This methodology of using variable trends draws on recent literature on trends' stochastic nature which attributes the classical cycle to the movement of the cyclical component around a stationary trend. This is generated by a stochastic process, and has its own fluctuations which contribute to the overall fluctuations observed (Beveridge and Nelson [4]; Nelson and Plosser [60]) (12). To account

---

(12) ZARNOWITZ [77] points out that since trends vary between different series and in time, the detrending procedure could reduce the cycles' time variability and their difference in extension. An international comparison shows that growth cycles are linked between the major countries and that the variability in the growth cycles' duration is generally less than that of economic cycles.

HARVEY [30] maintains that one should distinguish the period prior to 1970 from that following. In the preceeding period the cycle was an intrinsic part of the trend and

for this, there exists an alternative way of estimating the trend of a cyclical variable: to carry out recursive regressions of the series in question on a trend variable (generally using a linear or exponential function). The number of observations remains constant, and is sufficiently large to capture the period's trend while guaranteeing a certain degree of stationarity. Every observation of a trend so computed consists of the final value (initial or average) of each of the regressions carried out. However, this method is also very arbitrary as regards the length of the estimation period necessary to obtain a stationary trend. Nevertheless, the stationarity tests can be applied to guide the analyst towards choices which are more coherent with the assumption of a stochastic trend (13).

An alternative method of analysing growth cycles which avoids calculating the trend is to consider the cycle of the variation rate of the series, whose phases are characterised by the alternation of relatively high and low variation rates. This method was used by Friedman and Schwartz [25] to analyse fluctuations in monetary series. However, the direct measurement of variation rates implies some difficulties, the most important of which is detecting the cycle's turning points. In fact, growth tends to be more rapid after a period of recession or slowdown and tends to slacken late into the recovery when the expansion of the phenomenon is still in progress. If the turning points were located at the minimum and maximum levels, one would obtain considerable lags vis-à-vis the cyclical waves of the original series. To right this problem, instead of considering alternat-

---

not a separate component which could be subsequently added. After 1970, on the other hand, it could be appropriate to isolate a cyclical component.

In any case, after NELSON - PLOSSER'S article [60], the discussion concerning the trend's stochastic component would appear to have confirmed that the role of the permanent component (i.e., of the trend) in the business cycle is much greater than previously thought (CAMPBELL - MANKIW [9]).

However, for a correct understanding of the importance of this phenomenon see also LIPPI - REICHLIN [39].

(13) It should be noted that if one accepts the assumption that fluctuations in economic activity are generated to a large extent by fluctuations of the permanent component (trend), the procedure for separating the cycle and trend components using perequative functions, would lead to an overestimate (by frequency and size) of the growth cycle. Furthermore, in this case estimation of the trend could not ignore the evolution of the discussion on the methods suited to this purpose (HARVEY [30], WATSON [73], CLARK [10], COCHRANE [11], HAMILTON [29]).

ing increasing and decreasing variation rates, the average of the variation rates could be considered so that alternations of steps of high and low average rates are formed rather than continuous fluctuations. The procedure for correctly choosing the turning point, that is to say the extrema of each step, is however rather complex; on the other hand, step cycles do not furnish a complete description of growth cycles, even though they can be used to verify growth cycles obtained using other methods.

2.3 *Composite Indicators*

Composite (or synthetic) indicators, which synthesise the information contained in the single indicators, play a special role in the cyclical indicator theory.

The need to construct composite indicators derives from the attempt to minimise the risk of false signals generated by irregular movements in the indicator being considered. In this sense, composite indicators are more precise indicators than each of the series which go to make them up.

Synthetic indicators are generally merely weighted averages of the component indicators. However, several statistical problems are encountered when combining series with different intervals, different degrees of irregularity and different measurement units and the components should be transformed prior to aggregation. The series then have their irregular components removed using the MCD method indicated above (or a similar method) and are normalised to enable them to be compared.

Different methods have been tried to achieve this normalisation: in general the average sizes (i.e., the average variations in each time interval) are corrected on the basis of the average size for the period or the average size of a standard series (which can be the reference series or a series considered particularly important); the series are then transformed into indexes. An alternative method, used by the US Department of Commerce, is to make the average sizes for each time interval equal, thus reducing the importance of series with greater fluctuations (Zarnowitz and Boschan [78]).

Finally, the series are weighted; the choice of the weights is a decisive moment when constructing the synthetic indicator. To this end, various criteria can be assumed, including the use of the correlation coefficient with the reference series (taking into account an adequate lag), or the use of multivariate analysis (for example with the principal components or stepwise regression).

A more sophisticated and common method is to draw up a scoring system for the individual components; NBER has been developing this method since the end of the 1960s (Moore and Shiskin [55]), giving rise to a classification of the series on the basis of some criteria of their economic and statistical significance. However, the economic significance of the series, even though considered essential, is generally measured with reference to the degree of aggregation of the series itself, rather than to some theoretical model. Hence the series for new durables' orders in industry is awarded more points than that for new machinery orders (economic significance is examined in greater detail in the next Section).

The other criteria used include: irregularity, amplitude, reliability of measurement, and promptness with which current data are published.

In addition to these criteria one should add that of coherence with past business cycles; in particular an indicator's score depends on its correlation with the reference cycle and with the indicator's consistency as a leading, coincident or lagging indicator (14).

It is important to examine in greater detail how cyclical indicators are timed with respect to the reference series.

Leading indicators are mainly measurements of expectations or new orders; they are projected toward the future and are very sensitive to variations in the economic climate, or to the market's perception of such variations. Coincident indicators, as mentioned above, are general measurements of a country's economic performance, which is reflected in GDP in real terms, industrial production, employment, unemployment, income and trade. Finally, lagging indicators are characterised by a greater stickiness and hence they lag

---

(14) OECD uses a points model similar to that proposed by Moore and Shiskin. For a description of the methodology used by OECD see the article by R. Nilsson in this volume.

behind the economic climate. Nonetheless, this does not mean they are of secondary importance, since they are useful for confirming the variations in the cycle initially detected by the leading and coincident indicators. Moreover, the lagging indicators in turn act as leading indicators for the fluctuations which follow on the heels of those considered; hence they can indicate the presence of disequilibrium, and thus allow one to predict the behaviour of some leading and coincident indicators.

The choice of indicators is generally based not only on statistical properties, but also on the possibility of identifying the theoretical mechanisms which link them to the reference series. This does not mean that the economic variables considered important in detecting cyclical fluctuations do not have, at least in the available measurements, the properties necessary for use as components of a synthetic indicator; for example, fiscal policy variables are not generally good cyclical indicators, even though there is an extensive literature on their possible effects on growth and the business cycle.

It is, though, possible to identify some economic processes described by groups of indicators related to each other. This is necessary to avoid wasteful duplication of indicators which record the same event or phenomenon. As shown in Table 2, in the economic process regarding the determination of employment and unemployment, the number of hours worked is a component of the leading indicator, while the number of workers is part of the coincident indicator. The economic processes considered are: employment, output and income, consumption and trade, investments and stocks, prices and costs, money and credit. The theoretical bases of this methodology are discussed in the fourth Section.

3. - Recent Developments in the Cyclical Indicator Theory

3.1 *Applications of Time Series Analysis*

The method for constructing cyclical indicators illustrated above is widely used throughout the world, but can be criticised from both a statistical and economic point of view. These criticisms will be analysed in this Section and also in the following Section. The function of cyclical indicators, to detect the phases of the economic cycle and furnish short and very short-term forecasts, would suggest that alternative forecasting strategies should be evaluated on the basis of their ability to improve the degree to which they fulfil this function.

Many of the important developments in the cyclical indicator theory concern the method for selecting the leading series, constructing a composite leading indicator and identifying the turning points. These developments respond to a specific requirement: the present "classical" leading indicators, although capable of signaling all the inversions in the cycle which have taken place in the last 50 years in the US (where more attention is paid to these problems), often signal false turning points, and their lead time on the reference series has turned out to be rather unstable (Hymans [31]).

The recent literature has verified, for the entire business cycle and in proximity to the turning points, the statistical properties and forecasting capabilities of the traditional leading indicators; this literature generally refers to the indicators calculated by the Department of Commerce.

The main problems to emerge from the application of traditional methods are the stability and length of the indicators' lead; the former can vary considerably from cycle to cycle, while the brevity of the latter does not generally allow one to reliably detect a cycle inversion before it takes place (15).

This paper analyses whether these problems depend on the method used. Koch and Rasche [37] have shown that the weights used for constructing the DOC's composite indicator according to the classical method are not confirmed by multivariate regression. Neftci [58] and Auerbach [1], on the other hand used causality tests to underscore the loss of information implicit when the series used to construct leading indicators are seasonally adjusted.

The choice of the weighting system is a crucial point in construct-

---

(15) A rule generally applied, but absolutely arbitrary, lays down that a series has recorded a turning point if a succession of increases (decreases) is followed by three successive decreases (increases). However, it is rare for a composite leading indicator to have a lead of more than three months.

ing the composite indicators, and has been analysed in detail by Hymans [31]

Even if we accept the validity of the selection criteria for including time series in the synthetic indicator, it would appear optimal to obtain the weights through the linear projection of the reference aggregate on the series selected. Hymans applies this reasoning to the coincident indicator calculated by NBER using the component series as regressors. He obtains weights which are significantly different from those used by NBER. In Hymans' findings in fact, three of the component series are not statistically significant, while another five do not have the sign expected.

However, the importance of this result depends on the objective to be attained using the leading indicators. If one accepts the assumption that their usefulness depends on their correlation with the reference series at the turning points, but *not* necessarily during the entire period, then linear regression is not the optimal method for estimating the weights. In fact, in assigning a uniform weight to forecasting error for any of the sample's observations, linear regression minimises the error over the entire period. The behaviour of these series near turning points however should be differentiated from that observed at the other points of the cycle.

If we adopt Hymans' approach to leading indicators, then the usefulness of the indicators should be verified by analysing their behaviour at the turning points. It is appropriate to cite here an observation by Hymans regarding the hypothesis that the change in the phase of the general economic cycle (or of the reference series) is generally preceded by variations in an identifiable group of variables.

«This statement does not imply direct causality (if it did, one would attempt to estimate a behavioral or technological relation that could be expected to hold outside the sample, that would have directly interpretable coefficients and so on). Rather it implies something about the process through which those forces that do lead to turning points operate within the structure of the US economy. Thus a downturn that might result from a tightening of monetary policy would inevitably have an impact on some or all of the variables durable orders, plant and equipment contracts, profits, price-cost ratio, stock prices, building permits, and installment debt before it affected the aggregate level of production» (16).

To confirm this stance, Hymans analyses the forecasting capability of the turning points outside the sample. He shows that the forecasts obtained through linear regression on the components of the composite leading indicator selected by NBER are less precise than those provided by the indicator itself (17).

Hymans' method consists of developing a mechanism capable of providing a series of duplicative signals for the same event which, when suitably analysed, will reduce the possibility of false signals. Which of these series will be capable of anticipating the phase inversion will depend on the original cause of the fluctuations; it is therefore necessary to select a number of instruments able to represent (or rather record) the cause-effect mechanisms generated by the potential principal origins of the cyclical fluctuations.

The verification of the forecasting capability of leading indicators requires a further consideration. Since there is no single criterion for interpreting the signals provided by these indicators, it is necessary to determine a series of rules for recognising, or more precisely defining, the turning points. These rules should be able to filter out any false signals while remaining sufficiently informative to indicate the true ones. In addition, they should be sufficiently simple to render the information gathered from the indicators easy and quick to use. The evaluation of the forecasting capability can vary considerably depending on which set of rules has been chosen. Hymans compares the traditional definition of a turning point, (i.e., a series of increases/decreases) followed by a series of at least three decreases/increases with a set of more articulated rules.

Such a set considers two reductions in the leading indicator during the expansionary phase as sufficient to signal the maximum in the following month; the computation of the minimum is obtained through the same method.

This exercise shows that the leading indicators were less precise

---

(16) See HYMANS [31], p. 347.
(17) NEFTCI [58] takes an opposing stance. He emphasises that an examination of only the turning points implies that the model underlying the economy produces discrete variations in correspondence with the turning points.

than they would be if they had been evaluated using the interpretation criteria suggested by the traditional definition (used by the NBER). Using his alternative definition, Hymans calculates that the composite leading indicator published by the Bureau of Census (constructed in accordance with the NBER's methodology) furnished false signals 50% of the times it indicated a turning point, while it did not detect 33% of the peaks and 24% of the troughs which actually took place.

The traditional leading indicators' scant forecasting capability in detecting the turning points does not improve when one considers growth slowdowns, measuring growth rather than traditional cycles, instead of actual recessions.

If one wishes to reduce false signals, spectral analysis is very useful for constructing indicators. Spectral analysis analyses a time series as the sum of a certain number of non-observed variables, each of which is characterised by its own periodicity and amplitude. Hence, an observed series S is considered as the sum of three series, $S1$, $S2$ and $S3$, of which the first has a low periodicity and wide amplitude, the second greater periodic fluctuations but a narrower amplitude, and the third very frequent cycles with reduced amplitude. Assuming that the $S1$, $S2$ and $S3$ series are stochastic processes, the periodicity and amplitude of S are obtained from the weighted average of periodicity and amplitude of the three components, while $S3$ is the random error of the S series. Spectral analysis is therefore able to break the observed time series down into the "original" components and provide a measure ("power") of the amount of variability which can be attributed to each of the components. The periodicity and the power of the components into which the observed series are broken down form the series' spectrum. This analysis can also be applied to obtain the cross spectrum of the two series. Here one obtains a measurement defined as "coherence" which approximates the square of the correlation between the periodic components of the same series. One can also measure the lag between the turning points of the same periodic component in two different series.

The spectral analysis of both the reference aggregate and the series chosen as leading indicators can be used to construct a synthetic indicator which takes into account the spectral coherence between the series and has a minimal random error, thus reducing the possibility of false signals. Hymans [31], in particular, uses spectral analysis of single series to show that there is a trade-off between the probability of false signals and the lead time of the turning points when constructing a cyclical indicator.

The choice of evaluating the forecasting capability of an indicator solely as regards the cyclical turning points should be dealt with in further detail. Indeed, Hymans' position implies that the business cycle's ascendency and descendency phases should be treated differently.

The problem does not have a simple solution from either a theoretical or a statistical viewpoint since it is part of a more general problem. One should verify if it is possible to detect structural changes between the expansionary and recessionary phases which would justify the use of different rules for interpreting the signals furnished by the leading indicators. Nonetheless, it should be emphasised that regardless of the optimality of the estimation method, it could be very useful from an applicative viewpoint to construct a leading indicator with specific forecasting capabilities for the turning points (18).

An alternative method to that based on spectral analysis which takes into consideration all the cycle's points is that of impulse-response functions between the single indicators and the reference series (Box and Jenkins [6]). This technique, which requires the use of seasonally adjusted series (19), has the advantage of letting the data determine the form of the relation between the series considered as well as the average lag implicit in it for each moment of time.

The series are first filtered to extract an innovation series which presumably contains the important information for each indicator in addition to those furnished by the past. These variations are obtained with the appropriate *ARMA* models determined through the total and partial serial correlation functions; these models are then estimated with the least squares method. The innovation series thus obtained are compared with those obtained for the reference aggregate: the cross

---

(18) Among the attempts to construct synthetic indicators isolating the cyclical components of the series used one should make special mention of the contributions by BARAGONA [2] and BARAGONA - CARLUCCI [3].

(19) NEFTCI [58] and AUERBACH [1], using causality tests, showed that the usefulness of most of the leading indicators is greater when series which have not been seasonally adjusted are used.

correlation between the pairs of series provides the information desired regarding the relation between input and output and hence identify the form of the transfer function.

Koch and Rasche [37] use this approach to analyse the statistical properties of the series used to construct the DOC's composite leading indicator and compare them with those of the industrial production index.

Koch and Rasche's results confirm the explicative capability of eight of the nine leading indicators considered. However, four of them have no lead (average hours worked in industry, dismissal rate, new orders for consumer goods and materials and the variation in the raw materials price index) while another two anticipate the reference series by only two months (turnover and the share price index). Only two monetary series (percentage variation in total liquidity activities and real money supply, $M2$) have an average lead (in all the cycle's phases) of five months.

The authors also applied the same verification method (using a bivariate *ARIMA* model) to the composite indicator constructed using the new series considered and using the weight employed by DOC; the single components of the composite indicator could have a greater informational power (Zarnowit and Boschan [78]). What is noticeable is the absence of a true lead by the composite leading indicator with regard to the industrial production index. However, this does not necessarily imply that the composite indicator does not have a good forecasting capability. In fact it is useful for improving the industrial production forecast which can be obtained using only the past of the time series (the bivariate model's forecast errors are lower than those obtained using a univariate model with a single industrial production index).

It should nonetheless be stressed that the transfer function limits the techniques for constructing and selecting leading indicators: when first order difference series with monthly frequence are used, indicators constructed in this manner furnish information solely concerning the very short-term movements which could be influenced by other variables; in this case the cyclical components of the series considered would not be isolated. Hence this method means that an indicator need not show any lead vis-à-vis the reference cycle even though the cyclical components of the same series are stably correlated between themselves with a considerable time lag.

The relation between the leading indicator theory and time series analysis was formalised by Sargent and Sims [65] who prove that forecasts with the composite leading indicator can be interpreted as imposing a specific series of restrictions on the series' autoregression vector included in the index itself. Moreover, they point out that it is statistically incongruous to even consider a variable or a function of variables as a leading indicator. One can easily imagine the case of an exogenous variable x used to predict an endogenous variable y which nonetheless, thanks to a distributed-lag relation, can predict the variable x.

From the point of view of optimal forecasting theory, the choice of the synthetic indicator's components should be conditioned by the need to identify the direction of the causal relation using the Granger test [27] (20). In addition, the problem of discretionality in the choice of the weights for the synthetic indicator's components could be resolved by simultaneously estimating a system of the type:

(2)
$$y_t = a1_0 + a1_j y_{t-j} + \ldots + a1_k y_{t-k} + \\ + b1_j x1_{t-j} + \ldots + b1_k x1_{t-k} + \varepsilon_1 t$$

(3)
$$x_t = w_1 s1_t + w_2 s2_t + \ldots + w_n sn_t + \varepsilon_2 t$$

where y is the variation rate of the variable of the reference (or aggregate) series and x the variation rate of the indicator constructed with the series $s_1 \ldots s_n$ on the basis of the set of weights $w_1 \ldots w_n$. Hence the w parameters would be those which maximize the forecasting power of the composite indicator.

A similar methodoly is applied by Auerbach [1] to verify whether the set of weights used for constructing the composite leading indicator calculated by the Bureau of Economic Analysis (BEA) is optimal and if it is possible to identify a set of different weights to obtain better forecasts both in and outside the sample. Auerbach

---

(20) As regards causality analysis, NEFTCI [58] concludes that only six of the eleven series included in the indicators of the Bureau of Economic Analysis (USA) help predict the reference series with a significance level of 5%.

compares the results obtained using weights calculated using traditional methods to those obtained using the simultaneous system.

Auerbach also raises an important point regarding the control of the stability of the estimates which reflects on the forecasting capability outside the sample. In particular, he emphasises that the type of relations captured by the cyclical indicators, being more fundamental by nature, is less subject to the «Lucas critique» in the sense that these relations are less affected by economic-policy changes. The set of weights obtained by Auerbach is rather different from that used by BEA (which uses practically uniform weights) and consequently, given the optimal nature of the method employed, ensures that the indicator thus constructed has a better forecasting capability in the sample. Nonetheless, while the estimates of the equations with the BEA indicator are stable, those calculated by Auerbach are unstable. This in turn helps to explain another result: why the DEA indicator's forecasts outside the sample are better (in terms of lesser RMSE) than those obtained with simultaneously estimated variable weights. One interpretation of this evidence is that if there does actually exist a synthetic indicator capable of optimally predicting the economy's cyclical fluctuations, it is probable that it is considerably unstable in time. As a consequence, the procedure employed by BEA allows these structural changes to be damped.

Auerbach concludes that though only half of the twelve series considered were significant in explaining the reference series, the composite index was very significant.

3.2 *The Probabilistic Approach*

Despite the efforts of the last ten years, it is still difficult to imagine a formal probability model which engenders leading indicators and which can be tested to optimise the series selection and synthetic indicator construction processes. As we have seen, discretion plays an important role in traditional methods and in general the attempts to perfect, from the statistical viewpoint, some of the intermediate phases have met with little success.

Nevertheless, the attempts to reformulate the construction of indicators on the basis of a specified probabilistic model, represent a significant step forward in the advancement of cyclical indicator theory. One of the principal contributions in this sense is that by Stock and Watson [69] and [70] who start by asking themselves what leading indicators should anticipate.

As we have seen above, Burns and Mitchell ([8] and Mitchell and Burns [50]) provide a response in terms of "reference cycles" defined as significant shifts in economic activity.

There is a general consensus that the definition of an economic cycle cannot limit itself only to fluctuations in the GDP (Lucas [40]); rather it should refer to comovements observed and measured in a wide spectrum of macroeconomic aggregate variables such as production, employment and turnover. Important progress has been made in comprehending the possibility of this type of approach (Sargent and Sims [65], Singleton [67], Engle and Watson [24]; Engle and Granger [23]; King, Plosser and Rebello [32]). On the basis of this literature, Stock and Watson propose isolating these comovements and representing them with a single non-observed variable, which is however assessable (which they define "the state of the economy"). This variable would be a coincident indicator and serve as the base on which to construct a leading indicator.

Each series considered would therefore be formed by the non-observable component and an idiosyncratic component. The probabilistic model used by the authors is rather sophisticated; they assume that both the non-observed variable and the idiosyncratic components have a linear stochastic structure of the form:

(4)
$$Y_t = \beta + \gamma \Delta C_t + u_t$$
$$\phi(L) \Delta C_t = \delta + \eta_t$$
$$D(L) u_t = \varepsilon_t$$

where Y represents the growth rates of the variables considered (21), C the non-observed variable, i.e., the coincident index, u, v and e

---

(21) The authors use growth rates instead of levels so that the variables are individually integrated but not jointly co-integrated (as per ENGLE - GRANGER [23]). In other words, the series has a stochastic trend (see NELSON - PLOSSER [60]) but it is not shared by all the variables.

independent errors and $\phi(L)$ and $D(L)$ lag polinomials. The authors emphasise that caution should be exercised when interpreting this assumption to verify the existence of a common source of variations (shock) between real variables (Sargent and Sims [65], King et Al. [32]). The most correct interpretation should instead be that there are multiple sources of economic fluctuations but they have proportional dynamic effects on the real variables.

The authors use Kalman's filter to estimate the non-observed variable. Once the reference variable has been defined, the composite leading indicator is obtained as the estimate of its growth (and not of the levels as for traditional indicators), in the subsequent six months, on the basis of a set of series assessed as leading indicators of the business cycle. More specifically, the synthetic leading indicator, $C_{t+6|t}$, is estimated as the result of a vectorial autoregressive system which comprises the series selected as components (Y_t) and the non-observed variable of the economy C_t:

(5) $$\Delta C_t = \mu_C + \lambda_{CC}(L) \Delta C_{t-1} + \lambda_{CY}(L) Y_{t-1} + v_{Ct}$$
$$Y_t = \mu_Y + \lambda_{YC}(L) \Delta C_{t-1} + \lambda_{YY}(L) Y_{t-1} + v_{Yt}$$

where (V_{Ct}, V_{Yt}) are non-correlated errors. The leading indicator is therefore calculated as $C_{t+6|t} - C_{t|t}$ (22).

However, even a probabilistic model such as that formalised by Stock and Watson remains faced with the problem of how to identify the variables which are suited to being used in the construction of the coincident indicator. The authors first select a set of 55 series from a list of 280 variables using a selection method which is strongly influenced by discretionary criteria, such as the presence of expectation components, some theoretical base for the relation between variables and economic activity and their economic-policy content. These criteria are supplemented by statistical criteria such as spectral coherence, phase lead, the ability to cause the official index (DOC) in Granger's sense and the ability to improve the explicative and forecas-

---

(22) On the basis of this probabilistic model, Stock and Watson also calculate a recession indicator, defined as the probability that the economy will be in a recession over the coming six months. The authors define recession as a period of negative growth of the coincident indicator which lasts for at least six months.

ting capability of the coincident index (23). The authors further select a set of 11 series which go to make up the leading indicator on the basis of the capability to explain the growth (over the coming six months) of their composite coincident indicator (24).

3.3 Recessions and Recoveries

If recognising turning points is the main raison d'être of leading cyclical indicators, the decision to define the start of a recession (recovery) as a sequence of decreases (increases) in the levels (or in the growth rates) of the indicator would appear somewhat arbitrary (Zarnowitz and Moore [80]) (25). Neftci [59] has indicated a statistical criterion which, while not totally eliminating the criteria of discretionality, does make the content clear, quantifying it in a confidence interval.

The methodology proposed allows an optimal evaluation of the movement observed in the leading indicator through the use of three items of information: the probability that the most recent observation is part of an expansionary or recessionary phase; the probability of a recession (recovery) given the duration of the expansionary (recessionary) phase under way vis-à-vis the average recorded in the past; the estimation of the probability of a recession (recovery) relative to the previous observation. Neftci's models are based on the assumption that when a turning point is about to be reached economic activity rapidly decreases and the cyclical indicators register this dynamic (that is to say they decrease rapidly before a recession and increase rapidly before a recovery).

Thus structured, the optimal interruption theory can be applied

---

(23) Here we are principally interested in methodological questions. One should consult the works cited for a description of the results.

(24) Sims, in commenting the work of STOCK - WATSON [69], notes that a probabilistic model which does not use variable coeffcents and Bayesian estimation methods has little credibility.

(25) The debate on the appropriate definition of recession has seen more interest since the passing of the Gramm-Rudman-Hollings law in 1984 by the American Congress. This law, which limits federal government spending, envisages some exceptions in the event of recession (Section 254), which has been defined as a growth of less than one per cent for two successive quarters (ZARNOWITZ and MOORE [81]).

to the problem as part of a sequential analysis, obtaining a formula for calculating the probability that a recession (recovery) is imminent on the basis of the past history of expansions and recessions and an *a priori* distribution (Diebold and Rudebusch [19]). Define P_t as the (*a posteriori*) probability of a maximum (minimum) at time t, on the base of the observed data, R_t the probability of a maximum (minimum) at time t (the *a priori* probability), conditional on the fact that it has still not taken place and FU_t and FD_t, the values at time t of the density functions of the last observation if it had been generated, respectively, by an expansionary or recessionary phase of the specific cycle of the leading indicator. The recursive formula for calculating P_t is then given by:

$$(6) \quad P_t = \frac{(P_{t-1} + RU_t(1 - P_{t-1}))\, FD_t}{(P_{t-1} + RUt_1(1 - P_{t-1}))\, FD_t + (1 - P_{t-1})\, FU_t(1 - RU_t)}$$

When the cumulate probability exceeds the chosen level of confidence a turning point in the leading indicator is located. The relation between the latter and the turning point in the reference series depends on the lag structure detected.

Hence there remains an element of discretion in the choice of the confidence threshold above which a recession or a recovery will be detected. Nonetheless, Zellner [82] and Zellner and Hong [83] suggest that the optimal choice depends on the operator's relevant loss function. There is not necessarily any symmetry between the error of predicting a turning point when this does not take place and the error (potentially more serious) of not predicting the turning point when it instead does take place; applying the Bayesian method, these authors show how turning point forecasts are sensitive to asymmetry of the loss function.

The derivation of the cyclical indicator's probabilistic structure has been examined in more detail by F. Diebold and G. Rudebusch [19], [20] who developed an evaluation criteria for the capabilities of the leading indicators and different forecasting methods predicting the cycles' turning points. This criterion, the probabilistic equivalent of the mean squared error, and similarly defined as quadratic probability score, is given by:

$$(7) \qquad QPS = 1/T \sum_{t=1}^{T} 2(P_t - R_t)^2$$

where P_t represents the forecast of the probability of a turning point (with a determined lead). The QPS therefore varies between O and 2, with a score of zero in the case of a perfect forecast, and measures the gap between forecasts and realisations. It can be used to evaluate the validity of alternative rules for identifying the turning points with reference to the precision of the forecasts which can be obtained.

The method of calculating the probability of a turning point on the basis of the observed sequences in the periods immediately preceeding raises the problem of any possible asymmetry between the expansionary and recessionary phases of the business cycle. In fact, as we have seen, Neftci's formula requires the definition of an *a priori* distribution of the probabilities of a turning point given the duration of the cycle's ascending or descending phases. To this end, it would be useful to know: whether there exists any relation between the probability that a turning point is about to be reached and the number of months from the start of the corresponding phase; and whether this relation differs for recessions and recoveries (26).

McCulloch [43] has shown (with reference to the US business cycle) that once an expansion or recession has terminated its minimum duration, the probability of a turning point does not depend on the phase's age. This result has been confirmed by the analysis of Diebold and Rudebusch [20]).

---

(26) A problem which has received considerable attention is that regarding the irregularity of business cycles and their asymmetry between recessionary and expansionary phases. ZARNOWITZ [77] analyses business cycles observed in some industrialised countries over the last 150 years and finds considerable differences between the cycles in terms of both length and asymmetry in the two phases in each of the countries considered. The diversity of business cycles, with reference to the US, is also pointed out by BLANCHARD - WATSON [5].

4. - Cyclical Indicators and Economic Theory

4.1 *Measurement Without Theory*

The ambiguity existing between cyclical indicators and theory has been pointed out by many economists since their first appearance. The main criticism made of this methodology is that it constructs a "measurement without theory" in the definition coined by Koopmans [38] in his review of the volume by Burns and Mitchell [8]. More specifically, Koopmans maintained that a similar approach «which makes the least possible use of theoretical conceptions or hypotheses on the nature of economic processes» (27) would be useless for evaluating the probable effects of stabilisation policies. Koopmans' criticism emphasised that a methodology based solely on statistical regularities can provide information only on the phenomena observed, without any possibility of generalising to allow evaluation of other prediction methods or the forecasting power of alternative indicators to those used or how these indicators are influenced by structural changes (28).

Since then, economists have been divided between those who recognise an important role for cyclical indicators and those who consider them a sterile statistical exercise wiithout any theoretical foundation (29).

Macroeconometric models naturally play a leading role in business cycle forecasting. However, in view of the criticism of the lack of the theoretical foundations of cyclical indicators one cannot help but

---

(27) See Koopmans [38] reprinted in Isco: *Rassegna della letteratura sui cicli economici*, n. 1, 1962, p. 2.

(28) Koopmans' review gave rise to a debate with Vining [72] which, drawing on the probabilistic foundation of the cyclical indicator theory, emphasised that the statistical economy would be too limited in its range if it comprised only the estimate of the relations hypothesised.

(29) See Greenspan [28], in commenting a work by Saul Hymans, states his scepticism concerning the use of composite cyclical indicators, and in particular the method of selecting the components: «What underlying theory can be deduced from the choice of the indicators would appear to be hidden in some form of black box».
The position of Zarnowitz - Braun [79] is representative of the opposing faction. They recall that the choice of leading series is made also on the basis of criteria of economic significance, stating that, «The idea that the construction of leading indicators is purely measurement without theory is simply a myth».

observe that in macroeconometric forecasting exercises theory offers only an imprecise knowledge of the suitable model to be used (30). Human ignorance is compounded by the limited availability of observations and the stochastic structure of the economic variations in time which depend not only on economic policy, but also on changes in technology, consumer preferences, the availability of resources, etc. Furthermore, most of the macroeconometric models are not estimated simultaneously, but rather equation by equation, as deterministic models with measurement (and not stochastic) errors with least ordinary squares. Finally, as regards this type of model, it would be somewhat hazardous not to exercise a cautious judgement concerning the formulation of forecasts which are useful or significant (31).

Webb [75] analyses the capability for predicting a recession or a recovery in the short and very short-term (respectively one quarter and one year) of some of the more common macroeconometric models. The performance has been compared with those of two alternative forecasting methods in which economic theory has a limited role. These are an autoregressive model (*VAR*) for forecasting GDP (Webb [76]) and the sequential probability model proposed by Neftci and illustrated in the previous Section. In addition to these three forecasting methods the author also considers the standard rule for projecting the same value of the reference series on following periods, thus obtaining a forecast of no variation.

The precision (in terms of average absolute error) of the macroeconometric models in forecasting a turning point in the very short-term (one quarter) is no greater than that obtained using the *VAR* and the sequential probability models. Surprisingly, none of the models analysed provides a (average) forecast which is more precise than the standard rule (no turning point), indicating a high percentage of false signals. Nonetheless, when one considers a forecast with a more distant time horizon (four quarters) it turns out that the macro-

---

(30) The problems caused by the theoretical weakness of the macroeconometric models during simulation and forecasting are dealt with by DOAN - LITTERMAN - SIMS [21].
(31) Nonetheless, ONOFRI [62], emphasises that large-scale macroeconometric models are most suited to expressing operative propositions thanks to their flexibility in combining adherence to data and adherence to theory.

economic models are very imprecise (32), while the *VAR* methodology is able to forecast most of the turning points which actually did take place. Webb's analysis is subject to several qualifications, the most important of which is that he considers a relatively short estimation period (13 years, from 1971 to 1984) in which only three complete business cycles took place. However, the results obtained prove that a more solid theoretical foundation does not increase the precision of the model's forecasts.

In the light of these results the solidity of the cyclical indicators is less surprising even though they are constructed in large part using the same methods employed 40 years ago despite the considerable developments which have taken place in econometry and time series analysis.

This can be explained by the fact that the objective of cyclical indicators is not to comprehend economic phenomena and hence impose fewer constraints on the real phenomena to be verified. It is therefore possible that they measure an aspect of real phenomena which eludes time series analysis (Neftci [57]). In effect, as described above, cyclical indicators allow one to estimate the state of the business cycle, that is to say the probability that an expansionary or recessionary phase has begun. This is especially true when the stochastic processes which govern economic variables are characterised by sudden changes of regime (from expansionary to recessionary and viceversa). More specifically, let L define the synthetic leading indicator, S the state of the business cycle (i.e., the probability of a turning point), d the weighted sum of the serially correlated components of the series which compose L, and e the weighted sum of the stochastic processes which govern the single series. Then the variation in the synthetic indicator can be represented as:

(8) $$dL_t = S_t + d_t + e_t$$

If the stochastic processes are independent and if the number of the series comprising the synthetic indicator is sufficiently high, e_t is close to zero. The main problem could arise from d: if d is significant,

---

(32) In effect, they rarely provide a forecast of a turning point for a time horizon of four quarters.

i.e., if the series used to construct the synthetic indicator have components which are serially correlated between the series, the synthetic indicator would not be able to isolate the term S, the state of the business cycle.

The conditions which allow a synthetic indicator to act as a filter for the stochastic component of the series considered are therefore moderate variability and the series representing different economic phenomena. This would reduce the serial correlation between the causal factors.

4.2 The Economy of the Leading Indicators

If one rejects Koopman's thesis that cyclical indicators are a "measurement without theory", it is essential to analyse the economic mechanisms which are implied in the functioning of the leading indicators (Zarnowitz - Boschan [78], Moore [53], De Leeuw [14].

With reference to the series generally used as single leading indicators and as components of synthetic indicators, it is possible to identify some economic criteria which could justify their use (De Leeuw [14]).

A first criterion regards the times of the production process: for many goods several months pass between the decision concerning their production and the actual production. This criterion could justify the use, as leading indicators, of the series of new orders for consumer and intermediate goods, new contracts and orders for plant and machinery, and building licences for new constructions.

However this criterion would appear to assume some lack of information by the producers in forming their expectations regarding future demand; every new order is then a demand shock. An alternative, or complementary, interpretation could motivate the lead time of these variables on the basis of the cost of not satisfying an order in time vis-à-vis the cost of rapidly changing production. For some consumer goods which have a strong seasonal demand, it is reasonable to assume that the producers plan their production. However, this criterion can be valid in the case of products which are very complex and modelled according to the client's request and generally limited in volume. For example, a planned in advance production of an aircraft can cause many losses if, once produced, the aircraft remains unsold for a long time.

A second reason for the use of leading indicators could be identified in the greater speed of adaptation of some series vis-à-vis others when the economy is subject to shocks. This criterion could justify the use, as leading indicators, of the number of hours worked per week in industry and the speed of delivery of goods. It is in fact probable that producers react to an unexpected increase in demand by increasing overtime before hiring extra labour. Likewise, it is reasonable to expect that, at least in the short-term, producers are forced to reduce the speed of deliveries to respond to an unexpected increase in demand.

Nevertheless, the same objection as that raised above, namely producers' short-sighted expectations, can also apply to this second justification. Furthermore, this type of criterion cannot be applied indifferently to any type of shock, but only to demand shocks. A further objection is that the variation observed in this type of series, presumably following an unexpected shock, should coincide with a variation of the same sign in production and not anticipate it. On the other hand, they could actually anticipate a variation in employment; however, on the basis of this criterion, these indicators should return to their pre-shock levels as soon as employment has grown once again to its optimal levels.

A third criterion which could justify the use of some series as leading indicators (or their introduction in a composite indicator) regards expectations. Some series are more responsive to variations in expectations and hence move first (De Leeuw [15]); this criterion could justify the use of share prices or raw materials prices. The problem with this type of series is that their interpretation is somewhat ambiguous. Their increase is not in fact necessarily linked to an increase in economic activity. This is unarguably the case of an increase in prices caused by an increase in demand; nevertheless, when there is a supply shock (for example for the formation of a cartel which pushes raw materials prices up) there is no reason to expect an increase in production. Similarly, if the stock market is influenced by speculation it is probable that this does not affect economic activity.

This criterion could justify the use of sample surveys on consumer and company expectations even though their interpretation requires the definition of a common reference framework for all interviewees (D'Elia [16], Gennari [26]).

A fourth criterion different from the others for the economic significance is that the series considered are fundamentally responsible for short-term economic fluctuations. Such an interpretation would be discordant with the assumption, briefly mentioned above, that leading indicators can be considered solely as intermediate phases of the mechanisms which link economic fluctuations to the true causes which generate them. However, this criterion would appear appropriate for justifying their inclusion in the monetary series amongst the components of synthetic leading indicators. Recent economic literature on the effect of monetary policy would appear to specify that only unexpected variations in money are significant in determining the fluctuations of real variables (Sargent [64]; Stock and Watson [69]; Christiano and Ljungqvist [13]). However, even if we accept this causality relation, it still has to be proven that the effect of money on economic activity is realised within the time horizons significant for the construction of a leading indicator (that is to say several months). It would appear more probable instead that this effect is realised over a longer period and that it is subject to a high variability.

Even though most of the series used as leading indicators are less important economically than monetary variables, they are more easily and immediately available and hence are more useful as leading indicators. The role of this series is convincingly illustrated by De Leeuw [14] with an example. Let us suppose that our reference variable is the hour of arrival in office of a commuter and that we wish to obtain a forecast of this variable. In this case, the sanctions he would face in the event of late arrival can be compared to the fundamental variables on the basis of the fluctuations of economic activity while the time the commuter leaves home can be compared to the instrumental variables which form the intermediate mechanisms. In choosing the possible leading indicators, it is very probable that the second group of variables (time of leaving home) furnishes a relation with the reference variable (time of arrival) which is more direct and immediate than the first (the sanctions) even though it is very probable that the variables of the first group cause the variables included in the second. The causality relations can also be used to identify which of the intermediate mechanisms are more significant for forecasting purposes when there are important variations in the fundamental variables.

Finally, another criterion (of a statistical rather than economic nature) for selecting the variables to be used as leading indicators concerns the forecasting capability of the variations of some series vis-à-vis the levels. The series which have these characteristics are naturally those with a high serial correlation; variations in stocks and consumer credit would form part of this group.

5. - Conclusions

This paper has attempted to analyse the validity of the cyclical indicator method in short-term cyclical analysis.

In general this responds to the need to limit the wide margins of discretionality which characterise this methodology. In particular, our interest has been concentrated on two interrelated aspects: the possibility of improving the classical methodology developed in the 1930s and still applied in many industrialised countries and the possible determination of theoretical bases for the functioning of these indicators.

The principal result to emerge from the survey of the literature is that the validity of cyclical indicators depends on the way in which they are used and the researcher's objective. They do not describe causal relations, but rather reflect some mechanisms which characterise each single economy which can depend on factors such as technology, the institutions and market structure. It is through these mechanisms that the true causes of cyclical fluctuations are transmitted to the reference production aggregates. Hence the indicators only register the intermediate phases in this transfer process.

At least while we do not have a rather robust theory which illustrates these mechanisms, cyclical indicators will remain an empirical instrument and as such will be constructed on the basis of the needs it is desired to deal with. If the primary objective is that of anticipating turning points, the risk of false signals will probably be increased, while it can be minimised only by increasing the risk of not recognising (in useful time) that an inversion in trend is taking place. On the other hand, if the objective is that of having a forecasting instrument for all the phases of the cycle, it should be recognised that cyclical indicators are not the most appropriate instruments for this purpose.

With regard to the validity of cyclical indicators, G.H. Moore commented: «It is important to be clear about what these results do *not* mean, as well as what they do mean. They do not mean that one can get much advance notice that a general business contraction is beginning or is coming to an end. They do help one to recognize these events at about the time they occur. Even then there is some risk of error» (33).

It is therefore necessary to have a user's manual for cyclical indicators in order to fully exploit the statistical and economic relations (which are not easily distinguishable) synthesised by these instruments. At the same time it is necessary to analyse in more detail the mechanisms underlying each indicator so that they can also be used as a simulation tool. However, accepting the assumption that cyclical indicators reflect not the economic forces which generate the fluctuations but simply the intermediate mechanisms via which they are realised, one should be careful when using economic-policy variables since they can produce variations in the stochastic process which engenders the business cycle and (as emphasised in Lucas' critique) generate erroneous forecasts if based on past behaviour.

---

(33) See MOORE [52], p. 79.

BIBLIOGRAPHY

[1] AUERBACH A.J.: «The Index of Leasing Indicators: Measurement Without Theory, Thirty Five Years Later», *Review of Economics and Statistics*, n. 64, 1982.

[2] BARAGONA R.: «Una procedura per la costruzione di un indice sintetico del ciclo economico», *Atti della XXXIII Riunione scientifica* della Società italiana di statistica, Bari, 1986.

[3] BARAGONA R. - CARLUCCI F.: «Aggregating Cyclical Fluctuations in a Composite Index», Dipartimento di statistica, *Probabilità e statistiche applicate*, serie A, n. 16, 1989.

[4] BEVERIDGE S. - NELSON C.R.: «A New Approach to the Decomposition of Economic Time Series into Permanent and Transient Components with Particular Attention to Measurement of the Business Cycle», *Journal of Monetary Economics*, n. 7, 1981.

[5] BLANCHARD O.J. - WATSON M.W.: «Are Business Cycles All Alike?», *Working Paper*, n. 1392, 1984.

[6] BOX G. - JENKINS G.: *Time Series Analysis: Forecasting and Control*, San Francisco, Holden-Day, 1976.

[7] BRY G. - BOSCHAN C.: «Cyclical Analysis of Time Series: Selected procedures and Computer Programs», NBER, *Technical Paper*, n. 20, 1971.

[8] BURNS A. - MITCHELL W.C.: «Measuring Business Cycle», NBER, New York, Columbia University Press, *Studies in Business Cycle*, n. 2, 1946.

[9] CAMPBELL J.Y. - MANKIW N.G.: «Are Output Fluctuations Transitory?», *Quarterly Journal of Economics*, n. 102, 1987.

[10] CLARK P.K.: «The Cyclical Components of the US Economic Activity», *Quarterly Journal of Economics*, n. 102, 1987.

[11] COCHRANE J.H.: «How Big is the Random Walk in GNP?», *Journal of Political Economy*, n. 96, 1988.

[12] COMMISSIONE DELLA COMUNITÀ EUROPEA: *European Economy*, supplement B, July 1991.

[13] CHRISTIANO L.J. - LJUNGQVIST L.: «Money does Granger-Cause Output in the Bivariate Money-Output Relation», *Journal of Monetary Economics*, n. 22, 1988.

[14] DE LEEUW F.: «Toward a Theory of Leading Indicators», in LAHIRI K. - MOORE G.H. (eds.): *Leading Economic Indicators*, Cambridge, Cambridge University Press, 1991.

[15] —— - ——: «Leading Indicators and the "Prime Mover" View», *Survey of Current Business*, n. 69, 1989.

[16] D'ELIA E.: «La quantificazione dei risultati dei sondaggi congiunturali: un confronto tra procedure», ISCO, *Rassegna dei lavori dell'istituto*, n. 13, 1991.

[17] DE NICOLA E.: «Una nuova misura del grado di consistenza ciclica degli indicatori congiunturali: l'indice MDC», Isco, *Rassegna dei lavori interni dell'istituto*, n. 9, 1967.

[18] ——: «Cicli classici e cicli di crescita: analisi a doppio "binario" delle serie storiche», *Note economiche*, n. 2, 1981.

[19] DIEBOLD F.X. - RUDEBUSCH G.D.: «Scoring Leading Indicators», *Journal of Business*, n. 62, 1989.

[20] DIEBOLD F.X. - RUDEBUSCH G.D.: «Turning Point Prediction with the Composite Leading Index», in LAHIRI K. - MOORE G.H. (eds.): *Leading Economic Indicators*, Cambridge, Cambridge University Press, 1991.
[21] DOAN T. - LITTERMAN R. - SIMS C.: «Forecasting and Conditional Projection Using Realistic Prior Distributions», *Econometrics Reviews*, n. 3, 1984.
[22] EBANKS W. - BOSCHAN C.: «The Phase Average Trend: A New Way of Measuring Economic Growth», *Journal of the American Statistical Association*, 1978.
[23] ENGLE R.F. - GRANGER C.W.: Co-Integration and Error Correction: Representation, Estimation and Testing, *Econometrica*, n. 55, 1987.
[24] ENGLE R.F. - WATSON M.W.: «A One-Factor Multivariate Time Series Model of Metropolitan Wage Rates», *Journal of the American Statistical Association*, n. 76, 1981.
[25] FRIEDMAN M. - SCHWARTZ A.: «Money and Business Cycle», *Review of Economic and Statistics*, n. 45, 1963.
[26] GENNARI P.: «L'uso delle indagini congiunturali ISCO per la previsione degli indici della produzione industriale», ISCO, *Rassegna dei lavori dell'istituto*, n. 13, 1991.
[27] GRANGER C.W.: «Investigating Causal Relations by Econometric Models and Cross Spectral Methods», *Econometrica*, n. 37, 1969.
[28] GREENSPAN A.: «Commento a Hymans S.: On the Use of Leading Indicators to Predict Cyclical Turning Points», *Brooking Papers on Economic Activity*, n. 2, 1973.
[29] HAMILTON J.D.: «A New Approach to the Economic Analysis of Nonstationary Time Series and the Business Cycles», *Econometrica*, n. 57, 1989.
[30] HARVEY A.C.: «Trends and Cycles in Macroeconomic Time Series», *Journal of Business and Economic Statistics*, n. 3, 1985.
[31] HYMANS S.: «On the Use of Leading Indicators to Predict Cyclical Turning Points», *Brooking Papers on Economic Activity*, n. 2, 1973.
[32] KING R.G. - PLOSSER C.I. - REBELLO S.T.: «Production, Growth and Business Cycles I: The Basic Neoclassical Model», *Journal of Monetary Economics*, n. 21, 1988.
[33] KLEIN P.A.: *Analyzing Modern Business Cycles.: Essays in Honor of Geoffrey H. Moore*, New York, Sharpe, 1990.
[34] KLEIN P.A. - MOORE G.H.: «The Leading Indicator Approach to Economic Forecasting», *Journal of Forecasting*, n. 2, 1983.
[35] — - —: *Monitoring Growth Cycles in Market Oriented Economies*, New York, NBER, 1985.
[36] KLING J.L.: «Predicting the Turning Points of Business and Economics Time Series», *Journal of Business*, n. 60, 1987.
[37] KOCH P.D. - RASCHE R.H.: «An Examination of the Commerce Department Leading-Indicator Approach», *Journal of Business and Economic Statistics*, n. 6, 1988.
[38] KOOPMANS T.C.: «Measurement Without Theory», *Review of Economic and Statistics*, n. 2, 1947.
[39] LIPPI M. - REICHLIN L.: «Componenti permanenti e transitorie in macroeconomia», in AMENDOLA M.: *Innovazione e progresso tecnico*, Bologna, il Mulino, 1990.
[40] LUCAS R.E. JR.: «Econometric Policy Evaluation: A Critique», *Carnegie-Rochester Conference Series on Public Policy*, n. 1, 1976.
[41] — —: «Understanding Business Cycles», *Carnagie-Rochester Conference on Public Policy*, n. 5, 1977.

[42] MARRUCO E. - DE NICOLA E.: «Problematiche inerenti alla stima ottimale del ciclo-trend nelle serie storiche economiche», ISCO, *Rassegna dei lavori dell'istituto*, n. 23, 1978.
[43] MC CULLOCH J.H.: «The Montecarlo Cycle in Business Activity», *Economic Inquiry*, n. 13, 1975.
[44] MICONI G.: *Il metodo del National Bureau of Economic Research e la sua applicazione in Italia ai fini delle diagnosi congiunturali*, Roma, ISCO, 1961.
[45] MICONI G.: «Appunti di metodologia», *Congiuntura economica*, ISCO, March, 1968.
[46] MICONI F. - DE NICOLA E.: «Applicazioni del metodo del NBER», in ISCO: *Rassegna dei lavori interni dell'istituto*, n. 2, 1964.
[47] MINTZ I.: «Dating Postwar Business Cycles: Methods and Their Applications to Western Germany: 1950-67», NBER, *Occasional Paper*, n. 107, 1969.
[48] ——: «Dating American Growth Cycles», in ZARNOWITZ V.: *The Business Cycle Today*, New York, NBER, 1972.
[49] MITCHELL W.C.: «Business Cycles: The Problem and Its Setting», NBER, *Studies in Business Cycles*, n. 1, 1927.
[50] MITCHELL W.C. - BURNS A.F.: «Statistical Indicators of Cyclical Revivals», NBER, *Bulletin*, n. 69, 1938.
[51] MOORE G.H.: «Statistical Indicators of Cyclical Revivals and Recessions», NBER, *Occasional Papers*, n. 31, 1950.
[52] ——: *Business Cycle Indicators*, Princeton, University Press, 1961.
[53] ——: *Business Cycle, Inflation, and Forecasting*, Cambridge (Mass.), Ballinger, 1980.
[54] ——: *Leading Indicators for the 1990s*, Homewood, (Ill.), Dow Jones-Irwing, 1989.
[55] MOORE G.H. - SHISKIN J.: *Indicators of Business Expansion and Contractions*, NBER, 1967.
[56] MOORE G.H. - ZARNOWITZ V.: «The Development and the Role of the National Bureau's Business Cycle Chronologies», NBER, *Working Paper*, n. 1394, 1984.
[57] NEFTCI S.: «A Time Series for the Study of Leading Indicators», in LAHIRI K. - MOORE G.H. (eds.): *Leading Economic Indicators*, Cambridge, Cambridge University Press, 1991.
[58] ——: «Lead Lag Relations, Exogeneity and Prediction of Economic Time Series», *Econometrica*, n. 47, 1979.
[59] ——: «Optimal Prediction of Cyclical Downturns», *Journal of Economics Dynamic and Control*, n. 4, 1982.
[60] NELSON C.R. - PLOSSER C.I.: «Trends and Random Walks in Macroeconomic Time Series: Some Evidence and Implications», *Journal of Monetary Economics*, n. 10, 1982.
[61] OECD: «OECD Leading Indicators and Business Cycles in Member Countries 1960-1985», *Sources and Methods*, n. 39, 1987.
[62] ONOFRI P.:«Osservazione empirica e analisi economica: esperienze di indagine sulle fluttuazioni economiche», paper presented at: *Giornate di studio su crisi della teoria e degli indicatori*, Giardini Naxos, 24-25 ott. 1991.
[63] PASSAMONTI L.: «Analisi ciclica e indicatori ciclici», IBM, *Rassegna economica*, n. 1, 1988.

[64] SARGENT T.: *Dynamic Macroeconomic Theory*, Harvard, Harvard University Press, 1987.

[65] SARGENT T. - SIMS C.: «Business Cycle Modelling without Pretending to Have Too Much a Priori Economic Theory», in SIMS C.: *New Methods in Business Cycle Research*, Minneapolis, Federal Reserve Bank of Minneapolis, 1977.

[66] SCHLITZER G.: *L'approccio degli indicatori ciclici all'analisi della congiuntura: un'applicazione*, Roma, Banca d'Italia, lavoro preparatorio per la relazione del Governatore, 1992.

[67] SINGLETON K.: «A Latent Time Series Model of the Cyclical Behavior of Interest Rates», *International Economic Review*, n. 21, 1980.

[68] STOCK J.H. - WATSON M.W.: «Variable Trends in Economic Time Series», *Journal of Economic Perspective*, n. 3, 1988.

[69] ——: «Interpreting the Evidence on Money-Income Causality», *Journal of Econometrics*, n. 40, 1989.

[70] ——: «A Probability Model of the Coincident Economic Indicators», in LAHIRI K. - MOORE G.H. *Leading Economic Indicators*, Cambridge, Cambridge University Press, 1991.

[71] —— - ——: «New Indexes of Coincident and Leading Economic Indicators», NBER, *Macroeconomics Annual*, 1989.

[72] VINING R.: «Methodological Issues in Quantitative Economics - Koopmans on the Choice of Variables to be Studied and the Method of Measurement», Cowles Commision for Research in Economics, The University of Chicago, 1949; Italian translation in ISCO, *Rassegna della letteratura sui cicli economici*, n. 2, 1962.

[73] WATSON M.W.: «Univariate Detrending Methods with Stochastic Trends», *Journal of Monetary Economics*, n. 18, 1986.

[74] ——: «Using Econometric Models to Predict Recessions», Federal Reserve Bank of Chicago, *Economic Perspective*, November-December 1991.

[75] WEBB R.: «On Predicting the Stage of the Business Cycle», in LAHIRI K. - MOORE G.H. (eds.): *Leading Economic Indicators*, Cambridge, Cambridge University Press, 1991.

[76] WEBB R.: «Toward More Accurate Forecats from Vector Autoregressions», Federal Reserve Bank of Richmond, *Economic Review*, n. 71, 1985.

[77] ZARNOWITZ V.: «The Regularity of Business Cycles», NBER, *Working Paper*, n. 2381, 1987.

[78] ZARNOWITZ V. - BOSCHAN C.: «Cyclical Indicators: An Evaluation and New Leading Indexes», *Business Conditions Digest*, n. V-X, May 1975.

[79] ZARNOWITZ V. - BRAUN P.: «Major Macroeconomic Variables and Leading Indexes: Some Estimates of their Interrelations», NBER, *Working Paper*, n. 2812, 1989.

[80] ZARNOWITZ V. - MOORE G.H.: «Sequential Signals of Recession and Recovery», *Journal of Business*, n. 1, 1982.

[81] —— - ——: «Forecasting Recession under the Gramm-Rudman-Hollings Law», in LAHIRI K. - MOORE G.H. (eds.): *Leading Economic Indicators*, Cambridge, Cambridge University Press, 1991.

[82] ZELLNER A.: «Bayesian Estimation and Prediction Using Asymmetric Loss Function», *Journal of the American Statistical Association*, n. 81, 1986.

[83] ZELLNER A. - HONG C.: «Bayesian Methods for Forecasting Turning Points in Economic Time-Series: Sensitivity of Forecasts to Asymmetry of Loss Structures», in LAHIRI K. - MOORE G.H. (eds): *Leading Economic Indicators*, Cambridge, Cambridge University Press, 1991.

Leading Indicators for OECD, Central and Eastern European Countries

Ronny Nilsson (*)
OECD, Paris

Introduction

Business cycle analysis is an area in which central and eastern European countries (CEECs) have little experience at present, but which is likely to become increasingly important as they move to market economies. The OECD Secretariat has developed a "leading indicator system" for its member countries which is used by the Secretariat and its member countries for analysing business cycles and for predicting cyclical turning points. The first part of this paper explains how the OECD leading indicators are calculated and appraises the ability of these indicators to forecast changes in aggregate output.

The second part considers the possibility of applying the OECD indicator system in Central and Eastern European countries. Most of these countries already publish several series that may serve as leading indicators but there are generally little data from "business tendency surveys" which are widely used as leading indicators by OECD countries. The introduction of business surveys is, however, in progress in several CEECs today which will add to the pool of series among which leading indicators may be found in the future.

(*) The views expressed in this paper are the author's and do not necessarily reflect those of the OECD.

The selection of potential leading indicators for the CEECs during the transition period is outlined in a separate section. The criteria used to evaluate candidate series are broader than those normally used for cyclical analysis in OECD countries and incorporate criteria which are sensitive to the changing cyclical behaviour, statistical, problems and data availability in the pre-transition and transition periods. A final section looks into the selection of potential leading indictors in the long-term and possible candidate series are evaluated against the following criteria: economic structure, subject coverage and international linkages.

1. - The OECD System of Leading Indicators (1)

1.1 *The Reference Cycle*

The "reference series" is the economic variable whose cyclical movements it is intended to predict. Ideally, the OECD indicator system would use Gross Domestic Product (GDP) as the reference series, but for many countries GDP estimates are still available only on an annual basis and there is often a substantial time lag in their publication. Instead, the OECD indictor system uses the index of total industrial production (mining, manufacturing, utilities and construction) as the reference series. Indices of industrial production are available promptly for most member countries and industrial production constitutes the more cyclical subset of the aggregate economy. In addition, the cyclical profiles of industrial production and Gross Domestic Product have been found to be closely related as can be seen from Graph 1, so that the composite leading indicators for industrial production serve well as leading indicators for the GDP cycle.

Having identified the reference series, the next step is to identify its past cyclical behaviour. The "reference chronology" (the historical cyclical pattern) for total industrial production is shown in Table 1 for the 22 countries covered by the OECD system.

---

(1) This part is based on NILSSON RONNY: «OECD Leading Indicators», *Economic Studies* n. 9, Paris OECD, 1987.

GRAPH 1

CYCLES IN INDUSTRIAL PRODUCTION AND GDP
(percentage deviation from seasonally adjusted)

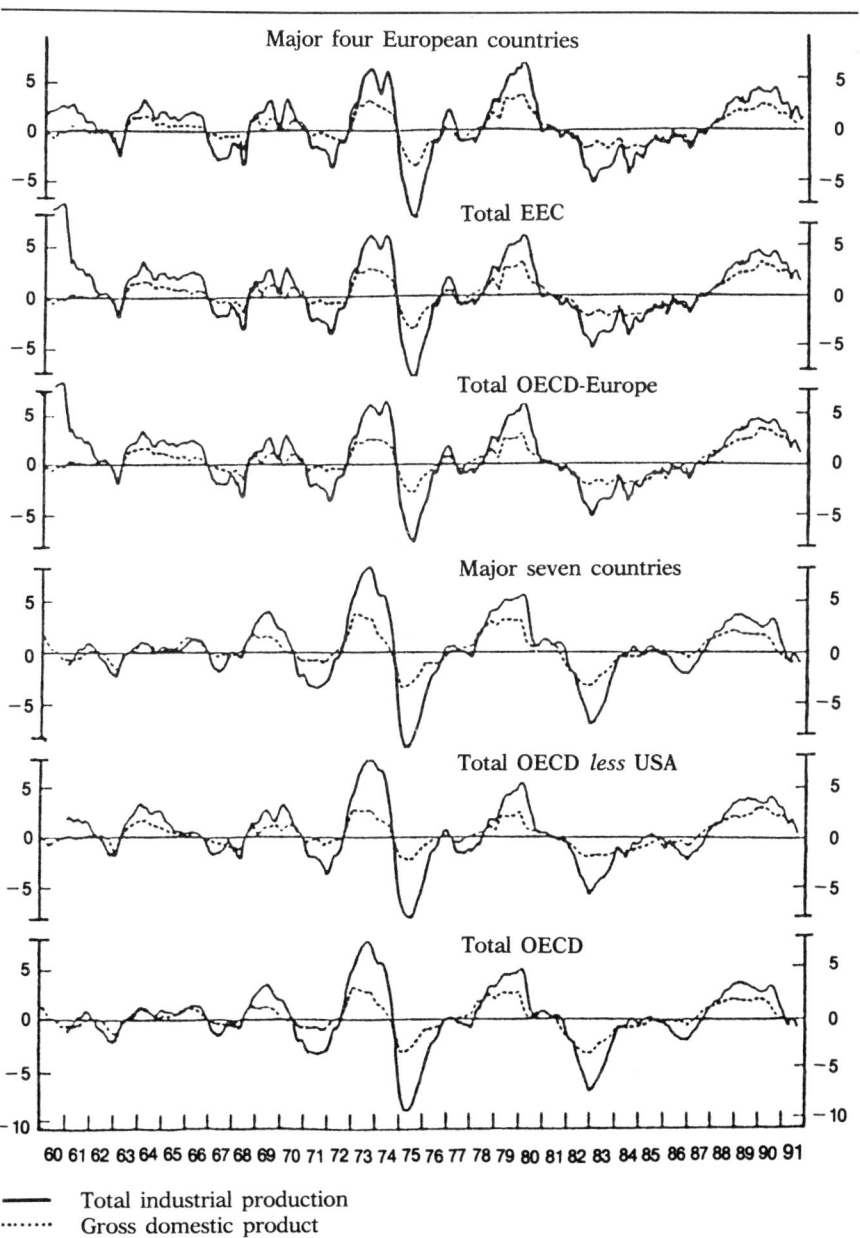

— Total industrial production
…… Gross domestic product

TABLE 1
REFERENCE CHRONOLOGIES 1960-1974
(Total industrial production)

Country	P	T	P	T	P	T	P	T	P	T	P
Canada	10/59	(3/61)	7/62)	8/63				12/65	3/69	2/68	10/70	1/74
US	1/60	(2/61)	12/61)	12/62				10/66	8/69	7/67	11/70	9/73
Japan			1/62	12/62	(5/63	10/64)	(11/67	9/68)	6/70		1/72	11/73
Australia					2/64	2/66	(2/67 | 1/68)	3/70		1/72	1/74
Austria	11/60				2/65	9/66						
Austria	11/60			2/63	1/65				2/70	8/67	12/71	4/74
Belgium			7/61	1/63	1/65				8/69	7/67	5/71	12/73
Luxembourg			8/61	2/63	2/65				11/69	2/68	2/72	8/74
Denmark									8/70		5/71	1/74
Finland			4/62	3/63	6/65				7/70	7/68	12/71	7/74
France	9/60			3/63	1/64	(1/65 | 7/66)		5/69	10/67	5/71	7/74
Germany			3/61	2/63	1/65				5/70	5/67	12/71	8/73
Greece					6/63	10/65	5/66		6/69	1/68	4/71	9/73
Ireland		Q4/60	Q2/61	Q2/63	Q3/64	5/66			1/69		3/72	3/73
Italy	(6/60	12/60)	(1/62	9/62)	9/63	3/65	(2/67	3/68)	3/70	5/67	4/72	1/74
Netherlands	12/60			2/63	3/64				8/69	11/68	12/71	8/74
Norway, mfg	12/60			3/63	(4/65 | 2/66)	1/67		7/71	4/69	11/71	10/74
Norway, tot	12/60			6/63	4/65	(12/65 | 1/67)				8/72	5/74
Portugal									12/69		3/71	1/74
Spain				7/73	(5/65 | 12/65)	10/66		2/70	8/68	9/71	8/74
Sweden			.12/61	3/63	1/65				7/70	2/68	1/72	6/74
Switzerland			3/61	(Q1/63)	Q3/63)				Q2/70	Q2/68	Q2/72	Q1/74
UK	3/60		Q4/61	1/63	5/65				6/69	8/67	2/72	6/73
Yugoslavia	6/60			5/62	11/64				(7/69	2/68	3/70)	12/74
Big 4 Europe			3/61	2/63	2/64	7/65	3/66		3/70	4/67	1/72	9/73
Major seven	1/60	(12/60)	12/61)	1/63	(2/64 | 9/65)	7/66		7/69	6/67	8/71	9/73
EEC				2/63	2/64	(7/65 | 1/66)		3/70	5/67	1/72	9/73
OECD Europe			3/61	2/63	3/64	(7/65 | 4/66)		3/70	5/67	1/72	6/74
N. America	1/60	(2/61 | 12/61)	12/62	(5/63	10/64	10/66		3/69	7/67	11/70	7/73
OECD Total	1/60	(1/61	12/61)	3/63	(2/64	8/65)	3/66		7/69	5/67	12/71	10/73

P = Growth cycle peak
T = Growth cycle trough

TABLE 1 continued

REFERENCE CHRONOLOGIES 1975-1991
(Total industrial production)

Country	T	P	T	P	T	P	T	P	T	P	T
Canada	10/75	(1/77)	9/77	9/79	(6/80)	6/81	12/82	(11/85)	9/86	4/88	3/91
US	3/75			3/79	(7/80)	7/81	11/82	(7/84)	6/86	4/89	3/91
Japan	3/75	(1/77)	7/77	2/80	(5/81)	10/81	2/83	11/84	5/87	10/90	
Australia	6/75	(10/76)	8/78	(9/79)	9/80)	5/81	1/83	2/86	1/88	8/89	
Austria	10/75	(1/77)	12/77	12/79			12/82	8/85	1/88	4/90	
Belgium	9/75	(10/76)	1/78	12/79			12/82	(12/85)	11/86	3/90	
Luxembourg	8/75			12/79	(1/81)	2/82	12/82	12/84	8/87	4/89	
Denmark	3/75	(6/76)	4/77	10/79	(11/80)	7/81	10/82	7/86			
Finland	(9/75)	12/76	7/78	7/80			10/82	4/85	4/86	11/88	
France	5/75	(1/77)	12/77	7/79			8/83			8/90	
Germany	7/75	(3/77)	3/78	12/79	(3/81)	1/82	12/82	(10/85)	2/87	6/91	
Greece	7/74	(11/76)	4/77	5/79	(9/80)	12/81	1/85	(10/85)	7/87	9/89	
Ireland	10/75			9/79			12/82	(12/84)	12/86	6/89	
Italy	5/75	(12/76)	12/77	4/80			6/83			11/89	
Netherlands	8/75	(9/76)	5/78	11/79			11/82	(2/86)	2/87	7/90	
Norway, mfg	(12/75)	1/77		7/80	(12/80)	9/81	11/82			2/87	
Norway, tot	1/75	8/76	5/77	2/80			10/82			8/89	
Portugal	2/76	(9/77)	8/78	1/80	(8/81)	3/83	9/85	(10/86)	8/88	9/90	
Spain	1/76	(3/77)	6/77	7/79			8/82			8/89	
Sweden	(1/76)	6/76	6/78	12/79			11/82	(12/84)	2/87	3/89	
Switzerland	Q1/75	(Q3/77)	Q3/78	Q1/80			Q4/82	(Q3/86)	Q2/87	Q2/90	
UK	8/75			6/79	5/81		4/83	(1/84)	8/84	6/88	
Yugoslavia	4/76			3/79	(7/80)	6/81				3/87	
Big 4 Europe	6/75	(1/77)	2/78	1/80			11/82			7/90	
Major seven	4/75	(3/77)	10/77	1/80	(8/80)	1/81	11/82	(5/85)	9/86	3/89	
EEC	7/75	(1/77)	2/78	1/80			11/82			7/90	
OECD Europe	7/65	(1/77)	2/78	1/80			11/82			7/90	
N. America	3/75			3/79	(7/80)	7/81	12/82	(7/84)	6/86	4/89	
OECD total	5/75	(3/77)	10/77	2/80	(9/80)	2/81	11/82	(5/85)	1/87	4/89	3/91

P = Growth cycle peak
T = Growth cycle trough
( ) = Turning points of minor growth cycles

1.2 *Selection of Indicators*

Once the underlying cyclical behaviour of the reference series has been established, the next step is to select economic time series whose cyclical movements typically predate those of the reference series. Candidate series are evaluated using the following criteria.

1.2.1 Relevance

1) Economic significance: there has to be an economic reason for the observed leading relationship before the series can be accepted as an indicator; 2) breadth of coverage: series with a wide coverage, in terms of the representation of the economic activity concerned, are preferred to narrowly-defined series;

1.2.2 Cyclical Behaviour

3) Length and consistency of the lead of the indicator over the reference cycle at turning points; 4) "cyclical conformity" between the indicator and the reference series: if the cyclical profiles are highly correlated, the indicator will provide a guide, not only to approaching turning points, but also to developments over the whole cycle; 5) absence of extra or missing cycles in comparison with the reference series; 6) smoothness, that is, how promptly a cyclical turn in the series can be distinguished from irregular movements;

1.2.3 Practical Considerations

7) Frequency of publication: monthly series are preferred to quarterly ones; 8) absence of eccessive revisions; 9) timeliness of publication and easy accessibility for data collection and updating; 10) availability of a long time series of the data with no breaks.

To determine how well candidate series meet criteria three through six, two separate tests are carried out (a peak-and-trough analysis and a cross-correlation analysis).

For-peak-and trough analysis, statistics are assembled on each series' behaviour at cyclical turning points: the mean or median leads, the mean deviation from the median and the number of extra or missing cycles when compared with the reference series. Usually these figures are not statistically significant in the usual sense because of the limited number of turning points available over the period investigated, and because most series contain irregular movements and double or multiple peaks and troughs. Peak-and-trough analysis therefore involves a substantial amount of judgement. Cross-correlation analysis is used to complement the peak-and-trough analysis concerning the average lead of the indicator, and to give information about the extent to which the cyclical profiles of indicator and reference series resemble each other.

Certain practical factors (criteria seven through ten) need to be considered too, if the indicator system is to be updated regularly and used for current analysis of the economic cycle. These factors refer to matters of data collection, updating and computation, so that the final composite indicator can be calculated quickly and, as far as possible, automatically.

1.3 Leading Indicators

The OECD system does not use a standard set of leading indicators for all countries, because of important differences between them in economic structure and statistical systems. Leading indicator series which perform well in both tracking and forecasting cyclical developments differ from country to country and may also change over time.

The different subject areas from which the leading indicator series are chosen are set out in Table 2. Certain types of series recur regularly in the list of leading indicators for different countries. Business survey series are among those most frequently used in the countries where they are available. These series concern business expectations on production, inflow of new orders, level of order books, stocks of finished goods and the general economic situation. The most frequently used other series are monetary and financial series such as stock-market prices, money supply and interest rates.

TABLE 2

LEADING INDICATORS USED IN THE OECD SYSTEM

Indicator series by subject area	1	2	3	4	5	6	7	8	9	10	11	12	13	14	15	16	17	18	19	20	21	22	23
Production, stocks and orders																							
Industrial production in specific branches		1			1												2					1	5
Orders																							4
Stocks																							
– materials	1															1							2
– finished goods	1		1													2							4
– imported products																1							1
Ratios, e.g. inventory/shipment			1																				1
Construction, sales and trade																							
Construction approvals				1		1	1					1					1						3
Construction starts	1	1				1	1																6
Sales or registrations of motor vehicles	1						1						1					1	1				5
Retail sales	1						1		1			1			1						1	1	5
Labour force																							
Ratio new employment/employment																			1				1
Layoffs/initial claims, unemployment insurance		1																	1				2
Vacancies																						1	1
Hours worked	1												1										2

TABLE 2 continued

Indicator series by subject area	1	2	3	4	5	6	7	8	9	10	11	12	13	14	15	16	17	18	19	20	21	22	23
Prices, costs and profits																							
Wages and salaries per unit of output	1																		1				3
Price indices		1																					6
Profits, flow of funds, net acquisitions of financial assets															1						2		2
Monetary and financial																							
Foreign exchange holdings								2															2
Deposits			1							1												1	2
Credit			1						1			2			1	1							4
Ratios, e.g. loans/deposits			1		1	1	1	1													1		1
Money supply	1		1			1	1		3	1			1	1	1				1	1	0		17
Interest rates		1	1	1		1			1	1		1	1	1	1				1	1	1		14
Stock prices	1									1		1	1		1	1			1	1	1		12
Company formation			1																				1
Foreign trade																							
Exports aggregates																							1
Exports components								2	1														2
Trade balance			1																				1
Terms of trade			1	1									1		1	1				1			6

Legend:

1 = Canada	9 = France	17 = Portugal	
2 = Usa	10 = Germany	18 = Spain	
3 = Japan	11 = Luxembourg	19 = Sweden	
4 = Australia	12 = Greece	20 = Switzerland	
5 = Austria	13 = Ireland	21 = UK	
6 = Belgium	14 = Italy	22 = Yugoslavia	
7 = Denmark	15 = Netherlands	23 = All countries	
8 = Finland	16 = Norway		

TABLE 2 continued

Indicator series by subject area	1	2	3	4	5	6	7	8	9	10	11	12	13	14	15	16	17	18	19	20	21	22	23
Business surveys																							
General situation				1				1	1			1				1							6
Production	1		1	1	1	1		2	1			1		1	1	1	1	1	1	1	1		15
Orders inflow/new orders	1			1		1	1	1				1		1	1	1	1		1	1	1		11
Orderbooks/sales					1				1	1		1		1	1		1	2	1		1		11
Stocks of raw materials										1			1								1		3
Stocks of finished goods	1		1						1	1			1		1			2	1	1	1		10
Capacity utilization																		1			1		2
Bottlenecks							1				2		1										2
Employment				1			1										1						3
Prices						1																	1
Economic activity in foreign countries	1				5						2				1								9
Indicators	12	9	11	8	9	7	9	10	11	9	2	9	9	7	11	11	6	7	12	7	10	4	190

Legend:

1 = Canada
2 = Usa
3 = Japan
4 = Australia
5 = Austria
6 = Belgium
7 = Denmark
8 = Finland

9 = France
10 = Germany
11 = Luxembourg
12 = Greece
13 = Ireland
14 = Italy
15 = Netherlands
16 = Norway

17 = Portugal
18 = Spain
19 = Sweden
20 = Switzerland
21 = UK
22 = Yugoslavia
23 = All countries

Series relating to stocks and orders, construction, retail sales, prices and foreign trade are also used frequently. Several series, such as stocks of finished goods, interest rates and prices, have to be inverted to obtain a positive correlation with the reference series.

1.4 *Turning Point and Trend Estimation*

In common with most similar systems, the OECD leading indicator system uses the "growth cycle" or "deviation-from-trend" approach. This is necessary because essential cyclical similarities between series may be obscured by different long-term trends. Trend estimation is thus a crucial step in detecting cyclical movements and identifying turning points.

The method of trend estimation adopted by the OECD is a modified version of the Phase-Average Trend method developed by the United States National Bureau of Economic Research (NBER) (2). This method has been designed specifically to separate the long-term trends from medium-term cycles, with the latter defined according to the criteria programmed in the Bry-Boschan computer routine (3) for selection of cyclical turning points.

The Phase-Average Trend (PAT) of a series is estimated by first splitting the series into *phases*, defined as the number of months between successive turning points. The means of the observations in each phase are then calculated and these *phase-averages* are used to compute a three-term moving average. The values obtained from the moving average are assigned to the mid-point of the three-phase period (known as a "triplet") to which they refer. The trend is then obtained by computing the slope between the mid-point of successive triplets. The trend is extrapolated from the last available triplet to the end of the series by a least-squares log-linear regression starting from the mid-point of the last triplet.

---

(2) The method is described in BOSCHAN CHARLOTTE - EBANKS WALTER: «The Phase-Average Trend, a New Way of Measuring Economic Growth», *Proceedings of the Business and Economic Statistics Section*, American Statistical Association, 1978.

(3) See BRY GERHARD - BOSCHAN CHARLOTTE: «Programmed turning point determination», *Cyclical Analysis of Time Series: Selected Procedures and Computer Programmes*, NBER, 1971.

It will be appreciated that the estimation of the peak and trough dates is a crucial step in the PAT procedure. First estimates are made using the Bry-Boschan routine, which begins by calculating a moving-average trend estimate for the identification of turning points. The routine then executes a series of tests on the deviations from this first trend estimate, so as to eliminate extreme values and turning points that are judged to be too close together; the Bry-Boschan routine specifies a minimum duration of five months for a phase and fifteen months for a cycle. These operations are applied to various smoothed curves in order to identify turning points which coincide more and more closely with observable variation in the original series. Last, the turning points are sought in the original series within the five months on both sides of the turning points found at the preceding stage. The points thus identified are taken as the preliminary turning points.

The main problem with the Bry-Boschan routine is that it tends to select too many turning points, thereby giving a long-term trend which is too variable; relatively minor fluctuations may be selected by the routine and given the same weight as more important cycles. The turning points finally chosen as input to the trend calculation are selected taking into account the relationship between the variables used in the indicator system. That is, care is taken to select the cyclical turning points corresponding to the reference chronology so that the trend estimation for each variable is done in a manner consistent with that for the other indicators and for the reference series itself. The same considerations apply in making the trend estimate for the reference series; here the main consideration is consistency between the turning points selected for a given country and the turning points for the other twenty-one countries included in the system.

1.5 The Phase-Average Trend Method

1.5.1 Objectives

The growth cycle programme based on the Phase-Average-Trend (PAT) method is designed 1) to select turning points (peaks and troughs) in raw (i.e. seasonally adjusted) data or in data adjusted for long-term trend; 2) to measure the long-term trend and its rate of change and 3) to produce trend-adjusted data. If trend adjustment is not desired, the turning point routine can be used on raw data alone, thus producing a chronology of turning points in "classical cycles". With the trend-adjustment option, the programme produces a chronology of "growth cycles". The successive steps in the programme of the iterative procedure used to obtain a "definitive" trend and the "definitive" turning points are explained in the following.

1.5.2 Programme Steps

The major steps in the programme are as follows: 1) data input; 2) calculation of *tentative trend* (section 1.4) and deviations from this trend. (Trend-adjustment option); 3) determination of *tentative turning points* using the Bry-Boschan routine (section 1.3) with input data from step 1 if detrending is not desired, or trend-adjusted data from step 2 if detrending option is in effect. (If the trend-adjustment option is not in effect, the programme stops at this stage); 4) calculation of the *PAT trend* (section 1.4) in raw with the tentative turning points as input and calculation of deviation from this *final trend*; 5) determination of *final turning points* using the Bry-Boschan routine (section 1.3) with detrended data calculated in step 4 as input.

1.5.3 Turning Point Selection

The programmed approach to turning point selection i.e. the Bry-Boschan routine is based on the traditional method of first identifying major cyclical swings in a series, then to search for areas of cyclical maxima and minima, and finally to determine turning points to specific calendar dates. The programme carries out a series of tests on the series, so as to eliminate extreme values, and points that are closer together than the minimum duration adopted for a phase i.e. the period between two peaks or two troughs. These operations are applied to various curves from the smoothest (*MA12*) to the raw curve as follows:

a) determination of *extreme values* and substitution of smoothed values in *Spencer curve* (15 points);

b) determination of cycles i.e. *potential turning points* in 12-month moving average curve (*MA*12) with, extreme values replaced. Turning points are identified on the basis of the following criterion: any month for which a value is higher or lower than any value during the 5 months on either side is a potential turning point. A further test is applied to ensure alternate peaks and troughs by selecting highest of multiple peaks and lowest of multiple troughs;

c) determination of *corresponding turning points* in the *Spencer curve*. This curve is used because its turning points are closer to those observed in the original series. The highest peak and lowest trough are identified within ± 5 months of selected turning points in the *MA*12 curve. Turning points within six months of the beginning or end of the series are eliminated. The programme also tests for the minimum duration of cycles (15 months) and eliminates peaks and troughs of shorter cycles. A further test ensures that peaks and troughs alternate;

d) determination of *corresponding turning points* in *short-term moving average curve* (3-6 months, depending on *MCD* (4)). Thus, turning points are identified in curves closer and closer to the original series. The highest peak and lowest trough are identified within ± 5 months of turning points identified in the Spencer curve. A test for minimum cyclical duration is also performed;

e) determination of *corresponding turning points* in *original series*. Identification of highest peak and lowest trough within ± 4 months or *MCD* term, whichever is larger, of turning points in short-term moving average curve. Final tests are performed to eliminate: 1) turns within 6 months of beginning and end of series; 2) peaks

---

(4) *Months for Cyclical Dominance*. MCD is defined as the shortest span of months for which the I/C ratio is less than unity. I and C are the average month-to-month changes without regard to sign of the irregular and trend-cycle component of the series, respectively. Although I remains approximately constant as the span of months increases, C should increase, thus the I/C ratio, itself a measure of smoothness, should decline, and eventually become less than unity. In practice there are some series for which the I/C ratio at first declines as the span in months increases, then starts to increase again without ever having dropped as low as 1. Thus, there is a convention that the maximum value of *MCD* should be 6. For quarterly series there is an analogous measure, *Quarters for Cyclical Dominance (QCD)*, which has a maximum value conventionally defined as 2.

(troughs) at both ends of series which are lower (higher) than values closer to end; 3) cycles whose duration is less than 15 months; 4) phases whose duration is less than 5 months.

The turning points identified are the *tentative turning points*.

1.5.4 Trend Estimation

The trend part of the programme uses the *tentative turning points* selected according to the Bry-Boschan routine as input for the calculation of the Phase-Average-Trend *(PAT)*. The tentative turning points are, however, determined in the deviations from a tentative trend (first trend) and used to break up the original series into segments (phases). This means that the *PAT* is a trend that allows for different length of successive cyclical phases, defined as the distance between two successive turning points. It is based on the principal that long-term growth rates are determined by short-term fluctuations with a duration shorter than three phases. The trend is then interpolated between the centered values of the averages of the data within these phases, and the programme selects turning points in the deviations of the raw data from the final trend. The major steps of the entire procedure are as follows: *a)* calculation of *tentative trend*: a 75 month moving average of seasonally adjusted data. The trend is extrapolated to fill in the first and last 37 observations. The extrapolation is performed by using the rate of change between the average of the first (last) 75 months starting two years later (earlier); *b)* calculation of *deviations* (ratios or differences) of individual observations from tentative trend; *c)* determination of *tentative cyclical turning points* (steps a) to e) in section 1.5.3), and thus expansions and contractions, in deviations; *d)* calculation of *phase averages* (i.e. averages during cyclical phases) of original seasonally adjusted data, for all expansions and contractions; *e)* calculation of three-term moving averages of phase averages *(triplets)*; *f)* calculation of "slope" of second approximation of trend by connecting *mid points of triplets*; *g)* adjustment of "*level*" of trend, to match the original series, by making the sum of each segment between two consecutive triplets equal to the sum of the original observations during that period in time; *h) extrapolation* of trend by calculation of slope from first (last) triplet mid point so that the trend values of the first (last) segment are equal to the sum of the original observations; *i)* calculation of twelve month moving average of the second approximation of trend to yield the *final trend*.

The last stage of the programme, the identification of *definitive turning points*, is carried out, using the final trend as input to the Bry-Boschan routine for selection of cyclical turning points (steps *a)* to *e)* in section 1.5.3).

1.6 *Composite Indicators*

Once a set of leading indicators has been selected, they need to be combined into a single composite indicator for each country. This is done in order to reduce the risk of false signals, and to provide a leading indicator with better forecasting and tracking qualities than any of its individual components.

The reason why a group of indictors combined into a composite indicator should be more reliable over a period of time than any of its individual components is related to the nature and causes of business cycles. Each cycle has its unique characteristics as well as features in common with other cycles. But no single cause explains the cyclical fluctuation over a period of time in overall activity. The performance of individual indicators will then depend on the causes behind a specific cycle. Some indicators will perform better in one cycle and others in a different cycle. It is therefore necessary to have signals for the many possible causes of cyclical changes (i.e. to use all potential indicators as a group).

A number of steps are involved in combining individual series to obtain the composite indicator. First, the detrended indicator series are all converted to a monthly basis. Most indicators used in the OECD system are in fact monthly series, but it is sometimes necessary to accept quarterly data. These are converted to monthly frequency by linear interpolation.

Next, it is necessary to ensure that all component series have equal "smoothness"; this is to ensure that month-to-month changes in the composite indicator are not unduly influenced by irregular movements in any one indicator series. The OECD procedure is to use the *Months for Cyclical Dominance (MCD)* moving average (5). This procedure ensures approximately equal smoothness between series, and also ensures that the month-to-month changes in each series are more likely to be due to cyclical than to irregular movements.

The third step is to normalize the series so that cyclical movements have the same amplitude; if this were not done series with particularly marked cyclical amplitude would have undue weight in the composite indicator. The method used to calculate normalized indices is, for each component series, to first subtract of the mean and then divide by the mean of the absolute values of the difference from the mean. The normalized series are then converted into index form by adding 100.

Finally, it may sometimes be necessary to lead or lag particular indicators. In the OECD system this is done only in one case, where the indicators selected for a particular country fall into two distinct groups of "longer-leading" and "shorter-leading" indicators. Combining the two types of indicators gave unsatisfactory results because of the interference between the two cycles. The alignment was improved by lagging the longer-leading group of indicators.

The indicator series having now been detrended, converted to a monthly basis, smoothed, normalized and, possibly, lagged to improve alignment, they are then ready to be combined into a single composite indicator. At this stage it would be possible to assign different weights to the component series depending, for example, on their past record in forecasting and tracking cycles or on their relative freedom from revisions. In the OECD system, equal weights are used almost invariably to obtain each country's composite indicator; this does not mean that there is "no weighting" in the OECD system, because equal weighting implies, by default, a judgement on appropriate weights, and the normalization process is itself a weighting system in reverse. However, when the composite indicators for individual countries are combined into indicators for country groups,

---

(5) See OECD «Leading Indicators and Business Cycles in Member Countries 1960-1985», *OECD MEI Sources and Methods*, n. 39, 1987.

each composite indicator is assigned the weight used in calculating group totals for the industrial production index.

1.7 Historical Performance

The performance of leading indicators can be evaluated in different ways. One is to examine the behaviour of the indicators in relation to the cyclical turning points of the reference series. Forecasting points is one of the main objectives of the leading indictor technique, because predicting the timing of cyclical turning points is one of the least reliable activities in economic forecasting. The OECD system of leading indicators is designed not only to pick out turning points, but also to give information about the likely rate and amplitude of movements in the reference series. Thus it is also useful to examine the "general fit" of the composite indicators in relation to the reference series at all stages of the cycle.

The historical performance of the composite leading indicators for all member countries covered by the OECD system is set out in Table 3. To check their performance at turning points the table shows the number of extra or missing cycles in the indicators, and the median leads at peaks, troughs and at all turning points, together with the absolute mean deviation from the median. The median, rather than mean, is usually used in this kind of analysis because there are relatively few observations (only 8 or 9 for some countries). These measures can be relied upon to give a true picture if the cycles are clear and irregular variation is not a problem. However, with a twin-peaked pattern, the choice of one date rather than another can alter these measures significantly. The classification of a cycle as a major cycle/no cycle at all can give such measures a spurious appearance of accuracy, and so Table 3 also shows how many out of all cyclical turning points have been successfully predicted since 1960. These figures should be treated with caution because an extra cycle is not penalised, but a missing cycle in the composite indicator is penalised twice: once for the peak and once for the trough.

A further desirable characteristic is that the mean of the absolute deviations from the median should not be too great in itself and

TABLE 3
SUMMARY OF HISTORICAL PERFORMANCE OF LEADING INDICATORS

Country	Start date year	Extra (x) or missing cycles (m)	Turning points analysis — Median lag (+) in months at peaks	troughs	all turning points	Turning points successfully predicted 1960/1985 — major	minor	all	General fit analysis — Mean absolute deviation around median	months lag	cross correlation R^2
Canada	1955		−11	−9	−10	9/10	5/6	14/16	3.8	−6	0.88
United States	1955	1m	−9	−3	−7	10/10	4/6	14/16	3.8	−6	0.85
Japan	1960		−4	−6	−5	10/10	5/6	15/16	2.9	−6	0.87
Australia	1966		−3	−2	−2	5/6	5/6	10/12	2.8	−6	0.85
Austria	1963		−6	−4	−6	7/8	2/2	9/10	3.4	−7	0.82
Belgium	1966		−7	−9	−9	7/7	2/2	9/9	2.8	−6	0.75
Luxembourg	1962		−6	−5	−6	8/9	1/2	9/11	2.6	−7	0.70
Denmark	1955	1x	−11	−5	−9	6/6	1/2	7/8	4.9	−6	0.85
Finland	1955		−10	−6	−8	10/10	2/2	12/12	3.6	−9	0.77
France	1963		−8	−6	−7	8/8	1/2	9/10	2.8	−7	0.81
Germany	1962		−7	−6	−6	8/9	—	8/9	2.0	−8	0.88
Greece	1963		−7	−9	−8	7/8	2/2	9/10	3.3	−8	0.80
Ireland	1967		−6	−5	−5	9/10	5/5	14/15	2.1	−5	0.88
Italy	1963		−3	−6	−4	6/7	4/4	10/11	2.5	−6	0.75
Netherlands	1962		−10	−7	−8	9/9	2/2	11/11	3.9	−6	0.81
Norway	1971		−5	−4	−4	4/5	3/4	7/9	3.9	−1	0.84
Portugal	1970		−3		−1	4/5	0/2	4/7	2.9	−6	0.79
Spain	1964		−9	−8	−8	10/10	0/2	10/12	4.3	−8	0.81
Sweden	1960		−4	−12	−9	8/9	1/2	9/11	5.1	−12	0.80
Switzerland	1966		−10	−15	−12	6/7	2/2	8/9	5.6	−11	0.77
United Kingdom	1959		−17	−10	−13	10/10	—	10/10	5.0	−6	0.75
Yugoslavia	1961	1/2m	−8	−4	−6	8/9	5/6	13/15	4.8		0.73
Big-4 Europe	1963	1x	−6	−6	−6	8/8	4/4	12/12	2.6	−8	0.92
Major-7	1960		−5	−4	−5	9/9	8/8	17/17	1.6	−6	0.94
EEC	1963	1x	−7	−6	−7	8/8	3/4	11/12	2.5	−7	0.93
OECD-Europe	1963	1x	−7	−5	−7	8/8	2/2	10/10	3.3	−6	0.94
North America	1955	1m	−9	−4	−5	10/10	4/6	14/16	3.3	−6	0.86
OECD Total	1960	1m	−5	−5	−5	9/9	6/8	15/17	1.9	−6	0.94

should not be too great in comparison to the median. Assuming that the distribution of the leads around the median is normal (which it is not), then the indicator can be expected to fail to lead at turning points no more than 1 in 40 times if the median lead is about double the mean deviation. This condition holds for most countries with the exception of Australia, Denmark, Italy, Norway, Portugal, Spain, Sweden and Yugoslavia. The mean deviation exceeds the median lead only for Portugal.

In testing the general fit, cross-correlation between lagged smoothed leading indicators and reference series is used. The number of months lag at which the correlation has the highest R^2 value is a guide to the average lead of the indicator over the reference series and the value of the correlation coefficient shows the extent to which the cyclical profiles of composite indicator and reference series resemble each other. There are limitations to this method however. First, it is a measure only of the linear relationship between variables, and second, the presence of extreme values can affect the estimate of the cross-correlation coefficient. The second problem is, however, generally solved by using *MCD*-smoothed series in the cross-correlation calculations.

From Table 3 it can be seen that, in general, the historical record of the composite indicators both at turning points and concerning closeness of fit has been rather good. There are very few occasions where the composite indicator does not reflect a cyclical fluctuation in the reference series at all. The most striking example of the failure of a composite indicator to show a cycle is in the 1963-1964 subcycle in the United States. The correlation coefficients give only a guide to the closeness of fit, but are high for all country groups, for a number of the major countries and also for some of the smaller countries.

The average lead of the composite indicator, as measured by the lag at which the closest correlation occurs, should not be too different from the median lag at all turning points if the composite indicator is to give reliable information both about approaching turning points as well as the evolution of the reference series. This difference has been four months for both Australia and Canada, and three months for Belgium, but for other countries it has been two months or less. In the case of Australia there seems to have been a genuine difference between the timing at turning points and the fit in general.

For most countries the composite indicators have in the past led the reference series by at least six months, taking both measures into account. The only exception is Portugal with a lead of only one month. The average lead of the composite indicators is rather long for some countries, notably Finland, Switzerland and the United Kingdom. However, these countries, as well as some others, are suitable candidates for the development of longer and shorter leading indicators, and when recombining these indicators into a total the lead time could be reduced to gain in precision and accuracy.

2. - A System of Leading Indicators for Central and Eastern European Countries

2.1 *Selection of Reference Cycle*

Fluctuations in output have been observed in the past in the CEECs, which had some of the cyclical characteristics of cycles in OECD countries. Future cycles in the CEECs are likely to follow much the same path as in OECD countries as they move to market economies and become more integrated in the world economy.

Economic fluctuations over the transition period may, however, be due to quite different reasons than in the post-transition phase. These differences in the mechanism of economic growth may make it difficult to establish cycles over a period that spans pre-transition and post-transition years.

The selection of reference series for the economic cycle in the CEECs is very much related to the availability of short-term statistics for variables representing aggregate economic activity. The only series available on a monthly basis for all CEECs is the index of total industrial production (ISIC 2, 3, 4). If a single economic variable is to be used as reference series for a leading indicator system in CEECs, the total industrial production index is obviously the best candidate. The index of total industrial production is shown in Graph 2 for five of the CEECs covered in this paper.

Total industrial production includes extractive industry and public utilities which may distort the general pattern of the reference

GRAPH 2

INDUSTRIAL PRODUCTION
1985 = 100

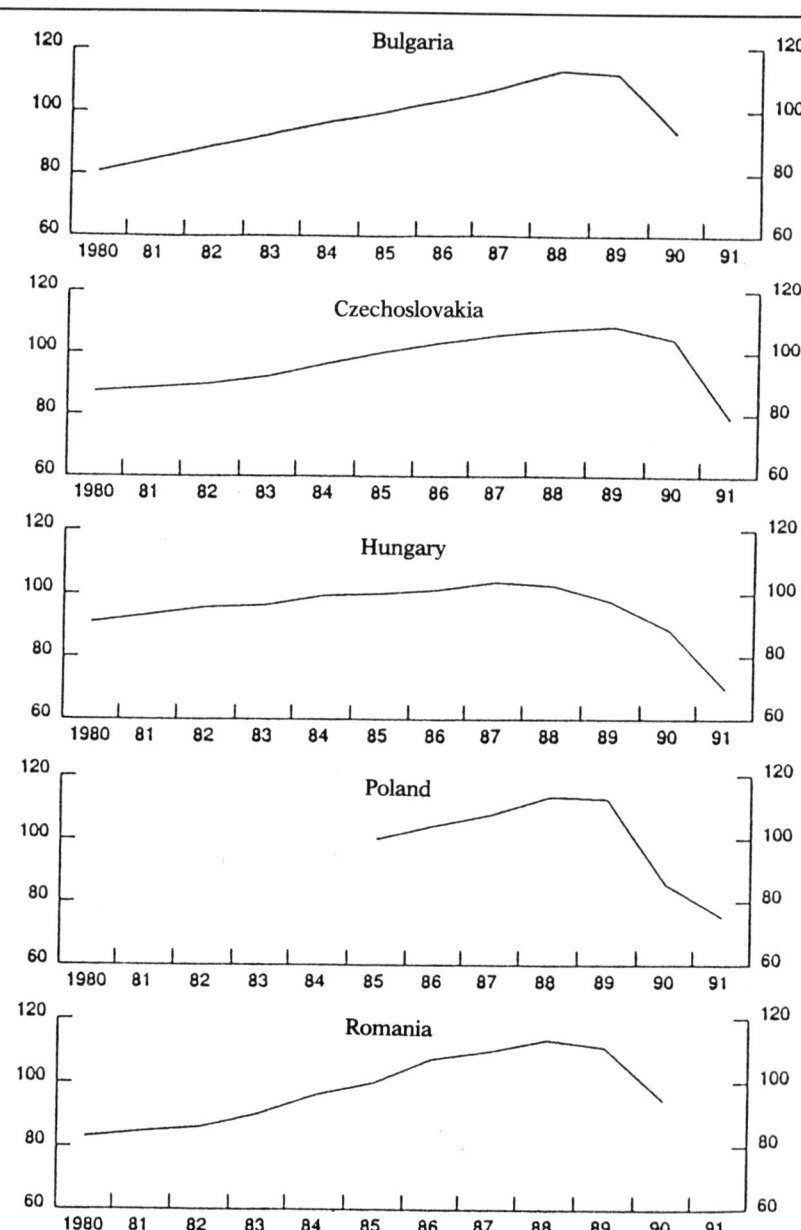

cycle. If this is the case, manufacturing production (ISIC, 3) could be used instead.

2.2 Statistical Problems and Data Availability

Not only differences in the mechanism of economic growth, but also statistical problems affecting the data in the past and over the transition period must be considered when analysing data over these periods. This section reviews some of the main statistical problems affecting short-term data for the CEECs.

2.2.1 Coverage

In the past, statistics for the CEECs covered state enterprises and cooperatives only. From 1989 onwards private enterprises became legal and their number has grown dramatically. Establishing and updating the business registers and devising sampling procedures in order to collect data on a sample rather than a census basis are major tasks that are unfamiliar tasks to the statistical offices in the CEECs. These are major innovations which will take time to implement fully and effectively.

Over the transition period, therefore, many series will still cover only the state and cooperative sectors and some part of the private sector will be missing. The extent of the omission will vary over time, from country to country and from sector to sector.

2.2.2 Recording

In the CEECs the practice in the past was very often to collect sales or output data in annual terms and the monthly or quarterly data were derived by subtracting the previously reported figure. This led sometimes to an error in the time at which activity was recorded because errors in previous reports would not be corrected explicitly but simply incorporated in a new cumulative total.

This practice introduced a distortion, at least in output data, because the data were used for monitoring production targets. These targets were expressed in quarterly or annual terms and many series show a larger than usual entry in the final month of each quarter and at the end of the year. This reporting practice resulted in a seemingly large seasonal component at these key dates.

2.2.3 Price indices

Prices in the CEECs were officially fixed by the State in the past and these prices were used in compiling the official price indices. One problem common to the compilation of price indices in all countries is the treatment of quality change. However, in the CEECs more of the increase in prices was, in the past, attributed to quality change than was justified in terms of the improved specification of the products. This under-statement of price rises led to an over-statement of volume increases when volume measures, such as indices of production, were derived by dividing current price data by price indices.

2.2.4 Volume Indices

In the past, index numbers in volume terms were calculated as current-weighted index numbers i.e. as ratios of current production at current prices to base-year production valued at current prices. The problem with this type of index is that while the index number for each period can be compared with the base period, comparisons between two other periods do not accurately reflect the change between the two periods.

Although prices did not change very much in the past, another problem affected index number compilation in the CEECs. This problem was related to the classification of the reporting enterprises. With changing government responsabilities, state enterprises were often reclassified from one sector to another. These changes were incorporated into the current-weighted index in such a way that comparisons between different periods were not always valid.

2.3 Classification of Existing Indicators

Table 4 summarises the ways in which OECD countries classify their short-term indicators between *coincident* (movements coincide with those of the reference series) *lagging* (movements follow the reference series) and *leading* indicators (movements precede those of the reference series so that they are of particular interest for the present purpose).

It should be noted that there is not always unanimity between OECD countries on the allocation of indicators between the three groups. Nevertheless, the classification in Table 4 seems a useful starting point, and it is used in Table 5 to classify the short-term indicators available for the CEECs. It should be emphasised that this is a highly tentative classification and more detailed analysis would be required to determine the precise relationship, for a given country, between movements of any particular short-term indicator and the reference series.

2.4 Potential Leading Indicators

The first criteria used when evaluating potential leading indicators is economic significance. There must be an economic reason for the observed leading relationship before the series can be accepted as an indicator.

The leading indicators used in the OECD system are classified in Table 6 according to 5 types of "economic rationale" (6): *(i)* early stage indicators; *(ii)* rapidly responsive indicators; *(iii)* expectation - sensitive indicators; *(iv)* prime movers; *(v)* other indicators.

The first category contains indicators which measure an early stage of production. The second contains indicators which respond rapidly to changes in economic activity. The third covers indicators which measure expectations or are sensitive to expectations. The fourth contains measures relevant to monetary and fiscal policies and foreign economic developments. The fifth category contains indicators

---

(6) This 5-way classification is taken from DE LEEUW FRANK: «Leading Indicators and the "Prime Mover View"», *Survey of Current Business*, US Department of Commerce, 1989.

TABLE 4

CLASSIFICATION OF SHORT-TERM INDICATORS IN OECD COUNTRIES
(classified by relationship to cycle and by "economic process") (*)

Economic process cyclical dating	Employment & unemployment	Production and income	Consumption, trade, orders and deliveries	Fixed capital investment	Inventories	Prices, costs and profits	Money & credit	Foreign position	Other indicators
Leading	hours of overtime worked period of work guaranteed by current order book (BS) (job vacancies)	production expectations (BS)	total new orders car registrations indicators of new orders (BS) (bankruptcies)	investment orders or commitments construction orders or commitments (construction output)	judgement on stock levels (BS) (changes in stocks)	raw materials prices share prices (profits) (unit labour costs)	changes in money supply changes in savings deposits credit commitments (interest rates)		business climate indicators (BS)
Coincident	(employment) (unemployment) (job vacancies)	GNP or GDP total industrial production output of a set of products income capacity utilisation	(purchase/sale of a set of goods) (bankruptcies)	(construction output) (investment expenditure)	(changes in stocks)	selling price trends (BS) (unit labour cost) (profits)		imports exports	(transport)
Lagging	(employment) (unemployment) (job vacancies)			(investment expenditure)	stock levels	wholesale prices (unit labour cost)	loans (interest rates) indicators of commercial debts		

(*) Bracketed items are those where classification seems doubtful *either* because they are only mentioned by a limited number of countries *or* because they are classified differently by different countries.
Non-bracketed items are those where classification to a particular category seems generally accepted.
Items marked (BS) are series derived from business surveys.

TABLE 5

POSSIBLE CLASSIFICATION OF SHORT-TERM INDICATORS FOR CEECs

Economic process cyclical dating	Employment & unemployment	Production and income	Consumption, trade, orders and deliveries	Fixed capital investment	Inventories	Prices, costs and profits	Money & credit	Foreign position	Other indicators
Leading	job vacancies	production in specific branches commodity output	car registration	construction of new buildings			money supply savings		
Coincident	employment unemployment job vacancies	total industrial production manufacturing production commodity output						imports exports	transport
Lagging	employment unemployment job vacancies					wholesale prices			

TABLE 6

OECD LEADING INDICATORS CLASSIFIED BY TYPE OF "RATIONALE" (*)

Type of rationale	1	2	3	4	5	6	7	8	9	10	11	12	13	14	15	16	17	18	19	20	21	22	23
Early stage indicators																							
New orders, amounts	1	1		1		1													1				4
New orders (BS)				1	1			1		1		1		1	1	1	1		1	1	1		11
Order books (BS)	1			1		1	2			1		1	1	1	1		1	2	1				11
Construction, approvals/starts	1	1								1		1							1		1	1	9
New company formation		1																					1
Vacancies																						1	1
Total: number	2	3	0	2	1	2	2	1	0	3	0	3	1	2	2	1	3	2	4	1	1	1	37
percent																							19
Rapidly responsive indicators																							
Average hours worked	1																						2
Profits		2										1	1								2		2
Stocks, amounts	2	1			1			1	1			1				4			2	1			8
Stocks (BS)	1							1	1	1			1	1	1	1	1	1	2	1	2		13
Production bottlenecks (BS)																		1					2
Total: number	4	3	0	0	0	0	1	1	1	1	0	0	2	1	1	5	1	1	2	1	4	0	27
percent																							14
Expectation-sensitive indicators																							
Stock prices	1	1		1	1	1	1	2	1	1									1	1	1		12
Raw material prices				1		1		1															2
Selling prices (BS)																							1
Production (BS)	1		1		1		1		1			1				1		1		1	1		15
Economic situation (BS)				1					1				1	1	1	1							6
Total: number	2	2	2	3	1	3	1	3	4	1	0	1	1	1	1	2	0	1	1	2	2	0	36
percent																							19

TABLE 6 continued

Type of rationale	1	2	3	4	5	6	7	8	9	10	11	12	13	14	15	16	17	18	19	20	21	22	23
Prime movers																							
Money supply	1	1	1	1	1	1	1	1	1	1		1	1	1	1				1	1		1	17
Deposits			1												1								2
Exports								2								1							3
Terms of trade			1	1		1	1		1	1			1	1	1					1			8
Indicators for foreign countries	1				5						2												9
Total: number	2	1	3	2	6	1	2	3	2	1	2	1	2	2	4	1	0	0	1	2	0	1	36
percent																							20
Other indicators																							
Production in specific branches					1		1					1	1		1							1	5
Retail sales																1	2					1	5

(*) Items marked (BS) are series derived from business surveys.

Legend:

1 = Canada
2 = Usa
3 = Japan
4 = Australia
5 = Austria
6 = Belgium
7 = Denmark
8 = Finland
9 = France
10 = Germany
11 = Luxembourg
12 = Greece
13 = Ireland
14 = Italy
15 = Netherlands
16 = Norway
17 = Portugal
18 = Spain
19 = Sweden
20 = Switzerland
21 = UK
22 = Yugoslavia
23 = Indicators

TABLE 6 continued

ratio	1	2	3	4	5	6	7	8	9	10	11	12	13	14	15	16	17	18	19	20	21	22	23
Motor vehicles registration	1						1		1									1			1		5
Layoffs/new hire/claims for unemployment insurance		1																	2				3
Price indices										1		2			1				1				4
Unit labour costs	1	1	1							1													3
Credit ratios		1	1			1															1		4
Interest ratios		1	1				1	2	3	1			1	1	1				1	1	1		14
Foreign exchange holidays								2															2
Foreign trade balances			1													1							2
Capacity utilisation (BS)																		2					3
Employment situation (BS)				1			1						1										3
Total: number	2	3	3	1	1	1	4	2	4	3	0	4	3	1	3	2	2	3	4	1	3	2	51
percent																							28
Grand total: number	12	9	11	8	9	7	9	10	11	9	2	99	7	11	11	6	7	12	7	1	0	1	190
percent																							100

Legend:

1 = Canada
2 = Usa
3 = Japan
4 = Australia
5 = Austria
6 = Belgium
7 = Denmark
8 = Finland
9 = France
10 = Germany
11 = Luxembourg
12 = Greece
13 = Ireland
14 = Italy
15 = Netherlands
16 = Norway
17 = Portugal
18 = Spain
19 = Sweden
20 = Switzerland
21 = UK
22 = Yugoslavia
23 = Indicators

of mixed types such as interest rates (stimulus to both consumption and investment), overtime and layoff rate and production in specific branches.

For the 22 countries included in the OECD indicator system, the total number of indicators are rather evenly split between the different categories. *Early stage* indicators, *expectation-sensitive* indicators and *prime movers* represent around 20% each of the total number of indicators. *Rapidly responsive* indicators represent around 14%, while *other indicators* represent about 28% of the total.

In three of the categories — *early stage, rapidly responsive* and *expectation-sensitive* indicators — business surveys provide most of the series used. These series concern new orders, level of order books and stocks and expectations about production. Two other frequently used series in these categories are construction approvals or starts and stock prices.

The most important series used in the *prime movers* category is money supply. Two series related to foreign trade and foreign economic developments are also well represented in this category, namely, terms of trade and indicators for foreign countries.

Among the *other indicators*, the most frequently used series are different types of interest rates. Series on production in specific branches and series related to retail sales or motor vehicles registration are also frequently used series.

Differences between countries in choice of indicators are, however, important. Available statistics and economic structure make it hard to find a common set of indicators for all countries. In the category, *rapidly responsive* indicators, no good indicators have been found for eight countries (United States, Australia, Austria, Belgium, Denmark, Luxembourg, Greece and Yugoslavia). For three countries (Japan, France and Luxembourg) no early stage indicators have been found and in the category expectation-sensitive indicators three countries are also missing (Luxembourg, Portugal and Yugoslavia). *Prime movers* are also missing for three countries (Portugal, Spain and the United Kingdom), while only one country (Luxembourg) is missing in the category *other indicators*.

Existing indicators for CEECs are set out in Table 7 using the same classification by type of rationale. This, of course, is based on

TABLE 7

INDICATORS FOR CEECs CLASSIFIED BY TYPE OF RATIONALE (*)

Indicators by type of rationale	Bulgaria	Czechoslovakia	German Democratic Republic	Hungary	Poland	Romania	USSR	All countries
Early stage indicators								
New orders, amounts								
New orders, *(BS)*								
Order books *(BS)*								
Construction, approvals/starts	1	1	1	1			1	5
New company formation					1			1
Vacancies	1	1	1	1	1	0	1	6
Total: number								12
percent		1				1	1	3
Rapidly responsive indicators								
Average hours worked								
Profits								
Stocks, amounts								
Stocks *(BS)*								
Production bottlenecks *(BS)*								
Total: number	0	1	0	0	1	1	0	3
percent								7
Expectation-sensitive indicators								
Stock prices								
Raw material prices								
Selling prices *(BS)*								
Production *(BS)*								
Economic situation *(BS)*								
Total: number	0	0	0	0	0	0	0	0
percent								0

TABLE 7 continued

Indicators by type of rationale	Bulgaria	Czechoslovakia	German Democratic Republic	Hungary	Poland	Romania	USSR	All countries
Prime movers								
Money supply					1	1		3
Deposits								1
Exports		1		1	1			5
Terms of trade	1	1	1	1	2	1	0	9
Indicators for foreign countries								
Total: number	1	2	1	2	2	1	0	9
percent								22
Other indicators								
Production in specific branches	1	1	1	1	1	1	1	7
Retail sales	1	1	1	1	1	1	1	7
Motor vehicles registration							1	1
Layoffs/new hire/Claims for unemployment insurance								
Price indices		1						1
Unit labour costs								
Credit ratios								
Interest rates				1	1	1		3
Foreign exchange holdings	1	1	1	1	1			5
Foreign trade balances								
Capacity utilisation *(BS)*								
Employment situation *(BS)*								
Total: number	3	4	3	4	4	3	3	24
percent								59
Grand total = number	5	8	5	7	8	5	4	41
percent								100

(*) Items marked *(BS)* are series derived from business surveys.

the assumption that a series which is a leading indicator for OECD countries is a potential leading indicator for CEECs as well.

In the category *early stage* indicators, construction starts is available for several countries and a series on vacancies is published by Poland. This leaves Romania as the only country with no series in this category. The only *rapidly responsive* indicator is a series on average hours worked. This is available in Czechoslovakia, Poland and Romania. *Expectation-sensitive* indicators are not available for any country, while prime movers are better represented. In this category, money supply is available for three countries (Hungary, Poland and Romania) and the USSR. A series on deposits is also available for Czechoslovakia. In the category, *other indicators*, three or more indicators are available for all CEECs. The different indicators are found among production series for specific branches or commodities, retail sales, interest rates and foreign trade balance.

2.5 *Development of New Indicators*

The previous section has tried to identify potential leading indicators from among the short-term statistics published in CEECs. This exercise has shown a lack of indicators in three categories: *early stage* indicators, *rapidly responsive* indicators and *expectation-sensitive* indicators. The easiest way to improve this situation would be to set up business surveys to collect information on new orders, orderbooks, stocks and production expectations.

In the area of *prime movers*, series on terms of trade and indicators for foreign countries could be developed. Money supply series could also be improved or developed. The coverage of *other indicators* could be improved by developing more employment indicators, price indices, motor vehicle registration series and interest rates series.

New information about existing and planned business surveys in CEECs has, however, become available since the first draft of this paper. This information was presented by participants from CEECs at a *Workshop on Opinion Surveys for Business and Consumers and Time Series Analysis* organised by OECD and Eurostat at the IFO-

Institute in Munich in June 1991. The *Workshop* revealed that business surveys had been implemented in Bulgaria and Czechoslovakia during Spring 1991 and that a draft questionnaire had been designed for Romania. Detailed information was also given about business surveys already established in Poland and Hungary.

Potential leading indicators for CEECs based on business survey data are set out in table 8 using the business survey series included in the OECD leading indicator system as the reference. The lack of indicators identified in the previous section, notably, in the categories expectation-sensitive indicators should not be a problem in the future. All CEECs cover all the business survey variables included in the OECD leading indicator system with the exception of orderbooks. The introduction of business surveys in CEECs has greatly improved the pool of indicators among which potential leading indicators may be found in the future.

2.6 *Data Needs and Cyclical Analysis*

The comments above are based on the assumption that the OECD leading indicator system is applicable to the CEECs. No data analysis has been carried out to test this assumption.

In order to identify the cyclical behaviour of the reference series and of the potential leading indicator series, data must be available on a monthly or quarterly basis for a period of at least 6 years. This is necessary in order to carry out seasonal adjustments and to detect cyclical movements. Two problems may arrive in connection with this. First, there may be statistical breaks in the data between the pre and post-transition periods. Second, even if there are no breaks of a statistical nature, there may be fundamental differences in the mechanisms of economic growth in the two periods; relationships discovered between the reference series and leading indicators in the pre-transition period may no longer apply after transition.

A final caveat: leading indicators are normally used to monitor cyclical fluctuations in *real* output and to do this it is essential to use, as far as possible, series adjusted for inflation. This means that it is necessary to have reliable price deflators as well as a broad range of leading indicators.

TABLE 8

FUTURE POTENTIAL LEADING INDICATORS FOR CEECs BASED ON BUSINESS SURVEY DATA

Business survey indictors	Bulgaria	Czechoslovakia	Hungary	Poland	Romania
General situation	X	X	X	X	X
Production/sales	X	X	X	X	X
Orders/demand	X	X	X	X	X
– export market	X	X	X	X	X
– domestic market			X		
Order books					
– export market					
Stocks:					
– raw materials		X	X	X	X
– finished goods	X	X	X	X	X
Purchases/supply:					
– raw material	X	X(1)	X(2)	X(3)	X(4)
Capacity	X		X		X
Capacity utilisation	X	X	X	X	
Production/Sales impediments:					
– demand	X	X	X	X	X
– equipment	X		X	X	X
Selling prices	X	X	X	X	X
Employment	X	X	X	X	X

(1) Total purchases or purchases of finished goods.
(2) Total purchases or purchases of imported goods.
(3) Purchases of finished goods or imported goods.
(4) Purchases of finished goods.

2.7 Selection of Indicators in the Short-Run

In the foregoing we have tried to identify potential leading indicators for the CEECs based on the assumption that a series which is a leading indicator for OECD countries is a potential leading indicator for the CEECs as well. During the transition period, however, several problems will make it difficult to identify leading indicators based on historical cyclical relationships between indicators and reference series. Some of these problems have been touched upon above and concern the changing cyclical behaviour, statistical problems and data availability over pre-transition and transition periods.

The selection of leading indicators in the short-run must be based on a broader range of criteria than what is normally used for cyclical analysis. A first criteria is cyclical sensitivity: series with a pure cyclical behaviour are preferred. This is important in a situation when the cyclical behaviour can not be estimated from historical data. A second condition is linked to economic significance in the sense that the leading relationship should be explained by the series ability to measure an early stage of the cycle, respond rapidly to changes in economic activity and measure expectations or be sensitive to expectations. The leading characteristics of the series should as far as possible be explained by their economic significance or their information content.

Problems in the transition period concerning coverage of the private sector and data collection mean that some practical criteria such as sound statistical basis, must also be taken into account when selecting indicators in the short-run. In the following we will examine to what extent indicators based on business tendency surveys fulfill the above requirements.

2.7.1 Cyclical Sensitivity

The statistical series derived from business surveys are by their very nature particularly suitable for business cycle monitoring and forecasting. The cyclical profile of the series are in many cases easier to detect because they contain no trend. While conventional statistics are focused on metric data, business surveys use ordinal scales for most varibles i.e. a three point scale with the preprinted answers up/same/down. This makes them very sensitive to the cyclical development.

2.7.2 Relevance

Compared to traditional statistical surveys, which only cover one or a few related variables from one area of the economy, business surveys collect information about a wide range of variables selected for their ability to monitor the business cycle. Priority is given to variables which measure the early stages of production (eg. new orders, order books), respond rapidly to changes in economic activity (eg. stocks), and measure expectations or are sensitive to expectations (eg. overall economic situation).

The range of information covered by business surveys also goes beyond variables normally covered by classical statistics. Qualitative information may be collected for variables which are difficult or impossible to measure by conventional methods, such as capacity utilisation and views on the overall economic situation. Business surveys in the CEECs cover as well variables that are sensitive to the transition period such as shortages of production or financial means.

2.7.3 Leading Characteristics

All the above types of variables give early information about changes in the cyclical development. In addition, variables related to judgements and expectations register a change in the cycle earlier than corresponding traditional statistics. This is because judgements and expectations lead to plans and only after these plans have been implemented will they be picked up by traditional statistical surveys.

2.7.4 Statistical Basis

A sound statistical basis is a crucial criterion when dealing with information in countries where the statistical system as well as the economic system are in transition. Recording of private sector activity and introduction of sample surveys to collect information from the growing number of private enterprises affect the reliability of basic statistics.

The *qualitative* nature of the information collected by business surveys means that a relatively smaller sample is sufficient to gain meaningful results on changes in the variables compared to data derived from *quantitative* surveys. This is explained in the first place by the fact that the sample size depends on the variance of the different variables and secondly, by the fact that the variance of changes in variables based on panel data is as a rule significantly smaller than in the case of data derived from surveys that measure levels.

The smaller sample size and the fact that qualitative information is easier for the enterprises to supply should give more reliable information in the sense that it should be easier to cover the expanding private sector and to reduce non-response. Business surveys also have some further advantages compared to traditional statistics when considering criteria normally used when evaluating leading indicators.

2.7.5 Consistency of the Lead

The length of the lead of business survey indicators is not among the longest compared to all types of leading indicators, the median lead range between 3.8 to 6.5 months for the most frequently used indicators, but the size of the lead is more stable (see Table 9).

2.7.6 Smoothness

In general, answers to business surveys are "seasonally adjusted" by the respondents and this adds to the relative smoothness of the indicators. For qualitative indicators based on business surveys, *MCD* statistics are usually significantly smaller than for corresponding quantitative indicators.

TABLE 9

CHARACTERISTICS OF LEADING INDICATORS MOST FREQUENTLY
USED IN THE OECD SYSTEM (*)
(Average of indicators)

Indicators	Number of countries	MCD	Median lag (+) at all T.P.	Mean deviation around median	Cross correlation lag (+) coef.	
Money supply	17	2.4	− 9.2	4.2	− 8.2	0.67
Stocks (BS)	13	2.6	− 3.8	3.6	− 4.3	−0.74
Production (BS)	12	3.3	− 5.6	4.1	− 6.0	0.70
Share prices	12	2.3	− 6.3	4.6	− 6.6	0.59
Interest rates	11	2.3	−13.5	5.1	−15.3	−0.71
Order book (BS)	10	2.5	− 4.1	3.1	− 4.8	0.75
Construction	9	3.7	− 6.4	4.6	− 6.6	0.60
New orders (BS)	8	4.0	− 6.5	4.2	− 8.0	0.71
Terms of trade	8	3.5	− 9.8	6.0	−11.8	0.57

(*) Items marked (BS) are indicators derived from business surveys.

2.7.7 Revisions

It is very important that the series are not revised to a significant extent in later periods if they are to be used for analysing the present economic situation and for forecasting. Business survey series rarely need to be revised while in many countries preliminary data for conventional statistics are released very quickly but later revised up to three times. For a few indicators — in particular indices of production and new orders — about 30-40% of the forecasting errors are due to revisions of the first published data in some countries.

2.7.8 Timeliness of Publication

Business survey results are usually available 2-3 weeks after the period under consideration is over. This is due to the fact that the information is qualitative in nature and the sample size relatively smaller for this reason.

The above arguments suggest that in the short-term period, business survey indicators are the best source for leading indicators. In particular, the fulfilment of the basic criteria, i.e. cyclical sensitivity, relevance, leading characteristics and statistical basis, may make these types of indicators the only alternative during the transition period.

The use of business survey indicators as leading indicators is also very common in OECD countries as noted in previous sections. The leading indicators most frequently used in the OECD System and their characteristics are set out in Table 9. They include four business survey series in the top nine series. These business survey series concern the following variables: stocks, production, order books and new orders. These variables could almost certainly be used as leading indicators in the CEECs.

2.8 Selection of Indicators in the Long-Term

The identification of potential leading indicators for the CEECs presented in previous sections will be used here in order to try to give some more information on the selection of possible leading indicators in the long-term. A definitive selection must, however, wait until it is possible to establish the cyclical behaviour of candidate series and reference series over a reasonably long period and to evaluate the indicator series using the normal criteria for cyclical analysis, i.e. relevance, cyclical behaviour and practical considerations (see section 1.2).

The business survey series proposed for use in the short-term will certainly pass these tests and are candidates for leading indicators in the long-term as well.

Among the other potential leading indicator series, the selection of possible candidate series to be included in the long-term will be evaluated against the following criteria: economic structure, subject coverage and international linkages.

2.8.1 Economic Structure

Differences in economic structure and economic conditions between countries make it difficult to obtain a standard set of indicators which can be used for all countries. The different subject areas from which the leading indicators are chosen in the OECD system are set out in Table 2 in section 1.2. In the following we will use this classification as a basis for the selection of possible future leading indicators for the CEECs.

Certain indicator series recur, however, regularly in the list of leading indicators for different countries. The most frequently used leading indicators and their characteristics are set out in Table 9. Four of the nine series concern business survey series and will not be commented on. The remaining five series are money supply, share prices, interest rates, construction starts or approvals and terms of trade. The series related to monetary and financial conditions are important policy instruments in OECD countries but, in the past, were considered irrelevant in the CEECs. This implies that it may be difficult to establish the cyclical relationship over the past and the future. They will, however, be strong candidates for possible leading indicators in the long-term.

The structural changes taking place in the CEECs will affect the cyclical behaviour in the different sectors of the economies. This will, however, mean instability in the cyclical relationship, but also a source to increased differentiation among indicators over the cycle. This latter effect will mean that leading indicator series may be found on a more disaggregated level by detailed activities and markets than is usually the case in OECD countries.

Series on production in specific branches may be good leading indicators in the CEECs. A first choice are those industrial branches which logically may be classified as leading branches such as intermediate goods, chemicals or basic metals industries. Structural changes and export intensities in different branches may, however, make other branches a better choice. Production data disaggregated by export and domestic goods and for domestic and export markets could be useful leading indicators in a country with a large export market.

Differences in economic conditions between state, cooperative and private enterprises will certainly exist over the transition period and may also persist over a longer period. This suggests that if indicators were available disaggregated by ownership and were presented separately for the different sectors it would be possible to monitor the transition process and it may be possible to find leading indicators among the private sector indicators.

The size structure of enterprises will certainly also undergo radical changes over the transition period and longer. In general there may be a more dynamic development among the small- and medium-sized enterprises and if indicators were disaggregated by size groups it may be possible to find additional potential leading indicators.

2.8.2 Subject Coverage

It is very important to have a broad range of indicators reflecting the cyclical development from different parts of the economy when analysing fluctuations in aggregate economic activity. The business survey indicators suggested for use as leading indicators in both the short-term and long-term cover variables mainly from the production area, i.e. stocks, orders and production series. The other series as possible leading indicators in the long-term refer to the monetary and financial area.

In the area of construction, sales and trade, several indicator series are candidates as leading indicators for the CEECs. Construction starts and retail sales series are available in the CEECs and these series are also used in the OECD system for many countries. Construction starts or approvals are among the top nine most frequently used leading indicator series. Series on sales or registration of motor vehicles are not available for many of the CEECs today, but may be developed in the future and will be leading indicators, as they are in several OECD countries.

Serie refering to marginal employment adjustments such as overtime and lay-off rate and other labour market series such as vacancies and hours worked were virtually irrelevant to the CEECs in the past, because they measured phenomena peculiar to market-economies. These types of series are not very well represented in the OECD system of leading indicators, but may prove to be leading indicators in the CEECs in the future.

The only series in the area of prices, costs and profits frequently used as leading indicators in the OECD system are series referring to wholesale prices or raw material prices. These series are not available for many of the CEECs today, but will probably be developed in the future and should be tested for leading characteristics.

Indicators linked to foreign trade developments are classified as "prime movers" and should be suitable leading indicators. Terms of trade series are also among the top nine most frequently used leading indicators in the OECD system. Series on terms of trade are available for all the CEECs and could prove to be good leading indicators for CEECs which have an important foreign trade sector. Changes in the recording of foreign trade statistics make it however, difficult to use historical data due to changes in coverage and timing. Series on different export aggregates or components are used as leading indicators in several OECD countries and should be tested for leading characteristics in the CEECs in the future.

2.8.3 International Linkages

Linkage via foreign trade is the most generally important method by which cyclical impulses can be transmitted between countries.

Other factors are, however, also important such as foreign investment, capital movements and other financial flows, tourism etc. particularly during the transition period in the CEECs. Leading indicator series are, however, difficult to find in these areas and, as noted above, the OECD system uses only foreign trade series as leading indicators.

Foreign trade development in one country is, however, dependent on economic activity in trading partner countries and cyclical indicators in major trading partner countries may prove to be good leading indicators for the dependent country. Indicators of economic activity in foreign countries are also used in the OECD system as leading indicators in several countries: the composite leading indicator for the United States is used as a leading indicator for Canada; a series on new orders in Germany and the OECD composite leading indicators for France, Germany, Italy and the United Kingdom are used as leading indicators for Austria; the IFO business climate indicator for Germany is used as a leading indicator for the Netherlands.

Indicators based on activity in foreign countries may be a source for potential leading indicators in the CEECs not only because of the above arguments, but also because they may be more reliable in the immediate future than indicators based on data from the CEECs due to statistical problems. Changes in trading patterns among the CEECs, i.e. shifts from east to west trade means, however, unstable relationships in the short-term, but also interesting possibilities for potential leading indicators.

A Monthly Model of the Industrial Sector for Business-Cycle Analysis

Enrico Giovannini
Istat, Roma

1. - Introduction

Without wishing to enter the debate on the existence of the business cycle and the methods for measuring its characteristics and intensity, there can be no doubt that the existence of so many applied economists who spend their life trying to furnish a "real-time" interpretation of the economy's various cyclical phases and forecast future trends is adequate proof of the importance of short-term analysis of the economic cycle. One could even venture that the type of growth which characterised the 1980s, in which the various technological shocks were accompanied by an increasing rapidity in the diffusion of information, and the consequent increase in the economy's flexibility, has made the role of business-cycle analysis even more important.

This increased responsibility together with the elaboration of new theoretical models has led to profound innovations in the diagnosis and forecasting instruments used by business-cycle analysts while also posing statisticians with new and increasingly complex challenges. If it is inevitable, given the costs of obtaining these data, that all "offical" statistics tend to some degree to represent a consolidated reality rather than inquire into its more innovative features, it is obvious that the statistician's task becomes even more arduous when an economic system is undergoing a profound transformation.

The increased flexibility of the production processes permits, amongst other things, businessmen more time in which to change their previously planned behaviour. This can have either stabilising or destabilising effects, depending on the complex play-off between expectations and realisations. It is therefore vitally important that those studying the economy's short-term dynamics should be able to observe and interpret the characteristics of the economic processes which respond to shocks of differing nature. In this regard, the business-cycle analyst's preferred instrument is disequilibrium analysis, that is to say observing how actions and reactions manifest themselves and not just the final outcome of the process.

As the papers in this volume convincingly demonstrate, there exist numerous instruments for analysing the business cycle which are heterogeneous as regards methodology. However, we believe we can affirm that the topics briefly mentioned have conditioned research and the development of new analytical instruments even within the different "fields" into which the research can be classified. Econometrics is no exception to this rule: it is no coincidence that in recent years much emphasis has been attributed to researching the correct dynamic specification of the relations between variables, as well as attempts to reconcile the representations of long-term relations between variables with the typically short-term ones.

The present paper intends to show that it is possible to construct an econometric model for analysing the short-term economic cycle and use it to evaluate some characteristics of the processes which govern the diffusion of demand and supply shocks within an economic system. The model, estimated on monthly data for the Italian economy for the period 1983-1989, examines, amongst other things, the mechanisms of formation of entrepreneurs' demand and inflation expectations which are then used to derive production plans, of production factors management and of selling prices. The model makes use of business survey data to avoid the use of "naive" models for the formation of expectations.

After a brief survey of the historical development of econometric models for short-term business-cycle analysis (Section 2), the paper examines the main features of the theoretical model on which econometric analysis is based (Section 3) and the results obtained (Section

4). The model is then used to simulate and evaluate the effects on the Italian industrial system of changes in international raw materials prices (supply shock) and (unanticipated) increases in foreign orders (demand shock).

The paper closes with the conclusions.

2. - Econometric Models for Short-term Economic Cycle Analysis

Alongside the "traditional" econometric models, i.e., the large-scale models which draw on the theoretical assumptions of the neoclassical synthesis, other types of models have been developed in recent years. These include longer-term models which use input-output schemes, continuous-time models and time series models (*VAR* and *VARMA*) which are now useful and perhaps necessary tools to integrate with the former for forecasting purposes and also for assessing economic-policy measures. In addition to the types of models mentioned above, models which are normally used for analysing the short-term economic cycle have also been developed. These models are characterised not only by the frequency (normally monthly) of the observations used for the estimates, but also by the use of indicators derived from business surveys. This enables, amongst other things, not only a more correct representation of the evolution of phenomena such as expectations (regarding inflation, demand, interest rates, etc.), but also the reduction to a minimum of the information lag which is a common feature of "official" evaluations of the various economic phenomena included in the national accounts system.

Research on constructing models for short-term economic cycle analysis dates back some ten years in Italy. In 1982 a monthly model of the balance of payments developed by the Bank of Italy (1) was presented. The declared purpose of the model was for use "as an operative instrument for analysis and forecasting exercises and simu-

---

(1) See BIAGIOLI *et AL* [4].
Advise: the numbers in square brackets refer to the Bibliography in the appendix.

lating economic policy measures", while in 1984 a first small, "complete" monthly model of the Italian economy was published (2). This model consisted of 13 stochastic equations and took into consideration both real (orders, inventories, industrial production, expected and actual prices) and monetary (monetary base, money supply, exchange rate, interest rates) variables for its analysis of the period 1973-1979. The model's specification derived from a causality analysis which paid particular attention to identifying the time-structure of the influences between the various variables, since correct representation of the model's dynamics was considered fundamental for a short term analysis to be used for economic-policy purposes; it is in fact common knowledge that an incorrect assessment of the lags of the influences between the instrument variables and the objective variables can produce undesired effects on the latter, effects which could transform an action conceived as anticyclical into a procyclical action.

It was in this period, when the traditional econometric models were being much criticised, that the first vector autoregressive (*VAR*) and vector *ARMA* models were developed, using in some cases data observed on a monthly basis (3). Despite their interest from the viewpoint of quantitative analysis, these models were never an efficient tool for short-term diagnosis or forecasting, which were carried out instead using the "traditional" annual or quarterly models.

Towards the end of the 1980s, the tendency to construct models for short-term economic cycle analysis had become well established. In fact, not only did the Bank of Italy present a monthly monetary model but (in the wake of the success of cointegration analysis) the use of monthly data became more common. This development is all the more evident if we examine the papers presented at the Bank of Italy's Biannual Conferences on quantitative models for economic policies. Of the works presented at the 1988 Conference, 40% used monthly data, against some 5% at the three previous conferences. It was at the 1988 Conference that the two new models developed for the Italian economy in the 1980s (4) were presented. These models derived from two different lines of research: the first, directed at

---

(2) See CARLUCCI - GIOVANNINI [9].
(3) Amongst others see CALLIARI - SARTORE [8], NOBILE [42], BARAGONA [3].
(4) See CARLUCCI [11] and GIOVANNINI [22].

A Monthly Model of the Industrial Sector etc. 231

constructing relatively aggregated models for the main industrialised countries (5) was designed to analyze the international transmission of the business cycle; while the second was directed at examining in greater detail (also on the theoretical point of view) the intersectorial linkages within a single economic system and the characteristics of the short-term management of industrial firms. These models were much more operational than those previously developed, even though their practical use was still very limited.

The international interest in these problems would appear to be very heterogeneous. In the Anglo-Saxon countries, macroeconometric models based on monthly data and survey indicators have not been deemed worthy of particular attention, perhaps due to the development of quarterly statistics for the national accounts. In Europe, on the other hand, surveys carried out amongst firms and families and harmonised at an EEC-level have stimulated greater interest. Since 1982, for example, the EEC has had an econometric model (named *BUSY*) in which information from surveys and "official" time series (consumption, investment, GDP, etc.) interact to produce short-term (one year) forecasts (6), while toward the end of the 1980s, in Switzerland, was developed an interesting project to construct a model which incorporated information from business surveys (7). In general, however, the models in question were estimated on data observed at quarterly intervals. Such information is much more frequently used in mono-equational models for forecasting specific macroeconomic variables (normally consumption and investment) or as part of procedures for the advance estimate of quarterly economic accounts (8).

The data contained in the business surveys carried out by the European Community have been widely used for microeconomic analysis of the behaviour of industrial firms. The most active in this field of study has been Nerlove, who has guided special research

---

(5) One of the reasons for the limited dimensions of such models is related to the use of the FIML estimation method. A first attempt to apply this technique is contained in CARLUCCI [10] with reference to the years 1973-1979.

(6) See CEE [12].

(7) See STALDER [47], FRANZ - SMOLNY [20].

(8) One example of this use is represented by GIOVANNINI [21]. See also DUDDEKEN - ZIJMANS [43].

groups in France, Germany and Italy, opening the way to similar detailed studies conducted for other countries (9).

Different, however, is the case of models which represent the monetary, financial and foreign-currency markets. The speed with which the fluctuations in interest rates, exchange rates and monetary variables take place has for some time now forced econometricians to use monthly models, even of medium dimensions. For several years now the central banks of various industrialised countries have had instruments of this sort, and even private study centres have models of varying complexity for forecasting monetary and financial variables (10). In general, however, these models have not linkages with similar models for "real" variables and hence these variables have to be extrapolated using simple *ARIMA* models for the operative use of these models.

3. - A Model for Analysing the Short-Term Economic Cycle: Theoretical Aspects

In order to overcome the shortcomings of the work carried out to date for the Italian case and construct a completely "operative" tool, the monthly econometric model presented in 1988 mentioned above was significantly extended and updated. While retaining the previous model's sectorial disaggregation and the basic theoretical framework, the new model (estimated for the period 1983-1989) provides a more detailed analysis of labour demand and endogenises the imports of goods which are classified by product groups (11). Finally, it should be noted that the real part of the model (that described here) is being completely integrated with the monetary part, which has to date been

---

(9) For Germany and France see NERLOVE [40]; again for Germany KONIG - NERLOVE [31] e [32], ARMINGER - RONNING [1]; for the United Kingdom MC INTOSH et AL [36]; for Switzerland ETTER et AL [19]; for Italy CHIZZOLINI [13].

(10) See, for example, THOMSON et AL [48], CLINTON - MASSON [14], JUDD - SCADDING [30], TINSLEY et AL [49], ESCRIVA et AL [18]. For the Italian case, see CALLIARI - SIRONI [7], COTULA et AL [15], BANCA D'ITALIA [2], GIOVANNINI - PALADINI [23] and the papers in GIOVANNINI [26].

(11) Even though the 'maintenance' work on aeconometric model is continuous, this paper refers to the version available at the end of 1991.

independent and has already established a name for itself as a forecasting tool (12).

The theoretical analysis starts by examining the behaviour of a single industrial firm which produces a single type of goods using three production factors (labour, raw materials and capital) and operates in a market open to foreign trade with monopolistic competition. It is hypothesised that this firm takes decisions concerning production and price policies in three successive phases: first, given the technology, the expected values of the exogenous variables and the evaluations of future demand for the goods produced by the firm are used to obtain the (desired) values of production, the production factors to be employed and the prices which maximise the expected profit. This phase does not take into consideration constraints of an organisational and commercial nature which can lead to adjustment costs and operative delays. The second phase considers these latter factors and any disequilibrium in the inventory stocks and unfilled orders dating from the previous period to obtain the planned values for production and prices. Finally, the real dynamics of the exogenous variables and orders received are used to determine the actual values of the afore-mentioned variables (13).

Once the model for a single firm has been obtained, one may proceed to aggregate the individual functions according to the economic destination of the firm's goods. More specifically, we considered three sectors of activity which embrace firms which produce intermediate goods, consumption goods and investment goods. By then considering a foreign sector and a commercial sector (in which the consumption goods are traded and the prices relevant for determining industrial wages are formed) one obtains an input-output model in which a sector's decisions are strictly dependent on those adopted by the agents operating in the other sectors.

In very general terms, the flow-chart of the model is shown in Graph 1. The sum of the (exogenous) orders from abroad (DE) and

---

(12) See GIOVANNINI [27].
(13) There is a very extensive literature on the behaviour of industrial firms as regards production, inventories management and price setting policies and demand factors. Models similar to those used by us are developed, amongst others, in MICOSSI - VISCO [37], MACCINI [34] and [35], PEARCE et AL [44], ROSSANA [45], DREZE - BEAN [17].

GRAPH 1

FLOW-CHART OF THE MODEL

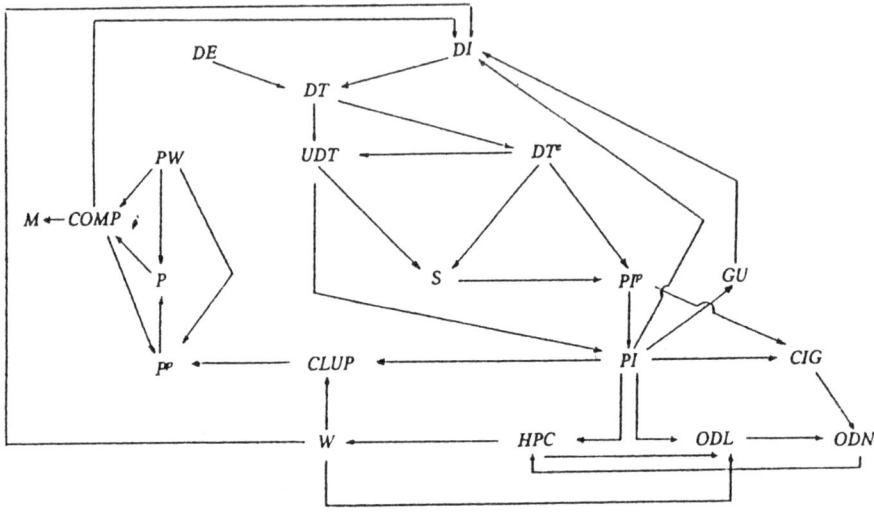

those from Italian firms (*DI*) gives the total demand for industry's products (*DT*). Since firms operate in conditions of uncertainty, in order to plan their activities they have to formulate their expectations regarding the tendency of this variable (*DT^e*) which depends, among other things, on the actual demand; there may of course be errors in forecasting demand (*UDT*), and these errors, together with the expectations, determine the evaluation of finished goods inventories (ΔS).

The planned production (*PI^p*) depends on the expected demand and changes in inventories, while the actual production (*PI*) depends on the plans drawn up in the previous months and on any errors which may have arisen when forecasting demand. The firm deals with the latter by altering the level of production, drawing on inventories and managing unfilled orders. The range of production factors at the firm's disposal means that each level of production corresponds to a certain degree of production capacity utilisation (*GU*) which is an important element when planning new investments and hence in the formation of domestic demand. The potential output which is the denominator for the indicator expressing the degree of production utilisation, is in turn endogenised in a simplified manner according to the production and imports of investment goods (14).

With a production function comprising three factors (raw materials, capital and labour) and a factor-interrelated demand model (15) it is possible to establish a causality relation between the level of production on the one hand and the demand for intermediate goods, capital goods and labour on the other. This means that domestic orders for these types of goods (*DI*) are endogenised according to the level of industry's economic activity (planned and real), the level of plant utilisation and other factors which we will mention below. As regards labour demand, given the rigidity of the Italian labour market, we modelled not the overall paid hours worked (*MORE*) but the components: per-capita hours (*HPC*) number of employees expressed in terms of labour units (*ODL*) and the number of employees temporarily laid-off (*CIG*) and hence not actively involved in the production process. The difference between *ODL* and *CIG* gives the number of active workers, that is to say net employment (*ODN*) (16). It should be noted that production expectations play an important role in the expression regarding the use of *CIG* (which, together with the per-capita working hours, is the tool firms resort to deal with very short-term fluctuations in labour demand) (17). The relation between per-capita worked hours and employment is negative and thus, while it is the first variable to adjust itself quicker in the short term, in the long term the two quantities almost completely swap places, with employment showing the most significant changes (18).

The dynamic of nominal wages per employee (*W*) is determined not only by the dynamic of consumer prices, using the *scala mobile*

---

(14) The importance of endogenising potential output even in a short-term model will become clear during the simulation. In commenting the results of the latter we will discuss this aspect.

(15) See NADIRI - ROSEN [38] and [39].

(16) This variable is coherent as regards definition with that contained in the national accounts schemes. As regards the aspects related to the construction of the data necessary for estimating the block of labour demand, see GIOVANNINI - ONETO [24].

(17) Examples of the use of expectations derived from business surveys in labour demand equations are given by WREN - LEWIS [50] and ILMAKUNNAS [29].

(18) It is interesting to note how the role of the per-capita working hours is often neglected when explaining the short-term adjustment of labour demand. Even the basic overview contained in NICKELL [41] leaves this issue more or less on the sidelines.

indexation system, but also by the evolution of hours worked (HPC) and retroacts (in real terms) on industrial firms' labour demand and (in terms of overall wages deflated by consumer prices) on the domestic demand for consumption. On the other hand, unity labour cost ($CLUP$), obtained by synthesising wage and production dynamics, influences the planned growth of selling prices which are also very dependent on the costs of the other production inputs (intermediate and investment goods) whether of domestic or foreign origin (PW).

The actual evolution of output prices (P) quickly adjusts to the planned one, while simultaneously feeling the effects of the changes in prices of foreign inputs not foreseen by the companies. In turn, prices determine (given the prices of foreign competitors) the competitiveness of industrial products ($COMP$) which not only influences the price plans but also determines domestic demand (DI) and imports (M).

4. - The Results of the Estimates

The lack of adequate statistical information with homogeneous definition forced us to use sets of time series obtained from different sources and characterised by different meaning. Many of these series were derived from business surveys carried out by the Istituto Nazionale per Studio della Congiuntura on a sample of industrial firms; since these data were expressed in qualitative form, it was first necessary to transform them into quantitative data by using the classical "balance" (19). On the other hand, the very particular nature of the answers given to these surveys, which refer to concepts of "normality" whose interpretation would require special preliminary analysis, made it necessary to restrict the range of the econometric analysis to the short-term aspects since this was the only solution which would enable one to overlook some elements deriving from the imperfect

---

(19) As shown in D'ELIA [16], if there are only three answers concerning the state of a phenomenon (i.e., "high", "normal" or "low"), the results furnished by the different procedures available (Carlson-Parkin, Pesaran, etc.) are very similar to those obtained by the balance.

TABLE 1

RESULTS OF THE ESTIMATES OF THE TRANSFER FUNCTIONS: R^2 AND LJUNG-BOX Q TEST ON THE FIRST 24 AUTOCORRELATIONS OF THE RESIDUALS (*)

Series	Trasform.	R^2	Q	Series	Trasform.	R^2	Q	Series	Trasform.	R^2	Q
DI2	—	0,945	24,17	DI3	—	0,932	13,56	DI4	—	0,924	19,16
S2	—	0,773	17,02	S3	—	0,733	11,53	S4	—	0,875	14,47
$DT2^e$	—	0,922	16,95	$DT3^e$	—	0,799	19,04	$DT4^e$	—	0,911	23,19
$PI2^P$	—	0,948	22,70	$PI3^P$	—	0,857	31,41	$PI4^P$	—	0,892	26,90
PI2	—	0,968	23,31	PI3	—	0,964	32,24	PI4	—	0,958	29,13
HPC2	log	0,985	19,78	HPC3	log	0,991	25,99	HPC4	log	0,973	27,77
CIG2	log	0,879	23,78	CIG3	log	0,915	18,94	CIG4	log	0,894	15,80
ODL2	log	0,998	24,95	ODL3	log	0,997	12,36	ODL4	log	0,999	15,83
W2	$(1-L^{12})\log$	0,813	21,21	W3	$(1-L^{12})\log$	0,823	14,17	W4	$(1-L^{12})\log$	0,840	15,26
$P2^P$	—	0,953	13,63	$P3^P$	—	0,946	20,10	$P4^P$	—	0,933	16,02
P2	$(1-L)\log$	0,783	21,22	P3	$(1-L)\log$	0,992	18,23	P4	$(1-L)\log$	0,684	16,76
M2	—	0,924	35,18	M3	—	0,920	14,18	M4	—	0,931	18,21
Pc	$(1-L)\log$	0,997	25,18								

(*) Sector 2 = firms producing intermediate goods; sector 3 = firms producing investment goods; sector 4 = firms producing consumption goods.

comparability of the statistics available. This consideration led us to suitably transform some of the time series taken from "offical" sources by filters for the differences (first or twelfth) which could reduce the weight of the long-term components and enhance those related to fluctuations of a cyclical character.

The model was estimated using monthly raw data for (in general) the period 1983-1989. For the equations regarding labour demand and (planned and actual) prices, the estimate period was cut-off at 1988 due to the unavailability of homogeneous time series for per-capita hours, employment and wages. Table 1 shows some characteristic statistics of the estimated equations, while Table 2 shows the symbols utilised and indicates the series to which they refer.

As regards the strategies followed for specifying the different equations, the order of the influence delays between the exogenous

TABLE 2

TABLE OF THE VARIABLES USED AND STATISTICAL SOURCES

DE	=	foreign orders (ISCO-ME survey)
DI	=	domestic orders (ISCO-ME survey)
DT	=	total orders (ISCO-ME survey)
S	=	finished goods inventories (ISCO-ME survey)
DT^e	=	orders expected for the coming three-four months (ISCO-ME survey)
PI^p	=	production planned for the coming three-four months (ISCO-ME survey)
PI	=	industrial production index (ISTAT, 1985 = 100)
GU	=	level of production capacity utilisation (our calculations from ISCO-ME survey)
HPC	=	per-capita hours worked (our calculations from Ministry of Labour and ISTAT data)
CIG	=	employees temporarily laid-off (our calculations from ISTAT data)
ODL	=	employees gross of temporary lay-offs (our calculations from ISTAT data)
ODN	=	employees net of temporary lay-offs (our calculations from ISTAT data)
W	=	wage per employee (our calculations from ISTAT data)
$CLUP$	=	unity labour cost (our calculations from ISTAT data)
P^p	=	planned increase in producer prices (ISCO-ME survey)
PW	=	index of average unit values for imports (our calculations from ISTAT and ISCO data, 1980 = 100)
P	=	index of producer prices (ISTAT, 1980 = 100)
$COMP$	=	P/PW
M	=	index of quantity of imported goods (our calculation from ISTAT and ISCO data)
Pc	=	general index of consumer prices (ISTAT, 1985 = 100)

variables and the endogenous was fixed by using the cross correlations on appropriately filtered series, wherever necessary since the specification could not be derived from the theoretical model. The use of this procedure allowed one to obtain extremely parsimonious specifications, while the results, as regards the serial correlation of the residuals, were also satisfactory. The ARMA structures on the residuals of the transfer functions (estimated with the non-linear least squares method) are in fact very rare and almost all induced by the need to represent seasonal phenomena or to correct the effects deriving from the use of twelfth-differences filters. Finally, it should be noted that the extremely erratic nature of the monthly time series considered necessitated using numerous dummies not so much out of economic considerations, but rather as a result of "statistical" causes, namely the anomalies in the observations deriving from the method used to gather the qualitative data.

5. - The Dynamics of the Different Sectors in Response to Demand and Supply Shocks

Table 3 shows the results obtained from a dynamic simulation of the model carried out on the period January 1983 - December 1989. As regards the model's capacity to represent the evolution of the endogenous variables, an examination of the simulation errors reveals a good quality for the interpolation obtained from the wages-price block while slightly higher errors are encountered for the real variables. In general, the results appear satisfactory if one also takes into account the duration of the simulation's period (seven years) with regard to the estimated model's short-term characteristics.

Since the series taken from the ISCO survey have both positive and negative signs, it would appear impossible to evaluate the errors in percentage terms. We will therefore limit ourselves to the other variables considered, which display a mean absolute percentage error of 3% for the general industrial production index and 1.4% for the general producer price index. As regards the per-capita compensations of the sectors as a whole, the error is instead equal to 1.9%, falling to 1.2% for net employment while that for imports by volume

TABLE 3

RESULTS OF THE DYNAMIC SIMULATION ON THE ENTIRE MODEL:
ME = MEAN ERROR, MAE = MEAN ABSOLUTE ERROR (*)

Series	ME	MAE	Series	ME	MAE	Series	ME	MAE	Series	ME	MAE
$DI1$	1,03	6,30	$DI2$	0,72	4,89	$DI3$	1,25	6,89	$DI4$	1,15	6,30
$S1$	−0,36	2,61	$S2$	−0,15	3,34	$S3$	−0,51	4,52	$S4$	0,44	5,02
$DT1^e$	1,01	3,61	$DT2^e$	0,04	3,95	$DT3^e$	0,78	4,39	$DT4^e$	1,71	5,02
$PI1^P$	1,03	3,24	$PI2^P$	0,37	3,53	$PI3^P$	0,83	4,44	$PI4^P$	1,41	4,53
$PI1^\bullet$	0,62	3,01	$PI2^\bullet$	0,73	2,93	$PI3^\bullet$	0,74	4,59	$PI4^\bullet$	0,46	3,67
$HPC1^\bullet$	0,10	2,14	$HPC2^\bullet$	−0,08	2,19	$HPC3^\bullet$	0,06	2,82	$HPC4^\bullet$	0,29	3,00
$ODN1^\bullet$	1,00	1,16	$ODN2^\bullet$	1,31	1,62	$ODN3^\bullet$	0,64	1,23	$ODN4^\bullet$	0,65	0,73
$W1^\bullet$	−1,15	1,87	$W2^\bullet$	−1,18	2,14	$W3^\bullet$	−1,26	2,71	$W4^\bullet$	−0,92	2,38
$P1^P$	2,21	3,66	$P2^P$	1,79	5,92	$P3^P$	3,70	6,23	$P4^P$	1,48	4,17
$P1^\bullet$	−1,31	1,41	$P2^\bullet$	0,14	0,91	$P3^\bullet$	−0,45	1,12	$P4^\bullet$	−0,80	0,92
$M1^\bullet$	0,01	5,45	$M2^\bullet$	1,25	5,70	$M3^\bullet$	0,03	7,89	$M4^\bullet$	−0,70	7,86

(*) Sector 1 = all firms; sector 2 = firms producing intermediate goods; sector 3 = firms producing investment goods; sector 4 = firms producing consumption goods.
For the variables marked with an asterisk the errors are given in percentages.

remains much higher (5.5%). When interpreting the latter result however, it should be borne in mind that until 1985 this variable was strongly influenced by delays of an administrative nature, which lead to the introduction in the series of a spurious erraticity which the model's structure obviously cannot repeat.

As regards the sectorial results, no clear "classification" of the quality of the simulation would appear to emerge, a shortcoming which is in part due to the high level of interdependence among the sectors considered in the model. We should note that the size of the errors is slightly lower in the intermediate goods sector, while the dynamic of some real variables of the investment goods sector would appear more difficult to represent.

We will now examine the results obtained from some of the model's simulations to assess the impact of demand and supply shocks on the variables taken into consideration. We will here examine two extreme cases: in the first simulation we assume a sustained increase of 10% in the import prices of intermediate goods (supply shock) for the purpose of highlighting above all the characteristics of the process of diffusion of inflationary pressure of foreign origin similar to that experienced by the Italian economy on various occasions (the last being in 1990). The second simulation on the other hand supposes a sudden and sustained growth in time of foreign orders which leads to a 10% increase in the total orders received by the firms (in each sector) (20).

The increase in import prices immediately affects domestic prices (Graph 2) in the intermediate goods sector, and six months later producer prices appear to cover almost 90% of the difference between the initial value and the new equilibrium level, while in the other sectors the maximum increase is recorded 18 months after the initial

---

(20) Since the demand for intermediate goods is affected by the existence of forecasting errors in other sectors, the initial shock on foreign orders in this sector was more limited.

It should be noted that the graphs show the differences between the disturbed and the control solution. Due to the different scales for prices, production, imports and employment the curves are obtained from the ratio between the two series of values, but as the difference between the series of values for domestic orders and inventories. Although the simulations were carried out on the period 1983-1989, for ease of consultation they only show the values for the first 24 months.

GRAPH 2

PRODUCER PRICES
(simulation *A*)

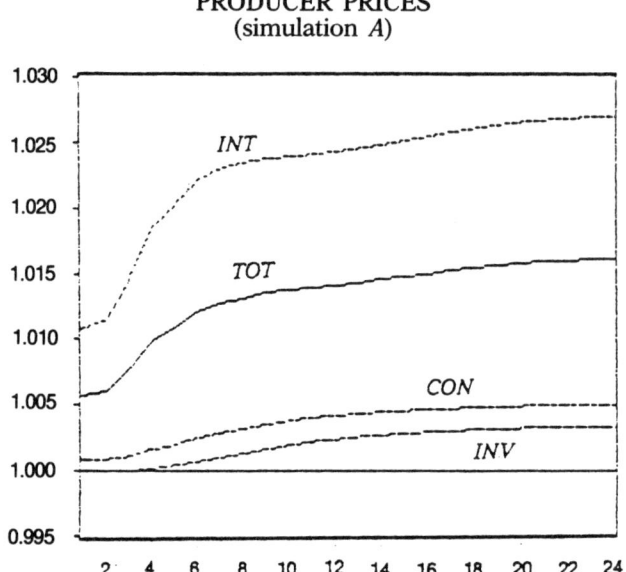

GRAPH 3

DOMESTIC DEMAND
(simulation *A*)

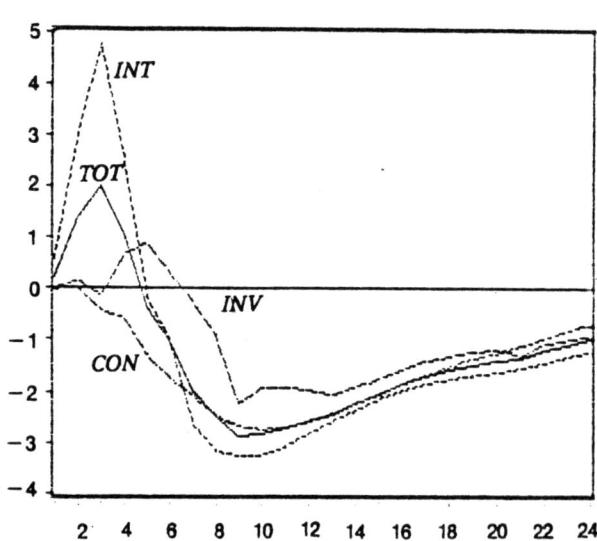

shock. For the purposes of the adjustment process, the general index increases by 1.5%, which is the average of the growth of some 2.5% for intermediate goods and 0.2% for consumption and investment goods.

The inflationary pressure produces an immediate, speculative increase in the domestic demand for intermediate goods and, to a lesser extent, for investment goods (Graph 3). Six months after the shock, there is a sharp fall in orders in all the sectors considered: this produces an increase in inventories of finished goods (Graph 4), more noticeable for consumption goods and a fall in production levels (Graph 5). Ten months after the initial impulse, this level is some 1.1% below the control level in all the sectors considered. A similar depressive effect is recorded for imported goods (Graph 6): here, however, the fall is much more marked, approaching 5% for intermediate goods and 1.5% for the other sectors. As time passes, however, production tends to rise back to its control values as do inventories and domestic demand. The initial equilibrium tends to be re-established with unchanged levels of activity and a higher level of producer prices. However, there persists a depressive effect on the imports of intermediate goods which can be estimated in the order of some 2%.

Labour demand expressed in terms of paid working hours basically follows the dynamics of production (Graph 7). Both the initial increase and the subsequent reduction of hours worked are satisfied in the short term by modifying the per-capita worked hours and by increasingly resorting to temporary lay-offs. The negative impulse affects the number of workers only after some time has passed and a reduction in worker numbers allows a return to the per-capita working hours recorded at the control level. Two years later, the fall in total employment (net of CIG) is much greater in the consumption goods sector, despite the sector's much more limited fall in production. The situation in the intermediate goods sector is the opposite; here the sharp fall in production is accompanied by a more limited decrease in worker numbers.

To conclude these comments on this simulation, we would note that in the sectors which produce investment and consumption goods, the increases in international prices of raw materials has negative

GRAPH 4

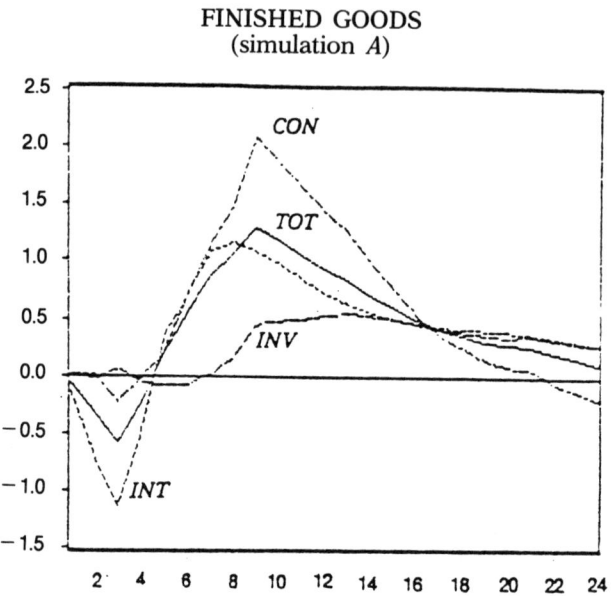

FINISHED GOODS
(simulation A)

GRAPH 5

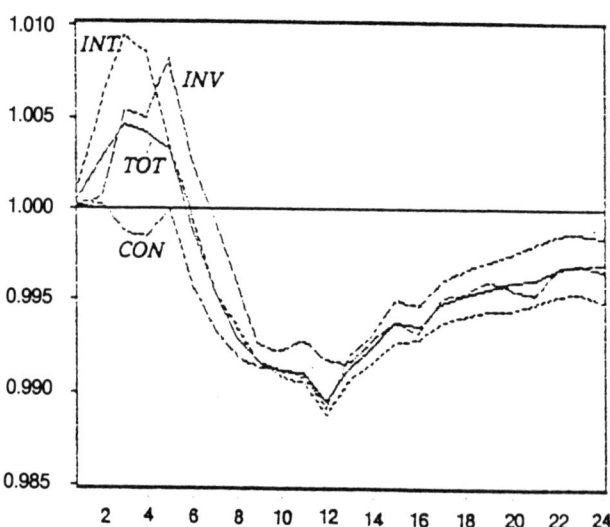

INDUSTRIAL PRODUCTION
(simulation A)

A Monthly Model of the Industrial Sector etc. 245

GRAPH 6

IMPORTS OF GOODS
(simulation A)

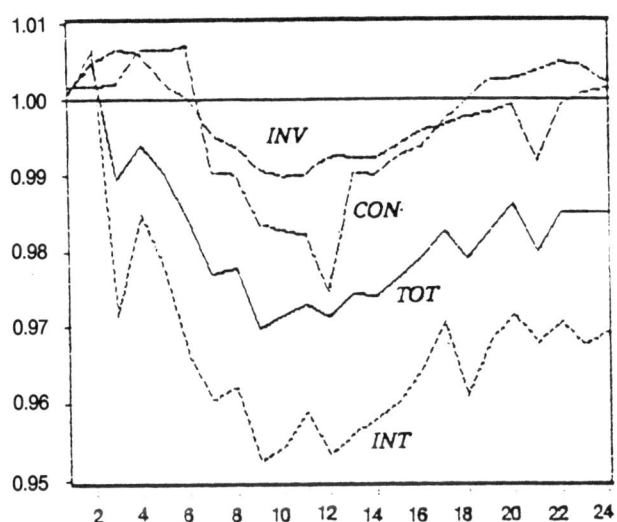

GRAPH 7

PER-CAPITA HOURS WORKED, EMPLOYMENT
AND TOTAL HOURS WORKED - ALL THE FIRMS
(simulation A)

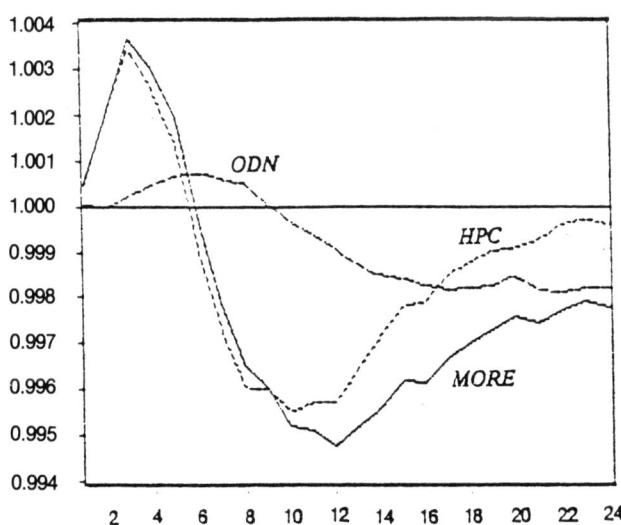

effects on expected demand. On the other hand, since the shock in question is punctual, the effect on this variable is one-off; therefore an inflationary pressure which alters the rate of change of international prices for a certain period would have a much more consistent effect than that measured here on total output and, as a result, on employment.

In accordance with theory, a demand shock produces in the short term an immediate fall in finished goods inventories (Graph 10) and an equally immediate increase in the production of industrial goods (Graph 11). This latter phenomenon in turn induces a significant increase in domestic demand (Graph 9), in particular in the intermediate and investment goods sectors. There is also a significant surge in imports (Graph 12) with a net prevalence, once again, in the capital and intermediate goods sectors (21).

The higher level of production leads to an increase in labour demand (Graph 13) which the firms initally cope with by increasing the hours worked per employee and reducing the number of workers temporarily laid-off. The increase in employment, which leads to per-capita hours worked returning to the pre-shock level, is slower. This process is in effect complete only in the case of intermediate goods while in the other two sectors it has a permanent effect on the level of per-capita working hours (22). The total hours worked increase in line with the increase in production, so that hourly productivity increases only in the short term.

Despite the higher level of per-capita wages, the unity cost of labour tends to fall, with beneficial effects on the dynamics of prices set by industrial firms (Graph 8). The intermediate goods sector is the most responsive in this regard, even though in absolute terms deflation would appear very limited (0.5 percentage points two years after the shock).

---

(21) It is interesting to note that when potential output remains exogenous, the quantitative evaluation of the effect on demand for investment goods is considerably underestimated. Thus, the utilised production capacity, which determines domestic orders and imports of investment goods, persists at a level which was permanently higher during the simulation period.

(22) Such an effect could be due to certain peculiarities of the Italian labour market regarding the rigidity of downwards employment and the relatively low cost of overtime work. On these aspects see GIOVANNINI - ONETO [24].

GRAPH 8

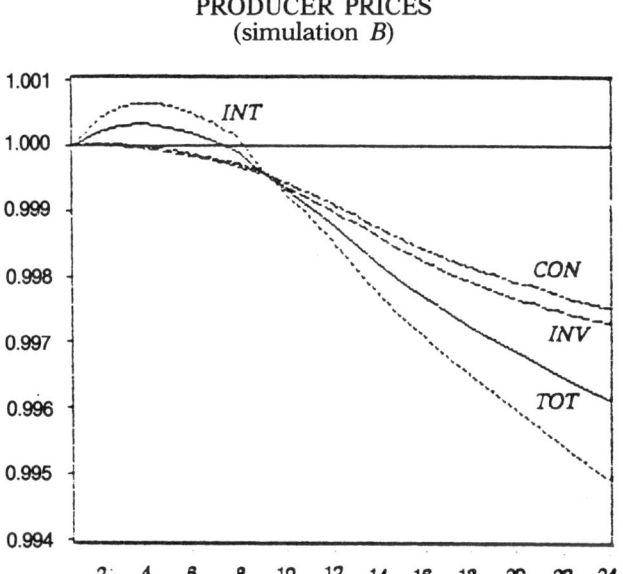

GRAPH 9

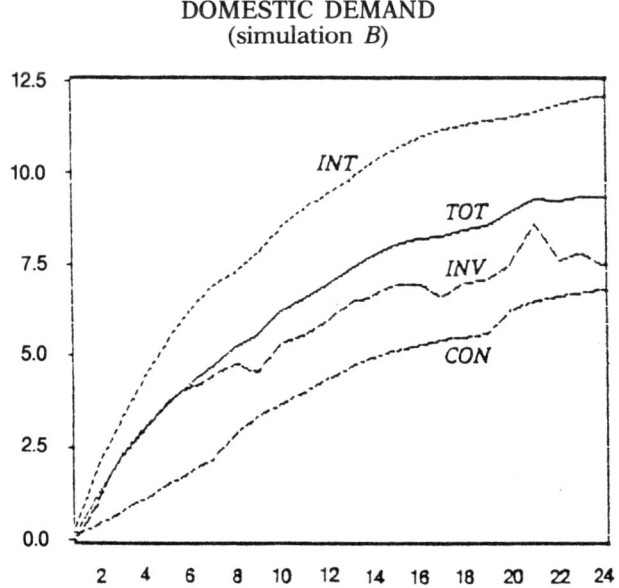

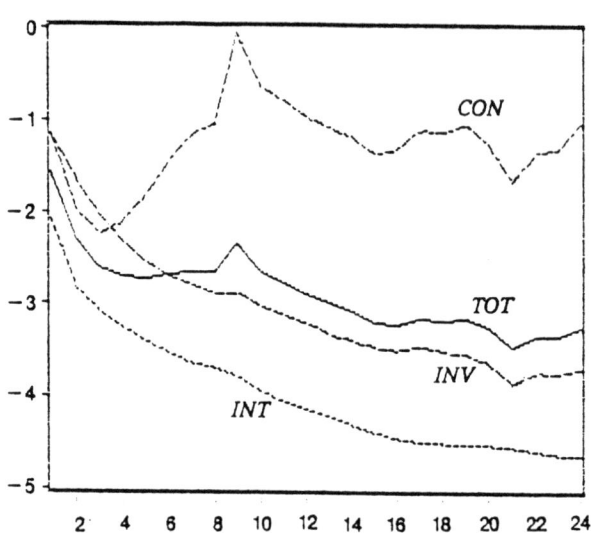

GRAPH 10

INVENTORIES OF FINISHED GOODS
(simulation B)

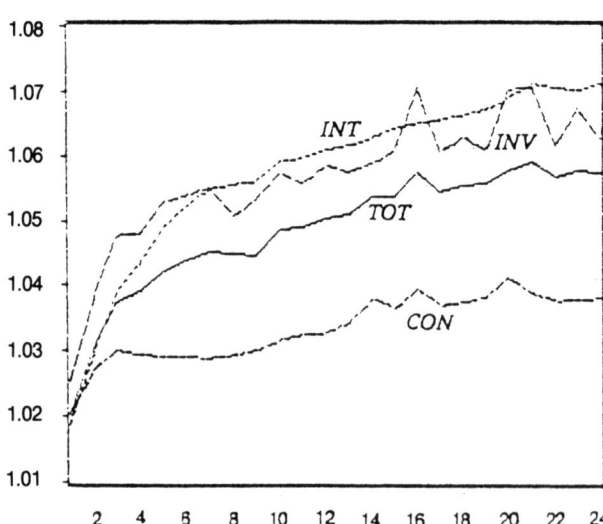

GRAPH 11

INDUSTRIAL PRODUCTION
(simulation B)

GRAPH 12

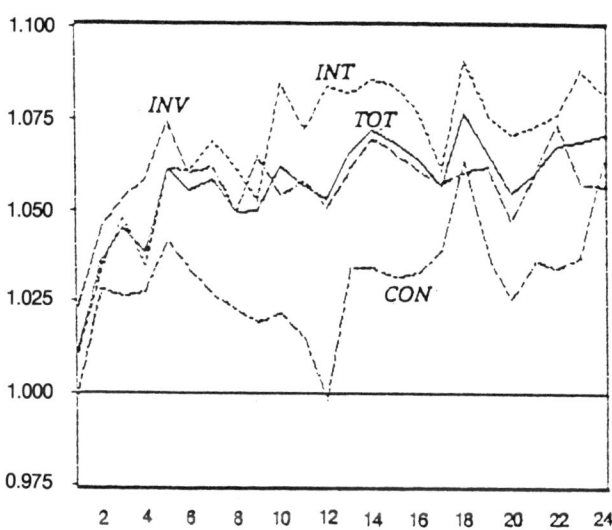

IMPORTS OF GOODS
(simulation *B*)

GRAPH 13

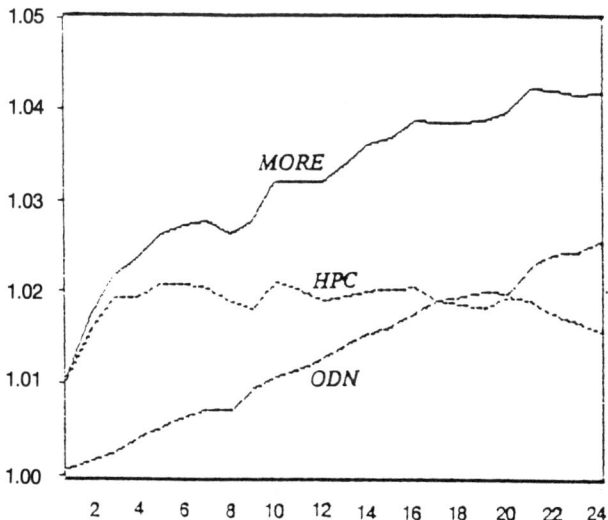

PER-CAPITA HOURS WORKED, EMPLOYMENT
AND TOTAL HOURS WORKED - ALL THE FIRMS
(simulation *B*)

The increase in production in the absence of significant effects on domestic prices produces an increase in wages in real terms which, given the greater sluggishness vis-à-vis the other sectors, stimulates a more sustained demand for consumption goods and thus prolongs the expansive effect on domestic demand. At the end of the adjustment process, total production appears to have grown by almost 6% while inventories tend to remain (even though by a small margin) below their initial value. Even without an accounting model which allows one to evaluate the coherence of the different multipliers, this result should imply a consistent increase in the imports of goods to compensate domestic production shortfalls. This phenomenon is reflected in the model and can be estimated in a permanent increase of circa 7% in purchases abroad.

Since similar simulation exercises were carried out with a model estimated for the years 1980-1985 (23), it would be interesting to compare the results obtained with the two models to assess any differences in the strategies adopted by industrial firms in the first and second halves of the 1980s. As regards the inflationary shock case, there is a basic similarity in the multipliers of intermediate and consumption goods, while the elasticity calculated using the 'new model for investment goods appears to be considerably lower. On the other hand, domestic demand appears to be decidedly more reactive, especially as regards the recessive phase induced by the increase in international prices: with the previous model, the initial increase of orders for intermediate goods was not followed by such a strong deceleration of demand in the months after the shock. Examining the experience of the 1990 Middle East crisis, the multipliers derived from the new model appear to be basically realistic.

In the new model, finished goods inventories would appear to play a less important role in absorbing the demand fluctuations which manifest themselves with greater rapidity and intensity on industrial production. This result is in line with what has been revealed by other statistical sources regarding the Italian case and would appear attributable to the greater production efficiency induced by the restructuring of industry in the early 1980s (24).

---

(23) See GIOVANNINI [25].
(24) See SESTITO - VISCO [46].

In the case of demand shock, a comparison of the two series of results basically confirms the "hierarchy" of the multipliers calculated vis-à-vis domestic orders and production levels. There is a clear surge in the demand for intermediate and investment goods after the initial shock, even though the reactivity of the production of consumption goods appears to be considerably higher in the second subperiod. As shown by the previous model, the intermediate goods sector is the quickest to cope with the excess demand by destocking, while the consumption goods sector is more hesitant to resort to this means.

Conversely, the effect of the multipliers calculated for prices is the opposite of that previously seen. In the model for the early 1980s, there was a positive link between the level of demand and inflation, above all in the investment and intermediate goods sectors. Observing the more recent years, however, there would appear to prevail a negative effect related to the reduction of labour costs which took place following the increase in productivity. This change of strategy can be attributed to the changed institutional set-up within which the monetary and exchange rate policies operated. Starting from 1988, the lack of internal alignment within EMS placed a strict constraint on companies exposed to foreign competition as regards price formation and the differences in firms' behaviour shown by the simulation are not all that unrealistic.

6. - Conclusions

The speed with which the markets react to the onset of real and monetary pressures would appear to have significantly increased during the 1980s and this has had important repercussions in the approach to modelling the various economic agents. As regards econometric models, much importance was placed on representing the dynamics of the relations between the different variables. To comprehend these aspects of reality more correctly we should construct models based on data observed with a higher time frequency which give adequate weight to expectations regarding the important variables and explicitly represent the dynamic adjustment processes.

The model presented in this paper originates from this line of research and represents the behaviour of the Italian industrial sector divided into three sectors which produce intermediate, investment and consumption goods. The model determines for each of these sectors the orders (expected and actual) which the companies receive, inventories, production (planned and actual), selling prices (planned and actual), hours worked, employment, wages and imports. For estimating the model, which refers to the period 1983-1989, much importance is attributed to the series derived from business surveys carried out by ISCO. The results obtained also via simulations of the model highlight its capacity to accurately represent even short-term fluctuations of the industrial system, thus confirming that this approach is also useful for analysing the current short-term economic cycle.

As regards their interpretation, the results presented show interesting asymmetries of strategies in the various sectors, in particular during the process of dynamic adjustment to the equilibrium positions of the quantity and price variables induced by demand and supply pressures. In this regard, the greater flexibility of management shown by the intermediate goods sector is significant while the consumption goods sector would appear to be slower to modify its dynamic. The results reveal significant differences in the industrial system's response to the shocks in the early 1980s and those in the latter part of the decade, when firms appeared to enjoy a greater flexibility in their production plans and their price policies were much more closely linked to the behaviour of their international competitors.

BIBLIOGRAPHY

[1] ARMINGER G. - RONNING G.: «A Structural Model for Price, Production and Inventory Decisions of Firms», paper presented at the *XX Conferenza CIRET*, Budapest, 1991.
[2] BANCA D'ITALIA: «Modello mensile del mercato monetario», Roma, Banca d'Italia, *Temi di discussione*, n. 108, 1988.
[3] BARAGONA R.: «Un modello ARMA vettoriale per l'analisi delle relazioni dinamiche tra prezzi e tasso di cambio», *Atti della XXXII Riunione Scientifica della SIS*, Napoli, Liguori, 1984.
[4] BIAGIOLI A. - CHIESA C. - GOMEL G. - PALMISANI F.: «Un modello operativo per l'analisi a breve termine della bilancia dei pagamenti», *Ricerche sui modelli per la politica economica*, Roma, Banca d'Italia, 1983.
[5] BLINDER A.S.: «Inventories and Sticky Prices: More on the Microfoundations of Macroeconomics», *American Economic Review*, vol. 72, n. 3, 1982.
[6] BLINDER A.S. - MACCINI L.J.: «Taking Stock: A Critical Assessment of Recent Research on Inventories», *Economic Perspectives*, n. 4, 1991.
[7] CALLIARI S. - SIRONI A.: *Un modello econometrico mensile dei mercati monetari e degli impieghi bancari*, Mimeo, 1984.
[8] CALLIARI S. - SARTORE D.: *Le cause dell'inflazione in Italia: un po' di evidenza empirica*, Mimeo, 1984.
[9] CARLUCCI F. - GIOVANNINI E.: «Un'analisi causale della congiuntura italiana degli anni '70», *Ricerche economiche*, n. 2, 1984.
[10] CARLUCCI F.: «Ciclo economico, analisi causale e modelli ARMA», CARLUCCI F. (a cura di): *Saggi sulla congiuntura italiana degli anni '70*, Milano, F. Angeli, 1988.
[11] CARLUCCI F.: «Un'analisi di breve periodo di tre economie della Cee», *Ricerche e metodi per la politica economica*, Roma, Banca d'Italia, 1989.
[12] CEE: «Les Principes Généraux Des Enquetes de Conjuncture», *Economie Europeenne*, supplement B., July 1991.
[13] CHIZZOLINI B. - NERLOVE M. - PUPILLO L.: «Demand Expectations. Production Plans, Prices and Inventories», *Rassegna dei lavori dell'Isco*, n. 8, Roma, Isco, 1986.
[14] CLINTON K. - MASSON P.: «A Monetary Monthly Model of the Canadian Financial System», *Bank of Canada Technical Report*, n. 4, 1975.
[15] COTULA F. - GALLI G. - LECALDANO E. - SANNUCCI V. - ZAUTZIK E.A.: «Una stima delle funzioni di domanda di attività finanziarie», *Ricerche quantitative per la politica economica*, Roma, Banca d'Italia, 1984.
[16] D'ELIA E.: «La quantificazione dei risultati dei sondaggi congiunturali: un confronto tra procedure», Roma, Isco, *Rassegna dei lavori dell'Isco*, n. 13, 1991.
[17] DREZE J.H. - BEAN C.: «European Unemployment: Lessons from a Multicountry Econometric Study», *Scandinavian Journal of Economics*, n. 92, 1990.
[18] ESCRIVÀ J.L. - ESPASA A. - PEREZ J. - SALAVERRIA J.: «A Short Term Econometric Model for Spanish Monetary Policy», paper presented at the *European Meeting of the Econometric Society*, 1986.
[19] ETTER R. - NERLOVE M. - WILLSON D.: *Swiss Inventory Behavior: A Recursive Simultaneous Equations Model*, Mimeo, 1989.

[20] FRANZ W. - SMOLNY W.: «The Use of Business Survey Data in a Disequilibrium Macroeconomic Model», paper presented at the *XX Conferenza CIRET*, Budapest, 1991.

[21] GIOVANNINI E.: «A Methodology for an Early Estimate of Quarterly National Accounts», *Economia internazionale*, vol. XLI, n. 3-4, 1985.

[22] ——: «Un modello per l'analisi della dinamica del settore industriale italiano nel breve periodo», *Ricerche e metodi per la politica economica*, Roma, Banca d'Italia, 1989.

[23] GIOVANNINI E. - PALADINI R.: «Fabbisogno, maturità del debito e tassi d'interesse, un modello econometrico del mercato dei titoli di Stato», *Moneta e credito*, vol. XLIII, n. 170, 1990.

[24] GIOVANNINI E. - ONETO G.: «Employment, Temporary Layoffs and Worked Hours: A Monthly Model of Labour Demand for the Italian Industrial Sector», paper presented at the *XXXI Conferenza internazionale dell'AEA*, Strasburgo, 1990.

[25] GIOVANNINI E.: «Squilibri settoriali e dinamica macroeconomica di breve periodo: il caso dell'industria italiana», Siena, Università di Siena, *Quaderni del dipartimento di economia politica*, n. 98, 1990.

[26] GIOVANNINI E. (ed.): *I mercati monetari e finanziari nel breve periodo. Modelli per l'analisi e la previsione*, IMI, Milano, Sole 24 Ore, 1992.

[27] GIOVANNINI E.: *Fabbisogno pubblico, politica monetaria e mercati finanziari*, Milano, Angeli, 1992.

[28] GORDON R.J.: «Output Fluctuations and Gradual Price Adjustment», *Journal of Economic Literature*, vol. XIX, 1981.

[29] KONIG H. - NERLOVE M.: «Micro-Analysis of Realizations, Plans and Expectations in the IFO Business Test by Multivariate Log-Linear Probability Models», paper presented at the *XIV conferenza Ciret*, Lisbon, 1979.

[30] —— - ——: «Price Flexibility, Inventory Behavior and Production Responses», in HELLER W. - STARR R.M. - STARRETT D.A. (eds.): *Equilibrium Analysis Essays in Honor of Kenneth J. Arrow*, vol. II, Cambridge, Cambridge University Press, 1986.

[31] ILMAKUNNAS P.: «Survey Expectations Vs. Rational Expectations in the Estimation of a Dynamic Model: Demand for Labour in Firms' Manufacturing», *Oxford Bulletin of Economics and Statistics*, n. 51, 1989.

[32] JUDD J.E. - SCADDING J.L.: «Liability Management, Bank Loans and Deposit Market Disequilibrium», Federal Reserve Bank of S. Francisco, *Economic Review*, n. 3, 1981.

[33] LOVELL M.C.: «Inventory Fluctuations and Macroeconomics», paper presented at the Conference on *Business Cycle, Inventory Fluctuations and Monetary Policy*, Siena, Certosa di Pontignano, 1992.

[34] MACCINI L.J.: «The Impact of Demand and Price Expectations on the Behavior of Prices», *American Economic Review*, vol. 68, n. 1, 1978.

[35] ——: «On the Theory of the Firm Underlying Empirical Models of Aggregate Price Behavior», *International Economic Review*, vol. XXII, n. 3, 1981.

[36] MC INTOSH J. - SCHIANTARELLI F. - LOW W.: «A Qualitative Response Analysis of UK Firms' Employment and Output Decisions», *Journal of Applied Econometrics*, n. 4, 1989.

[37] MICOSSI S. - VISCO I.: «Scelte reali e scelte finanziarie dell'impresa: un modello di disequilibrio», Roma, Banca d'Italia, *Contributi alla ricerca economica*, n. 8, 1978.

[38] NADIRI I. - ROSEN S.: «Interrelated Factor Demand Functions», *American Economic Review*, n. 59, 1969.
[39] —— - ——: «A Disequilibrium Model of Demand for Factors of Production», *American Economic Reiview*, n. 64, 1974.
[40] NERLOVE M.: «Expectations, Plans and Realizations in Theory and Practice», *Econometrica*, n. 53, 1983.
[41] NICKELL S.: «Dynamic Models of Labour Demand», in ASHENFELTER O. - LAYARD R. (eds.): *Handbook of Labour Economics*, Amsterdam, Elsevier Science Publisher, 1986.
[42] NOBILE A.: «Un modello in spazio di stato di indicatori mensili dell'economia italiana», *Atti della XXXIII riunione scientifica della SIS*, 1986.
[43] OUDDEKEN F.E.M. - ZIJMANS G.M.: «The Use of Tendency Surveys in Extrapolating National Accounts», *Review of Income and Wealth*, n. 2, 1992.
[44] PEARCE J.F. - TRIVEDI P.K. - STROMBACK C.T. - ANDERSON G.J.: *A Model of Output, Employment, Wages and Prices in the UK.*, Cambridge, Cambridge University Press, 1976.
[45] ROSSANA R.: «Buffer Stocks and Labour Demand: Further Evidence», *Review of Economics and Statistics*, n. 67, 1985.
[46] SESTITO P. - VISCO I.: «Indicators for Finished Goods Stocks and Business Cycle in Italy», paper presented at the Conference on *Business Cycle, Inventory Fluctuations and Monetary Policy*, Siena, Certosa di Pontignano, 1992.
[47] STALDER P.: «Excess Demand and Capacity Utilization - An Empirical Analysis Based on Swiss Business Survey Data», *Applied Economics*, n. 21, 1989.
[48] THOMSON D.T. - PIERCE J.L. - FERRY R.T.: «A Monthly Money Market Model», *Journal of Money, Credit and Banking*, November 1975.
[49] TINSLEY P.A. - FARR H.T. - FRIES G. - VON ZUR MUEHLEN P.: «Policy Robustness: Monthly Money Market Model», *Journal of Money, Credit and Banking*, November 1982.
[50] WREN-LEWIS S.: «An Econometric Model of UK Manufacturing Employment Using Survey Data on Expected Output», *Journal of Applied Econometrics*, n. 1, 1986.

Business Cycle Analysis and Industrial Production Forecasts

Pietro Gennari
Istituto Nazionale per lo Studio della Congiuntura, Roma

1. - Introduction

The industrial production index is still one of the favoured indicators for assessing the short-term trend of an economic system. Despite the increased influence of tertiary activities on the overall economies of the industrialised countries, a phenomenon which has contributed to stabilising the dynamics of their GDP, cyclical fluctuations continue to remain an ever-constant characteristic of market economies and the industrial cycle remains the predominant component of the aggregate one (1).

The aim of this paper is to analyse the literature regarding multivariate models for short-term forecasting of the volume of industrial production. Few studies on this subject have been published in international journals, while it is obvious that short-term economic analysts are very interested in being able to forecast, even for a very limited time horizon, the size of the quantitative variations in industrial activity.

There are various reasons for this lack of fortune. Firstly, the delay in publishing industrial production data varies from country to country. In the United States, for example, the Bureau of Census publishes preliminary estimates for this index with very little delay, thus removing much of the practical interest in developing the procedures being studied here. In Italy on the other hand, the Istituto

---

(1) See SCHLITZER [42] for a recent review of Italian experience.
Advise: the numbers in square brackets refer to the Bibliography in the appendix.

nazionale di statistica (ISTAT) furnishes the provisional estimates of the monthly volume of industrial production some 50 days after the month to which they refer; as a result, numerous econometric models have been proposed and there has been much lively debate on the issue.

Furthermore, although many of the institutes carrying out short-term economic analysis have probably developed their own methods for forecasting the level of industrial activity, the results tend to be for internal use as a consequence of both their insufficient accuracy and the continuous need to "update" the methods used. For such a short time period, there is a somewhat high risk of incurring in large forecast errors which, unlike those generated by long-term forecasting models, cannot be explained by a change in the exogenous environment.

Finally short-term quantitative prediction models of the industrial production cannot be based on specific propositions of economic theory. Indeed, the nature of the problem rules out the possibility of building structural models, the values of necessary variables being known only after the production data to be forecasted are published.

The difficulties which have hindered the development of an extensive international discussion on the different methods for advance estimation of the volume of industrial activity do not justify the little attention paid to this issue. The use of multivariate models for short-term forecasting of the industrial production generally results in a considerable improvement in the prediction accuracy with respect to univariate models (*ARIMA* or extrapolative), in particular at cyclical turning points. It should be pointed out, on the other hand, that the official index, while remaining the benchmark for any type of forecasting accuracy analysis, embodies errors which increase in entity with its level of provisionality (2) and decrease according to its level of cover (3).

---

(2) In Italy, for example, ISTAT elaborates each mid-month a provisional index which refers to the actual data of two months back. Subsequently, some two weeks later, ISTAT communicates a new index value which should be considered only partially definitive since it can be revised some months after the publication of the provisional data. BODO - CIVIDINI [4] have shown that in the period 1984.1-1988.12 the provisional index was distorted, inefficient, and strongly underestimated *vis-à-vis* the value of the definitive index.

(3) Again in the case of Italy, ISTAT calculates the industrial production index by an extended direct survey of the companies above a certain minimum threshold (20

Two different streams of research can be distinguished in the literature, the difference being the type of predictors (either quantitative or qualitative) introduced in the models. In the case of the former, the forecasting models include quantitative indicators which are directly or indirectly related to the industrial production and are published quickly. In the second case, the explicative variables are represented by the firm's expectations, qualitative in nature, which are gathered with the business surveys. The main contributions belonging to these two types of models will be presented in the next two sections paying particular attention to the extensive debate that has taken place in Italy; there then follows a concluding section which attempts to outline some summary considerations and propose some areas for future research in this field.

2. Models for Industrial Production Forecasting Based on Quantitative Indicators Collected in Real Time

The basic characteristic of these methods is that they forecast the industrial production data on the basis of quantitative indicators collected in real time. The interest in these techniques, as already noted in the Introduction, has developed above all in those countries, such as Italy, where the delay in publishing the preliminary index is considered overly long by business cycle analysts.

A first group of models, developed in particular by IRS (Istituto per la ricerca sociale) and Banca d'Italia, uses a single predictor derived from the data concerning the amount of electricity produced by ENEL (Ente nazionale per l'energia elettrica) for the national grid. The statistics on the quantity of energy distributed satisfies the fundamental requisite of timeliness, since it is gathered daily and available with only one day's delay. Some problems arise however when these statistics are compared with the industrial production index. The amount of electricity produced by ENEL, in fact, does not

---

employees). Given the structure of the Italian industrial sector with its myriad of small companies, the industrial production index can, in some business-cycle situations, provide a biased estimate of the manufacturing's level of activity.

correspond exactly to the total energy distributed (4) and does not allow one to distinguish between the industrial and civil uses of this energy. Furthermore, this aggregate indicator does not permit one to discern between variations in energy consumption due to changes in the composition of the output and simple variations in production levels, since the incidence of the various sectors on the industrial production index is not proportional to their electrical-energy input coefficient. It should also be borne in mind that the relation between industrial production and energy consumption tends to change over time according to electricity price changes and to tecnological progress. Even large discrepancies in the cyclical dinamics of the two variables are determined by these underlined differencies.

The models based on the electrical-energy data differ according to the type of solutions proposed for the problems related to the information source employed. In one of the first studies by Lippi and Saraceno (Lippi [30], Ranci [40]), the relation between the raw industrial production index and the electricity data was specified by an *ARMA* vectorial function (16.12), applied on variables previously made stationary (by a double, sequential and seasonal, differentiation and by logarithmic transformation). The general form of the model is:

$$(1) \quad \begin{bmatrix} A(L) & 0 \\ A'(L) & B(L) \end{bmatrix} \begin{bmatrix} y_t \\ \varepsilon_t \end{bmatrix} = \begin{bmatrix} C(L) & 0 \\ C'(L) & D(L) \end{bmatrix} \begin{bmatrix} u_t \\ v_t \end{bmatrix}$$

in which:
$y_t = (1-L)(1-L^{12}) \log Y_t$
$\varepsilon_t = (1-L)(1-L^{12}) \log E_t$
Y_t = raw industrial production index
E_t = electrical energy produced by ENEL for the national grid
$A(L), A'(L), B(L), C(L), C'(L), D(L)$ are polynomials in the lag operator L.
$(u_t \ v_t)$ = white noise vector

The model estimated on the period 1968.1-1982.12 yielded one lead forecasts for the period 1983.1-1984.6. The model's forecasting

---

(4) To the total amount of electrical energy produced by ENEL for the national grid one should also add the energy produced by the municipal energy utilities and the own consumption declared by private energy producers.

performance was not completely satisfactory since the mean absolute error (MAE) of the forecasts was slightly above 3%. In this work, however, the authors indicated some areas of future research for improving forecast accuracy which were later developed in subsequent studies. On the one hand, they proposed using a three-variable model which replaced the aggregate industrial production index by the indexes for the energy-intensive and non energy-intensive sectors, to enable variations in the composition of industrial output to be taken into consideration. On the other hand, they also suggested introducing a climatic variable so as to reduce the variance of energy for non-industrial uses.

This was the direction subsequently taken by Bodo and Signorini ([7], [8]); they included the average national temperature in the elettricity-production relation according to a quadratic specification, so as to remove the "non-industrial" components from the overall data on electrical energy. Household electricity consumption, in this case, would tend to increase progressively both when the temperature rose above the average (due to the greater use of cooling and conditioning units) and when it fell below the average (due to the increased need for heating).

The linear model was specified as follows (5):

(2) $$Y_t = a + \Sigma_j b_j E_t^j + c_1 \; Temp_t + c_2 \; Temp_t^2 + \\ + dt + eY_{t-12} + \Sigma_i f_i S_i + u_t$$

where Y_t is the industrial production index corrected for trading-day variations, E_t the energy produced for the national grid by ENEL in area j (also adjusted in a similar way), $Temp_t$ the average national temperature, t a linear trend, S_i a dummy variable for the i-th month of the year and finally u_t a casual error for which the standard assumptions of zero mean, homoscedasticity and absence of serial correlation hold.

---

(5) The article compares two types of specification for the model: dynamic regression and transfer function. On the basis of considerations concerning both the forecasting performance and the absence of significant cross correlations between the variables beyond a zero-order lag, they prefer the former method.

The linear trend and the electricity data disaggregated by geographical district were included in the model in order to correctly evaluate the influence of non-industrial uses on total electricity consumption, given the different weights of this component in the various areas of the country. The authors also introduced this trend to represent any effects of technological change on industry's global electricity intensity. The area data, on the other hand, would furnish the approximate sectorial distribution of the energy consumed. As regards the dynamic specification of the endogenous variable, the twelfth-order lag would appear to be the only significant term, indicating a possible modification in the seasonal pattern not picked up by the dummy variables.

This monthly model was estimated for each region employing the *OLS* method. The results refer to the period 1978.1-1985.4: in general, the fit is rather good, with a very small standard error and no evidence of incorrect specification. The forecasting performance of model *(2)* was assessed calculating one-lead and two-lead predictions for the period 1984.1-1985.4. On the whole the multivariate models performed significantly better than the univariate models used as benchmark. The results compared favourably also with those obtained by Lippi and Saraceno, since the mean absolute error was respectively 2.1% for one-lead and 2,3% for two-lead forecasts.

In a later article Bodo, Cividini and Signorini ([5] and [6]) retained the structure of the preceding model but extended its forecast horizon (from one and a half months to 2 months ahead of the provisional index) on the basis of electrical energy data for the first half of the month. In passing from the monthly model to that based on half-monthly electrical energy data, almost no loss of accuracy in the forecasts was noted with the mean absolute error remaining at 2,3%.

Gutierrez and Saraceno [26] suggested slightly different solutions to the multiple problems posed by the variable utilised as leading indicator. They substituted the indirect indicators of non-industrial electrical energy, such as temperature, with direct indicators so as to limit the number of variables to be collected. In their opinion, furthermore, the use of a quadratic function specification for modelling the relation between temperature and household electricity consumption, assuming a symmetric effect in the case of both a temperature increase and decrease, was a considerable simplification of the actual state of affairs. The non-industrial component was thus approximated by constructing a special variable based on electricity consumption for Sunday, which is not a working day for most of the manufacturing sector.

Moreover, in order to resolve the aggregation problems, Gutierrez and Saraceno chose to insert a variable expressing the relation between the intermediate-goods and the aggregate industrial production indexes, on the assumption that the sectors upstream of the production process had a higher energy input coefficient.

The equation, which was estimated using the ordinary least squares method for the period 1978-1981 and 1981-1987, takes the form:

$$(3) \quad Y_t = a + \Sigma_j A_j(L) E_t^j + bRAP_{t-3} + cED_t + \\ + dt + eY_{t-2} + \Sigma_i f_i S_i + gDUM_t + u_t$$

where:

E_t^1, E_t^2, E_t^3 = electrical energy distributed on trading-days (E_t^1), Saturdays (E_t^2) and Sundays (E_t^3);

RAP_t = the ratio between intermediate goods and the aggregated industrial production indexes;

ED_t = monthly electricity consumption calculated by multiplying the average holiday demand for energy by the number of calendar days in the reference month.

This model allowed the obtainment of one and two lead forecasts for the raw industrial production index. The results refer to the period 1986.6-1987.7: the mean absolute error is respectively 1,6% for one lead and 2% for two lead predictions. The forecasting accuracy of this model is generally greater than that of similar models studied in the past.

Schlitzer's recent contribution [41] should be viewed as part of a general move to update and revise the economic models used by Banca d'Italia's servizio studi (6).

---

(6) As pointed out previously, there are two models, one based on monthly electrical energy data, the other on half-monthly data.

Schlitzer started out by noting the progressive deterioration of the forecasting performance of the model developed by Bodo and Signorini, which tended to considerably overestimate the level of production activity starting from 1990, in concurrence with the strong economic-cycle slowdown experienced by the Italian economy. Evident anomalies were also noted when analysing the estimates' results: the usual diagnostic tests revealed first order serial correlation and heteroscedasticity of the residuals in addition to considerable problems of collinearity. Furthermore, the signs of the coefficients were not always those expected. The trend's parameter was positive, not what one would expect assuming this variable should represent the growing influence of the non-industrial component on overall electricity consumption. Similarly, the coefficients of the temperature variables in the quadratic function which links them to the electricity consumption both had a positive sign, which was in contrast with the U-shape assumed for household electricity uses.

Schlitzer introduced two main innovations to the original model: firstly, instead of the simple linear trend he adopted a cubic trend to allow for the non-monotonic evolution of non-industrial electricity consumption in the estimation period; and secondly, he reselected the subset of the ENEL districts so as to eliminate more completely the effects of the composition of industrial output from the electricity data.

To conclude, the Banca d'Italia's model corrected with the aforementioned indications, takes the following form:

(4) $$Y_t = a + \Sigma_j \, b_j \, E_t^j + c_1 \, Temp_t + c_2 \, Temp_t^2 + \\ + d_1 t + d_2 t^2 + d_3 t^3 + e Y_{t-12} + \Sigma_i \, f_i \, S_i + u_t$$

The new version of the model, estimated for the period 1985.1-1990.12, passed most of the diagnostic tests it was subjected to. All the variables included were significant and have the expected signs and there was no indication of the relation being incorrectly specified. As regards the forecasting performance, the results obtained on a one-year time span (1991.1-1991.12) show that for one-step forecasts the mean absolute error decreased to 1.5% and there was almost no overestimation of the predictions *vis-à-vis* the actual realisations. The half monthly model revised along the same lines, yielded two lead forecasts with no distortion and a mean absolute error of 2.1%.

A different kind of methodological approach was followed by Teräsvirta's contribution [43]. He considered six monthly series published in a timely manner which, thanks to their direct or indirect relation with the industrial production index, he used simultaneously to improve the *ARIMA* model forecasts. These indicators are: electricity consumption; export volume; the number of automobiles transported by rail; the index of advertising space in newspapers; the number of vacancies and the number of unemployed. All the variables were subject to logarithmic transformation to make them stationary in variance: in addition, the industrial production index was seasonally differentiated, to make it stationary on average.

Given the potentially large number of parameters the problem was to reduce the dimension of the input vectors without any loss of information. The author considered two ways of achieving such a reduction: the principal component transformation and the frequency domain method, as suggested by Box and Jenkins.

Following these two distinct procedures two different models were identified:

(5) $$(1 - L^{12}) \log Y_t = a + b \log p_t^1 + (c_1 + c_2 L^6) \log p_t^2 + (1 - dL^4) u_t$$

in which p_t^1 and p_t^2 are the two principal components to which the explicative variables vector is reduced; and

(6) $$(1 - L^{12}) \log Y_t = a + b \log E_t + c \log A_t + (1 - c_1 L - c_2 L^2 - c_3 L^3)^{-1} (1 - dL^4) u_t$$

in which A_t is the number of automobiles transported by rail per month at time t. In the estimation procedure, conducted on monthly data referring to the period 1970.1-1980.12, model *(5)* fitted better than model *(6)*, the standard error being 3.7% against 3.9%. However, for forecasting purposes the transfer function models are not inferior to principal component models. The forecasting performance was separately assessed on three consecutive years, 1979, 1980 and 1981. For one-lead forecasts the first model's mean absolute error increased from 2.6% for 1979, to 3.4% for 1980, to then decrease to 2.4% for 1981; for the same three years, the mean absolute error of the second model's forecasts, on the other hand, fell progressively from 3.7% to 1.9%.

Both the models estimated performed better than an *ARIMA* (3, 1, 0) used as benchmark. Nevertheless, the methodology proposed by Teräsvirta, consisting in modelling the volume of industrial production on the basis of several quick indicators not functionally related to it, does not seem very fruitful. The results obtained in fact are not completely satisfactory: they do not compare well (7), in particular, with those yielded by the models developed in Italy.

3. - Models for Industrial Production Forecasting Based on Firm's Expectations

Today, business surveys on manufacturing industry are carried out on a periodic basis in more than 50 countries. The information gathered is generally qualitative in nature and consists of enterpreneurs' assessment on past demand, production and stocks as well as on expected output, demand and price trends. The expectations data, in particular, make it possible to forecast the volume of industrial production with at least a three months lead.

However, the use of business data for forecasting purposes has to date been rather limited. Few papers on the subject have appeared in international journals or have been presented at the CIRET conferences since 1960 (8).

---

(7) The comparison can only be very approximative, given the diversity of the economies studied and the period considered for the simulations outside the sample.
(8) CIRET (Centre for International Research on Economic Tendency Surveys) holds a conference every two years on the most recent developments and applications of business surveys which enables specialists from the more than one hundred Institutes which now conduct business surveys throughout the world to compare experiences in this field.

Many of the researches who have extensively worked on business survey results consider that the information is very useful in tracking cyclical movements and in forecasting turning points (9), but not in predicting the monthly (or quarterly) volume of industrial production (Anderson - Strigel [1], Öller [35], Piatier [38]).

One of the most important obstacles which has hampered the use of business survey results for forecasting has undoubtedly been the problem of "quantification", that is to say the transformation of qualitative information into summary quantitative indicators. The most traditional quantitative indicator is given by the balance between the percentages of favourable and unfavourable replies. The assumptions implicitly underlying the use of the balance are that the replies are uniformly distributed over the number of possible options, and that these options are divided in turn into classes of equal size. These assumptions are extremely restrictive and in conflict with the empirical evidence. Moreover, the reduction of the replies to the balance alone means that some of the initial information is lost: in particular, for a given balance, the varying percentage of "unchanged" replies may indicate a varying degree of uncertanty among managements. In order to overcome these limitations, other summary indicators which either incorporate more complex assumptions concerning the managers' behaviour (the probabilistic approach) or else compare the survey series with the corresponding quantitative statistics (regression approach) (10), have been proposed.

Many of the papers on the subject tend to consider the problem of the quantitative interpretation of the surveys settled when they have elaborated a quantified indicator of managers' replies. Nonetheless, the quantified indicator merely expresses the deviations of the phenomenon being studied from "normality", that is to say the reference term for the subjective assessments of the managers. The use of the quantified indicators as a proxy for the corresponding quantitative

---

(9) The cyclical indicator approach to business cycle analysis has engendered an extensive literature on the subject, starting from the very first works by NBER in the early 1930's: there has been recent renewed interest in these works as a result of the recession which affected the economies of most of the industrial countries in 1990 (LAHIRI - MOORE [29], SCHLITZER [42]).

(10) For a survey and empirical comparison of the different procedures, see D'ELIA [16].

statistics, cannot justify neglecting the search for "normal" or "stationary " values, as they tend to modify themselves over time, producing similar survey results even when the objective situation is different (D'Elia [16], Gennari [19]).

Further difficulties in interpreting the business survey data arise due to ambiguities in the formulation of some of the questions and to managers' incorrect interpretation of the questions. In other words, when examining the replies it is not always possible to identify the relevant time interval, to decide whether the data refers to levels or variations, to differentiate between *ex-ante* and *ex-post* judgments, etc. Because of these difficulties the use of business surveys data for forecasting purposes has not always produced satisfactory results.

An industrial production forecasting model based on business survey results was tested for some time by Banca d'Italia's servizio studi (this experience is documented in Bodo and Signorini [7] and in Palmieri and Signorini [36]). In both these papers the possibility of using ISCO survey data for quantitative forecasting purposes is judged negatively because of the high volatility of the subjective factors which "irreparably" influence the managers' qualitative assessments. The impossibility of formalising these subjective factors within econometric models would lead to highly unstable estimates of parameters and to forecasts which rapidly deteriorate the further they are from the estimation period.

The survey series examined in Bodo and Signorini's paper to test the fit with the profile of industrial production are the order-book level, the demand expectations for the coming 3-4 months, the stocks of finished goods, the production level, its monthly rate of variation and the production expectations for the next 3-4 months. The qualitative judgments are quantified by the simple balance, as other more complex quantification methods do not provide dissimilar results.

After having suitably treated the quantified series to make them stationary on average (through double differentiation, both sequential and seasonal), the authors used a transfer function model, which is normally more restrained in describing dynamic relations. To determine which survey variables provided the short-term trend of the industrial production index, they separately modeled the endogenous and exogenous variables of the transfer function with ARIMA models and then analysed the correlation between the residuals of the univariate model of production and the residuals deriving from the survey series models, using the Haugh-Box approach [27]. The only variables to show significant correlations at zero lag vith the ISTAT index were the level and the month-to-month variation of production (11). Both series were then simultaneously inserted in the transfer function, so that the final form of the model is:

$$(7) \quad (1-L)(1-L^{12})\,Y_t = \frac{b_1}{(1-\delta_3 L^3 - \delta_4 L^4)} (1-L)(1-L^{12})\,VP_t +$$

$$+ b_2 (1-L)(1-L^{12})\,SP_t + (1-\varphi_1 L - \varphi_3 L^3 - \varphi_{12} L^{12})\,u_t$$

where: VP_t = month to month variation of production (12).
SP_t = production level.

The estimation exercise encompassed a six-year period, from 1978.1 to 1984.12, while the one-lead forecasts for the interval 1984.1-1985.4 were calculated in the simulation phase. The predictions from this model ($MAE = 2.4\%$) compare well with those from the models based on electrical energy data, developed by the same authors. However, with the passage of time, this model has started to show evident signs of incorrect specification (with little significant and/or highly unstable coefficients), while forecasting accuracy has progressively deteriorated; the model has therefore been abandoned, also in view of the short lead of the *ex-post* ISCO series *vis-à-vis* ISTAT's provisional indexes (only 15-20 days).

The following work of Palmieri and Signorini [36] pointed out that the previous model contained a rather complex lag structure which it was possible to rationalise only relying on purely statistical

---

(11) The best results as regards estimation and simulation are obtained by using the raw indicator for industrial production and not that adjusted for the different number of working days. This leads the authors to deduce that when replying to the survey questions, industrialists implicitly discount monthly calendar variations.

(12) The authors point out that the ISCO series for short-term variations of production is, contrary to what might be expected, more correlated to production levels than to the corresponding ISTAT indicator.

considerations (13). These authors then implemented a simpler model which was easier to interpret and was supposed to be more stable over time. In particular, the month to month variation of production was eliminated due to its negligible contribution in explaining the total variance of the endogenous variable. Furthermore, it was decided to include only the production level without any autoregressive structure as a regressor to the IMA production model (with first and twelfth order MA terms).

$$(8) \quad (1 - L)(1 - L^{12}) Y_t = a + b(1 - L^{12}) SP_t + (1 - \varphi_1 L - \varphi_{12} L^{12}) u_t$$

On the basis of this new specification, an *ex-ante* simulation was carried out with a rolling regressions procedure on a sample of observations of fixed length (equal to eight years) to obtain one-lead forecasts for the period 1986.1-1988.8. Once again the results were not totally satisfactory: on the one hand, the reduction in the mean absolute error *vis-à-vis* the univariate model, even though significant, was less than that obtained with the more complex model previously developed; on the other hand, the estimates of the parameters did not turn out to be stable and, in particular, those regarding the survey variable were not significant in some iterations.

As in the previous work, the authors attributed the low forecasting performance of the model mainly to the high level of instability in the managers' replies. They concluded that, since the normal value varies in time in a rather erratic and unforeseeable manner, it cannot be included in the econometric models; in their opinion it is not possible therefore to explain the differences in the cyclical trends between the ISTAT indexes and the survey series.

Other examples of the simultaneous use of multiple survey variables in a forecasting model for the volume of industrial production have been furnished for the French and Finnish experiences respectively by Fanouillet and Salanie [18] and by Teräsvirta [44]. In

---

(13) As already pointed out by GIOVANNINI [22], the model developed by BODO - SIGNORINI [7] had also some statistical problems since, on the one hand, the sum of the autoregressive parameters was greater than the one and, on the other, autocorrelation of the first order of residuals had not been completely eliminated.

the former, the authors inserted as leading indicators the quarterly balances of exports orders, stocks of finished goods and production expectations for the following quarter. The survey series were regressed on the annual variation of the industrial production index; it was therefore implicitly assumed that the balances express the deviations from their previous year value. The authors also maintained that in the case of some variables, such as production expectations, managers tend to confuse levels and variations not replying coherently to the questionnaire. The model was specified by a very simple functional form based exclusively on survey variables, without any lag structure on the endogenous variable:

(9) $\quad (1 - L^{12}) Y_t = a + bLOE_{t-1} + cLS_{t-1} + dTP_{t-2} + u_t$

where: LOE_t = export order-book level against the previous quarter;
$\quad\quad\quad\ LS_t$ = stock levels against the previous quarter;
$\quad\quad\quad\ TP_t$ = production expectations for the following quarter.

The relation was estimated using the ordinary least squares technique on quarterly data for the period 1979.1-1988.4. The multiple determination coefficient was equal to 0.71, while the Durbin-Watson test of serial correlation of residuals gave a value of 1.7. The variables were all significant except for the production expectations, which was in any case maintained in the model: the signs were those expected. The mean absolute forecasting error was equal to 1.7%, slightly higher than the value provided by a fourth order AR model used as a yardstick. Putting aside the simplicity of its formulation, the model indicates that the introduction of several variables from the same information source generally creates problems of multicollinearity, which reduce the significance of those series which should furnish a better representation of industrial production trends.

As part of a methodological study on techniques for selecting between different econometric models, Teräsvirta elaborated a model for forecasting the output of the Finnish engineering sector which combined several business survey series. The series which contributed the most in explaining the variance of the endogenous variable were the expected rate of capacity utilisation, the stock of finished goods, the export order-book levels and the industry's climate of opinion. Once again, the production expectations in conjunction with other survey series proved not to be significant and was not inserted in the final model. As regards the treatment of qualitative data, the author used no quantification procedure for the managers' evaluations, considering the quotas of replies "increasing" or "decreasing" as separate variables (14); the latter, in particular, should provide a more reliable leading indicator *vis-à-vis* the balance method, given that managers are less reluctant to report a downturn than an upturn.

Given the potentially very high number of variables *vis-à-vis* the observations, the author spent much effort on drawing up a hierarchical procedure which could efficiently select the series to be inserted as leading indicators in the final model. Using this procedure, Teräsvirta managed to estimate a model with a rather good fit and more accurate in predicting the industrial production index than simpler univariate models. He, nonetheless, pointed out that if a different criterion was used to select the variables, the model's specification would be completely different. Forecasting performances no worse than those generated by the chosen model were also obtained by constructing a new equation based on the two best single leading indicators for industrial production (one of which being the production expectations for the following quarter).

The equation estimated on quarterly data for the period 1978.1-1984.4 is:

$$(10) \quad (1-L)\log Y_t = a + b_1(1-L)CAP^-_{t-3} + b_2(1-L)LS^-_{t-1} +$$
$$+ b_3 TX^-_{t-4} + b_4 TE^-_{t-2} + A(L)(1-L)\log Y_t + \Sigma_i d_i S_i + u_t$$

where: CAP^-_t = excepted downturn in the rate of capacity utilisation in the next two quarters;
LS^-_t = decrease in stock levels against previous year;
TX^-_t = reduction in the volume of exports against previous quarter;
TE^-_t = worsening of the sector's climate of confidence.

---

(14) Following the suggestion of ANDERSON - STRIGEL [1] and PESARAN [37].

The forecasts for the years 1981, 1982 and 1983 taken separately, are very close to the actual realisations in terms of both *MAE* (which ranges from 1% to 1.7%) and *RMSE* (2.3%; 1.9%; 3% respectively for the three years considered), even if it should be noted that these results refer to quarterly data, generally less erratic than monthly data.

Returning to the debate in Italy, a first attempt to revaluate the information content of the business surveys — also for forecasting purposes — was carried out by Giovannini in some of his papers (Giovannini [22], [23]). In his inital study (Giovannini [22]) he elaborated transfer functions in which a single explicative variable is included and, more precisely, the production expectations for the next 3-4 months.

This variable allows the obtainment of predictions of the industrial production index which are more timely than those based on *ex-post* survey series.

In order to apply the transfer function methodology, the survey data (quantified with the method proposed by Carlucci [9]) and the ISTAT indexes were made stationary on average and variance through logarithmic transformations and twelfth-order differences; the author did not consider it necessary, however, to sequentially differentiate the series, despite the model's estimate period being almost identical to that chosen by Bodo and Signorini. Modelling with univariate models was also carried out solely for production indexes, by applying an *AR* model of the second and third order, while the explicative variable was inserted within the transfer function without any dynamic structure. The model in its general form is:

(11) $(1 - L^{12}) \log Y_t = a + b(L)(1 - L^{12}) \log TP_{t-1} +$

$+ \Sigma_i c_i S_i + (1 - \varphi_1 L - \varphi_2 L^2 - \varphi_3 L^3)^{-1} u_t$

where Y_t represents average daily production.

The author carried out his analysis on both the general index and the indexes for the three main economic sectors (consumer goods, investment goods and intermediate goods), obtaining, on the one hand, more complete short-term information and, on the other, through the suitable aggregation of the sectorial projections, more accurate forecasts for the general index.

This functional specification of the model, partly different from the one elaborated by Banca d'Italia, was explained by the better statistical performances regarding both estimation and simulation ($MAE = 2.4\%$ for two-lead forecasts). This first contribution made no reference, instead, to a possible specification of the normal value, nor the choice to regress the production expectations on the production indexes of the following quarter is explained; in fact, according to the questionnaire, this variable should represent the quarterly variations of industrial activity.

The problems not completely solved in the above contribution were examined in greater detail in a subsequent paper (Giovannini [23]), as part of the presentation of a structural model for analysing the short-term dynamics of the Italian industrial sector.

In this paper, the author stated, firstly, that the "normal" value should be identified with the long-term value of the statistics examined (15). Since hypothetically expectations are realised in the long-term, the managers' production forecasts should tend to coincide on average with the actual volume of production in this time span. The ISCO series of production expectations would therefore represent the cyclical fluctuations over the long-term growth path of industrial production. In order to compare the ISCO series with the ISTAT indexes, the industrial production should then be detrended. As for the period examined (1978.1-1985.12) the ISTAT series was not characterised by a clear long-term trend, the "normal" value was omitted from the model on the basis of strictly empirical reasons.

Moreover, unlike the models developed in the previous paper, the equation for average daily production contained, not only the production expectations, but also other explicative variables (16), some of which however could only be considered within the context of structural models.

---

(15) A similar hypothesis has been used with regard to the stocks of finished goods by CONTI - FILOSA [14].

(16) Some of variables being the errors in forecasting demand, the amount of hours lost in strikes and the correction coefficient for the number of working days per month.

Some indications contained in these works were subsequently developed by Gennari [19]. The paper firstly pointed out that survey series (contrary to what could be assumed on the basis of the formulation of the questionaire) had a seasonal nature, and confirmed that managers confused levels and variations as regards the variables being surveyed.

Particular attention was then paid to identify the "normal" value so as to correctly specify the forecasting models. Given the lack of objective and constant points of reference in the managers' replies, Gennari concluded that the tendency to be considered normal could only be deduced *ex-post* by comparing the survey data with the actual evolution of the phenomena. In particular, in assessing the current level of production, or that expected in the following three-four months, managers would base their assessments on the data recorded for the same period of the previous year. This initial evaluation would then be corrected on the basis of the production trends in the months immediately preceeding the survey. Hence, in addition to the business survey data, the industrial production forecasting models also include a non-constrained autoregressive structure for the endogenous variable, with a twelfth-month lag and a suitable number of terms for lesser lags.

Finally, it should be noted that no attempt was made to estimate relationships containing different survey series to avoid the possible presence of collinearity. On the basis of these hypotheses, five models, differentiated by the survey variables utilised, were constructed: the first was based on industrialists' assessments of activity levels for the present month, the second comprised the month to month variations of production while the third, fourth and fifth included production expectations for the upcoming two, three and four months respectively, according to the time horizon implicit in the industrialists' replies.

The general form of the linear regression models estimated on the period 1979.1-1989.12 using *OLS* was therefore:

(12) $\log Y_t = a + B(L) \log Y_t + c IND_t + d \log DAY_t + \Sigma_i e_i S_i + u_t$

where Y_t represents the raw industrial production index, IND_t the survey variable and DAY_t the number of trading days, should the managers be in part unable to quantify the effects of variations in the calendar on production levels.

The models so specified were used to obtain forecasts of the raw industrial production indexes for the period 1988.1-1989.12, both aggregate and disaggregated by sector according to their economic purpose. The models based on *ex-post* leading indicators (levels and monthly variations of production) yielded forecasts one-lead ahead of the official provisional data; the models which used production expectations as an explicative variable generated two, three, four and five-lead predictions. The forecasting performance of the models decreased in proportion to the lengthening of the time lead over the official data: the mean absolute error progressively rose from 1.3%, for one-lead forecasts, to 2.4% for five-lead forecasts.

The results obtained were quite satisfactory. In particular, predictions were significantly more accurate than those achieved with other models based on survey variables; they compared favourably also with those yielded by the models based on electrical energy data.

The problems of the structural instability of the parameters, which would appear to affect many of the models based on survey data (17) have led some scholars to call for the use of variable-parameter models. This was the direction of the research carried out by Gennari, Giovannini and Sartore [21].

An attempt to use the Kalman-filter algorithm to forecast the quarterly production index of the Finnish timber industry was made also by Rahiala and Teräsvirta [39]. This algorithm, thanks to its iterative procedure, allows information on process innovations obtained from business surveys to be optimally combined with forecasts generated by a univariate model based on the dynamic characteristics of the process itself. The authors however, having noted that the production series, once transformed using first-order logarithmic differences, becomes stationary starting from 1981, ended up limiting the estimation period and adopting conventional dynamic regression techniques.

---

(17) Similar problems of parameter instability were noted in works which used electrical energy data as leading indicator. Various authors have sought to remedy this problem by using rolling regression techniques in the simulation phase.

The model is:

$$(13) \qquad (1 - L) \log Y_t =$$
$$= a + B(L)(1 - L) \log Y_t + cSP^+_t + \Sigma_i d_i S_i + u_t$$

In this equation SP^+_t represents the share of firms which report an increase in output vis-à-vis the previous quarter. Forecasts for the upcoming quarter were obtained by extrapolating the *ex-post* series on the basis of some *ex-ante* variables (18) and subsequently substituting the estimated value of SP^+_t in equation *(13)*.

In their article, Gennari, Giovannini and Sartore presented two variable parameter models, each of which was based on a single variable of the ISCO survey. The series considered were the production level in the reference month and the production expectations for the next three-four months both quantified using the balance method: the *ex-ante* variable was inserted in the model with a four-period lag thus allowing the industrial production index to be forecast some five months ahead of ISTAT's publication of the provisional data.

The estimated equations contain only one variable parameter, the one associated with the survey series considered. A structural specification of the variable parameter equation was provided, including a lagged variable of the series to be forecast as an explicative component. In this way the authors intended to verify the hypothesis that the latent variable indicating the notion of normality could be approximated by a weighted average of the most recent realisations of the phenomenon being observed (D'Elia [16], Gennari [19]).

The identification phase was conducted with reference to the period 1979.10-1990.9, while the simulations outside the sample were carried out on the time horizon 1990.10-1991.9. The final form of the models, obtained by comparing the results given by different specifications of the variable-parameter equation, is:

$$(14) \quad \log Y_t = a + bIND_t + C(L) \log Y_t + d \log DAY_t + \Sigma_i e_i S_i + u_t$$
$$b = \alpha + \beta b_{t-1} + \sigma (1 - L^{12}) \log Y_{t-1} + \delta S_8$$

---

(18) The *ex-ante* variables considered are, more specifically, the quota of firms which foresee an increase in output and the proportion of those which expect a worsening of economic prospects in the short-term.

As can been seen in *(14)*, the final specification of the variable-parameter equation comprised the rate of variation of production over twelve months with a one-period lag and a seasonal dummy for the month of August. A positive and a significative coefficent was associated to both these: hence the industrialists would seem to assess the "normality" of the production situation according to the industrial sector's speed of growth recorded in the recent past; in addition to that, their evaluations would appear to be also influenced by changes over time of the seasonal pattern.

The models' forecasting performances were compared with the results obtained from constant-parameter equations estimated by *OLS*. The inability of the variable-parameter models to improve the forecasting accuracy of the standard models probably indicates that the equations still contain an imperfect specification. The presence of an autoregressive structure for production in the equation of the endogenous variable is somewhat perplexing, even though this dynamic form could be simply due to the aggregation effect (Lippi [31]). However, the considerable improvements in forecasting performances obtained by switching from a non-stationary stochastic specification of the variable-parameter equation, to a structural one, seem to confirm that the research is heading in the right direction.

4. - Concluding Remarks and Hints on Possible Future Research

The use of multivariate models for short-term forecasting of industrial production generally results in a considerable improvement in the prediction accuracy with respect to univariate models; this is due to the informational content incorporated in the indicators which are included as explicative variables in such models. The extrapolative and *ARIMA* techniques resort exclusively to information contained in the series to be predicted; as a result, their forecasting performance is not completely satisfactory, especially in proximity to cyclical turning points. However, numerous difficulties are encountered in developing multivariate models due mainly to the type of information sources available in time. These difficulties also help to explain the lack of an extensive literature on this subject.

Our overview has examined a series of contributions, mostly originating from Italy, which use either quantitative indicators available in real time or qualitative series taken from business surveys. Among the quantitative indicators, the most favoured is undoubtedly data on electricity consumption, which has the advantage of being gathered on a censual base, of having a very fine time disaggregation and for which it is possible to hypothesise the existence, at least at a sectorial level, of a closed function relation with the volume of industrial production.

However, like other quantitative indictors, it provides an actual information advantage only when the official data is published with considerable delay. In addition, its direct link with the level of industrial activity tends to be weakened by a number of methodological problems. Firstly, in the case of Italy at least, the timely indicator actually gathered is not industry's electricity consumption, but the total amount of electrical energy produced for the national grid by ENEL. This is compounded by the problems of aggregation which arise because the electricity inputs for the various sectors are not proportional to their weights in the general industrial production index. In order to remove the above mentioned distortional factors other indicators are usually included in the estimated relationships. However, as the additional indicators are often transformations of the electrical energy data, the models proposed tend to suffer from multicollinearity, with consequent instability in parameter estimation.

Finally, with regard to the identification phase of the models, it should be noted that both the presence of lagged variables and the dynamic specification of error terms are decided on the basis of exclusively statistical criteria, as there is no theoretical reference framework.

The second information source, namely firms' expectations taken from business surveys, allows one to predict the industrial production with at least a three months lead on the official data. The qualitative information is also very useful for more detailed business-cycle analysis since it allows one to calculate the industrial production indexes in a disaggregated manner by either sector and/or region.

On the other hand, the principal obstacle to the use of business survey data for forecasting the volume of industrial production is the transformation of qualitative information into quantitative indicators. Various synthetic indicators have been proposed and there has been extensive debate on the potential and limits of each technique.

The problem of quantitatively interpreting the survey data cannot be resolved simply by adopting one quantification procedure rather than another: the meaning of the "normal" or "stationary" value, used by managers as a term of reference for their individual assessments, has still to be clarified. Many of the authors who have developed forecasting models based on firms' expectations do not seem to be fully aware of this interpretative problem: therefore the results achieved have not been completely satisfactory and, in any case, worse than those obtained through quantitative indicators. The use of survey series in conjunction with a autoregressive structure on the endogenous variable, which tends to capture the evolution of the "normal" value, allows one to explain the trend of the reference indicators with a precision which would not appear to depend on the quantification method used. The forecasting performance of these models would appear comparable if not, in some cases, better than that of the models which use electricity data as leading indicators.

The econometric methodology used in the various contributions generally includes the conventional techniques of dynamic regression based on *OLS* and non-linear *OLS* methods. More sophisticated methodologies, such as variable-parameter models or vectorial *ARMA* models, have still to produce totally satisfactory results. The path followed in the final contribution analysed in this survey (Gennari, Giovannini and Sartore [21]) — which used a structural specification of the variable-parameter equation associated to the survey variable, in an attempt to identify the factors which explain the evolution in time of the "normal" value — seems to be promising, even though still at an early stage of development.

A final observation concerns the difficulties of the multivariate forecasting models in further improving the results obtained to date, given the impossibility to exhaustively take into account the limits of the informational sources available. The attempts to insert in the models several indicators would not appear to have been very fruitful.

On the other hand, empirical evidence demonstrates that the combination (even by simple arithmetical average) of two or more indipendent forecasts tends to be more accurate than the best single one. Even for forecasting industrial production, further improvements in prediction accuracy can be achieved by combining several series of independent forecasts (19) based on the different information sources available at the time.

---

(19) BODO - SIGNORINI [7], for example, combine forecasts based on electrical energy consumption with those obtained from qualitative series, thus achieving a reduction of some 10% in average absolute error *vis-à-vis* the best single forecast. See SCHLITZER [41] for a different result.

BIBLIOGRAPHY

[1] ANDERSON O. - STRIGEL W.H.: «Business Surveys and Economic Research: a Review of Significant Developments», *15th CIRET Conference*, 1981.

[2] BANCA D'ITALIA: «Ricostruzione storica e depurazione stagionale degli indici di produzione industriale», *Bollettino statistico*, n. 3-4, 1985.

[3] BODO G.: «Un modello previsivo dell'andamento della produzione industriale», *Rapporto Progetto DESEC*, n. 12, 1984.

[4] BODO G. - CIVIDINI A.: *Stime efficienti di dati provvisori di produzione industriale*, mimeo, 1991.

[5] BODO G. - CIVIDINI A. - SIGNORINI L.F.: «Stime in tempo reale della produzione industriale», *Temi di discussione*, n. 104, 1988.

[6] ——: «Forecasting the Italian Production Index in Real Time», *Journal of Forecasting*, vol. 10, n. 3, 1991.

[7] BODO G. - SIGNORINI L.F.: «Uno schema per la previsione a breve termine della produzione industriale», *Temi di discussione*, n. 55, 1985.

[8] ——: «Short Term Forecasting of the Industrial Production Index», *International Journal of Forecasting*, n. 3, 1987.

[9] CARLUCCI F.: «La costruzione di una serie mensile di aspettative d'inflazione», *Note economiche*, n. 2, 1982.

[10] CHIURAZZI L. - TRESOLDI C. - VALCAMONICI R.: «Andamento congiunturale dei consumi di energia elettrica e dell'indice della produzione in Italia», *Atti del XXXII Convegno della società italiana di statistica*, 1984.

[11] CIPOLLETTA I. - MARZANO G. - TRESOLDI C. - SIGNORINI L.F.: «L'analisi congiunturale attraverso i dati elettrici», in ENEL: *Rapporto sull'attività del Comitato tecnico-scientifico per la programmazione elettrica nel biennio 1983-84*, Roma, 1985.

[12] CLÒ E. - GAMBETTA G.: «Analisi e previsioni di indici settoriali della produzione industriale», Appendix to *Rapporto di Prometeia*, 1981.

[13] COMMISSION OF THE EUROPEAN COMMUNITIES: «The System of Business Surveys in the European Community: an Effective and Widely Respected Instrument», *European Economy*, supplement B, special edition, July 1991.

[14] CONTI V. - FILOSA R.: «Offerta interna, importazioni di manufatti e scorte in un modello di disequilibrio», *Contributi alla ricerca economica*, n. 2, 1980.

[15] CONTI V. - VISCO I.: «The Determinants of Normal Inventories of Finished Goods in the Italian Manufacturing Sector», *II Simposio internazionale sulle scorte*, Budapest, 1982.

[16] D'ELIA E.: «La quantificazione dei risultati dei sondaggi congiunturali: un confronto tra procedure», *Rassegna di lavori dell'Isco*, n. 13, 1991.

[17] DIEBOLD F.X. - PAULY P.: «Structural Change and the Combination of Forecasts», *Journal of Forecasting*, n. 1, 1987.

[18] FANOUILLET J.C. - SALANIE B.: «Prévoir la Consommation et la Production Grace Aux Enquêtes de Conjoncture», *Economie et Statistique*, n. 234, 1990.

[19] GENNARI P.: «L'uso delle indagini congiunturali Isco per la previsione degli indici della produzione industriale», *Rassegna di lavori dell'Isco*, n. 13, 1991.

[20] ——: «Forecasting Industrial Production Indexes: the Italian case», *20th CIRET Conference*, Budapest, 1991.

Business Cycle Analysis and Industrial Production Forecasts 283

[21] GENNARI P. - GIOVANNINI E. - SARTORE D.: «L'impiego di modelli a parametri variabili per la previsione della produzione industriale», *Quaderni di statistica ed econometria*, forthcoming, 1992.
[22] GIOVANNINI E.: «La previsione degli indici mensili della produzione industriale mediante l'uso dei sondaggi d'opinione», *Quaderni dell'istituto di studi economici e sociali*, Università di Camerino, n. 4, 1985.
[23] —— : «Un modello per l'analisi della dinamica del settore industriale italiano nel breve periodo», in BANCA D'ITALIA: *Ricerche e metodi per la politica economica*, vol. II, 1989.
[24] GRANGER C.W.J. - NEWBOLD P.: *Forecasting Economic Time Series*, London, Academic Press, 1977.
[25] GRANGER C.W.J. - RAMANNANTHAN R.: «Improved Methods of Combining Forecasts», *Journal of Forecasting*, n. 3, 1984.
[26] GUTIERREZ L. - SARACENO P.: «Un indicatore di attività in tempo reale per orientare le decisioni di politica economica», *Politica economica*, n. 1, 1988.
[27] HAUGH L.D. - BOX G.E.P.: «Identification of Dynamic Regression (Distributed lag) Models Connecting Two Time Series», *Journal of the American Statistical Association*, n. 72, 1977.
[28] ISTAT: «La destagionalizzazione degli indici della produzione industriale», *Note e relazioni*, n. 2, 1987.
[29] LAHIRI K. - MOORE G.H.: *Leading Economic Indicators. New Approaches and Forecasting Records*, Cambridge, Cambridge University Press, 1991.
[30] LIPPI M. (ed.): *L'energia elettrica immessa in rete come indicatore anticipato dell'indice aggregato della produzione industriale*, Mimeo, 1984.
[31] LIPPI M.: «Sulla dinamica delle relazioni tra variabili aggregate», *Politica economica*, n. 2, 1985.
[32] MAKRIDAKIS S. - ZINKLER R.L.: «The Combination of Forecasts», *Journal of the Royal Statistical Society*, Serie A, 1983.
[33] MALHOMME C.: «L'influence du Passé Dans les Enquêtes de Conjoncture. Un Essai de Correction», *9th CIRET Conference*, Madrid 1969.
[34] MENEDIAN C.: «The Business Survey as an Instrument for Forecasting the Index of the Industrial Production», *14th CIRET Conference*, Lisbon 1979.
[35] ÖLLER L.E.: «Forecasting the Business Cycle Using Survey Data», *International Journal of Forecasting*, n. 6, 1990.
[36] PALMIERI G. - SIGNORINI L.F.: *Analisi congiunturale: un'applicazione degli strumenti SAS*, mimeo, 1990.
[37] PESARAN M.H.: «Formation of Inflation Expectations in British Manufacturing Industries», *Economic Journal*, December 1985.
[38] PIATIER A.: «Business Cycle Surveys: their Utilization for Forecasting», *14th CIRET Conference*, Lisbon, 1979.
[39] RAHIALA M. - TERÄSVIRTA T.: «Forecasting the Output of Finnish Forest Industries Using Business Survey Data», *20th CIRET Conference*, Budapest 1991.
[40] RANCI P. (ed.): «L'utilizzazione dei dati di consumo elettrici per l'analisi economica», in ENEL: *Rapporto sull'attività del Comitato tecnico-scientifico per la programmazione elettrica nel biennio 1983-84*, Roma 1985.
[41] SCHLITZER G.: *Stime della produzione industriale in tempo reale: una revisione del modello basato sui consumi di energia elettrica*, mimeo, 1992.
[42] —— : *L'approccio degli indicatori ciclici all'analisi della congiuntura: un'applicazione*, mimeo, 1992.

[43] TERÄSVIRTA T.: «Short-term Forecasting of Industrial Production by Means of Quick Indicators», *Journal of Forecasting*, vol. 3, n. 4, 1984.

[44] —— : «Model Selection Using Business Survey Data: Forecasting the Output of the Finnish Metal and Engineering Industries», *International Journal of Forecasting*, n. 2, 1986.

Death and Rebirth of the Business Cycle

Innocenzo Cipolletta
Confindustria, Roma

1. - The Peaks and Troughs of Business Cycle Theory

The business cycle was "discovered" (in the nineteenth century) when the idea of a static economy which did not progress was abandoned and that of a dynamic economy which developed, grew and experienced phases of difficulty or crises gained ground. It would appear to be the characteristics of growth which determine the fluctuating trend of the economy, which tends to draw near or away from a given equilibrium point which is not stable but dynamic, that is to say it increases or decreases depending on the specific trend.

As was often the tradition in early economic science, it was a French doctor, Clement Juglar, who in the mid-nineteenth century likened the dynamics of economic systems to those of the human body in a physiological approach which would lead him to state that economic systems follow a cycle of birth, development, adulthood and decay similar to that of human life. Again like man, during its life an economy will experience moments of great physical strength and equilibrium just as it will experience moments of weakness and periods of crisis of varying degrees of seriousness.

According to this approach, business cycles are nothing more than the alternation of these physical states. Illness cannot be excluded, it cannot be accurately predicted and, in general, clears up by itself after a period of time. As a good doctor, Juglar knew to shift the attention of those studying economics from the moment the illness manifests itself (the recession) to that preceeding (of expansion) in which it is likely that it caught the illness. An illness, Juglar explained, should be studied not when its symptoms manifest themselves, but before, when the human body appears healthy.

This shifting of attention from the symptoms to the causes of the recession was something of a revolution. Up until then, it had been assumed that a recession (or economic crisis) was the result of a chance event, unpredictable and inevitable, and one could intervene only to mitigate the effects (the symptoms) and thus allow the economy to bear and rid itself of the crisis situation as soon as was possible.

Juglar opened the way to studying the business cycle as the interaction between external facts and internal workings, in other words he laid the foundations for studying how the economy functions: how it reacts to external phenomena (illnesses) and how the latter can be prevented, or else their consequences mitigated.

It was E. Wagemann in Germany between the two world wars who theorised studying the business cycle and short-term economic trends as the interaction between two separate fields: that of external stimuli and that of the economic organism. While the study of external stimuli is important for understanding the causes and forms of a cyclical fluctuation, it is the study of the economic organism and its functioning which can furnish the more interesting replies. The latter study allows one not only to understand how and why economic fluctuations take place as a result of action of specific stimuli, but also to seek to modify the organism (the economic system) so that it does not react to negative stimuli and also to prevent economic fluctuations as well as striving to strengthen the organism when it is attacked by illness so that it makes a quick and complete recovery.

The physiological growth of an organism, illness and crises of varying degrees of seriousness, small incidents are all elements which, when they concern an economic system, indicate that it is moving with waves of different length and intensity. J.A. Schumpeter divided business cycles into: short cycles (or Kitchin cycles) which last for no more than forty months; medium cycles (or Juglar cycles) which last from five to seven years and long cycles (or Kondriateff cycles) with an almost secular duration.

This tendency to fluctuate in recurrent but not periodic cycles — irregular regularity was J.A. Schumpeter's definition — led to the construction of many indicators which could predict the cycle. Among the first were the Harvard barometer (W.M. Persons) which drew on the leading characteristics of interest rates; E. Wagemann's business-cycle indicators; and the works of W.G. Mitchell, A.F. Burns, G.H. Moore of the National Bureau of Economic Research of New York, who continued the research started by W.C. Mitchell which led to the construction of diffusion indexes as well as the systematic drawing up of leading indicators either in step or deferred *vis-à-vis* the business cycle.

These works engendered many techniques and definitions of the business cycle. In particular, referring to the model of the US economy surveyed by the NBER it was concluded that a recession entailed a continuous series of decreases in output levels: at least two quarters of decrease in GDP in the USA. This affirmation, based exclusively on the empirical observation of twentieth-century business cycles in the US, has for a long time influenced business-cycle theory and has often served to separate those who maintain the existence of a recession in a given moment and those who deny such. In the 1960s, which were characterised by a strong and continuous expansion in the industrialised countries — it was very difficult to identify a business cycle on the basis of NBER's classical formulation. While the latter strove to modify definitions and methods of estimating the cycle with the discovery of *growth cycles*, that is to say cycles which arise around a basically strong growth trend, as I. Mintz defined it — doubts began to be expressed concerning the existence of the cycle, thus sentencing its demise, if it had ever existed that is. At a conference held in London in 1967 discussion revolved around whether "the cycle was obsolete", which created panic amongst the supporters of the business cycle, who hastily described its changes in the post-war period so as to prove that it was still alive and kicking.

"Fortunately", the following years of the decade 1970-1980, characterised as they were by the oil crisis and serious fluctuations in production activity, belied the death of the business cycle while the works of R.E. Lucas jr. and the theories of New Classical Macroeconomics rehabilitated cyclical evolution as an intrinsic component of the market economies which was irremovable, at least with the weapons in the arsenal of classical Keynesian short-term economic policies.

But the progress of the western economies, even though they began once again to experience recession and expansion in the 1970s, also threw up numerous and varied "forms" of the business cycle which drove the 'classical' researchers up the wall. *Stagflation* in the 1970s, that is to say a mixture of production stagnation and inflation which belied the supposed procyclical trend of prices, gave way to "W cycles" with two successive recessions interposed by a brief expansion (the US in the early 1980s and again in the early 1990s), and then to "double recovery" expansion phases as was the case in the early 1980s when the initial recovery of 1983 was followed by another stimulated by the fall in oil prices to conclude with the more recent stepped trends and, today, another stagnation phase without, however, inflation.

There is enough material here to affirm, yet again, that the business cycle is dead and some observers once again maintain this, backing their claim with the arguments we will examine in the following section.

On the other hand, there have been studies and theories which have aimed at defining a 'new' business cycle: the theoretical school of the *real business cycle* would appear to have discovered that the trend is not stable but varies considerably even in the short term, which in turn gives rise to continuous modifications in the short-term cycle calculated as a residual from the *trend*: in other words, the business cycle is still with us, but it should be seen as the deviation of a random walk trend due to continuous shocks of a stochastic nature. This theory, which we will briefly discuss in the third section, leads us to enquire about the relationships between the cycle and *trend* and, hence, in the relationships between the economy's short-term cycle and its structure.

The latter topics imply a reconsideration of our traditional division of economic policies in short-term and medium to long-term policies: we will deal with this in the final section which concludes this short paper.

2. - The Reasons for the Present Demise of the Business Cycle

Those who assert the passing of the business cycle do not claim that it has never existed, but place it in a specific phase of the development of the industrial economies and do not consider it an intrinsic feature of the economy.

In general, the "opponents" of the business cycle are to be found amongst those who have faithfully followed the works of the NBER and the US Department of Commerce, who, with an almost fanatic attention, have decreed that a recession should be preceded by a certain number of successive decreases in the leading indicators and by at least two successive quarterly decreases in GDP. When this does not take place for some time, there inevitably appears an article which announces the passing of the business cycle.

What are the principal arguments used to justify these death sentences? They can be grouped into three categories: *a)* the existence of built-in business-cycle stabilizers; *b)* the changed composition of the GDP (or rather the increased importance of the tertiary sector for the economy); *c)* changes in production processes.

We will examine each of these three reasons below. The first attributes the responsibility for the end of economic fluctuations to built-in stabilizers and more generally to the burden of public works and the construction of a "welfare state". This argument is not totally unfounded. Since study of the business cycle began and the Keynesian macroeconomic approach developed, the public-sector budget has been recognised as acting as a stabilizer for the economy: a variation, in one sense or the other, in public spending could compensate some excesses of the cyclical phases.

Although Keynesian policies are essentially discretional, implying a careful analysis of the short-term prospects and the choice of the specific intervention instruments, it should nonetheless not be underestimated how this propensity to intervene has ended up by shaping many budget-policy instruments which in fact act automatically as full-blooded stabilizers. The public-sector finances of the industrialised countries are replete with examples of this.

As regards public spending, it is unarguable that much spending is anticyclical, that is to say it contains the negative (or positive) repercussions of the business cycle. A typical case is that of unemployment benefit which every country has, albeit with a different name (in Italy there is the Cassa integrazione guadagni); this spending increases during a recession and decreases during an expansion. Moreover, almost all the industrialised countries have organised flexible systems of professional training and pensions (with various types of early retirement schemes) which serve to safeguard earned income in the event of recession. All these mechanisms supply income and transfer during an economic slowdown and recession and are curtailed when the economy is expanding. In fact they act as business-cycle cushions and, when they are dictated by understandable criteria of equity and social solidarity, constitute built-in business cycle stabilizers because they block, or at least mitigate, the negative consequences of an economic slowdown or recession.

It is therefore no surprise that the present-day recessions are less severe and less evident than those in the past when the lack of such stabilizers magnified every business-cycle fluctuation.

Business-cycle stabilizers do not only comprise unemployment benefit, but the entire public budget and more generally the *'Welfare State'* are manipulated to have an anticyclical effect. Taxes are progressive and rise with income and hence increase more than proportionately *vis-à-vis* income during the cycle's acceleration phases. If the latter are also characterised by inflationary processes (prices generally have a procyclical trend), then the gap between income and taxation tends to widen thanks to fiscal drag; the opposite holds during recessions, when the reduction in taxation is more than proportionate. Much public spending is, however, independent of the cycle which often gives it an anticyclical character, precisely because it is likened to taxation which instead closely follows the twists and turns of the business cycle.

Finally automatic cushions also exist outside the public budget. For example, in all the industrialised countries, the banking system is sustained by explicity or implicity guarantee institutions which avert bank failures or at least mitigate their consequences for account-holders, avoiding those traumas and risks which led to the great depression of 1929.

These mechanisms therefore limit the effects of cyclical fluctuations, reducing their size, modifying their form and duration and helping the more minor fluctuations to disappear.

The second cause for the passing of the cycle is the increased importance of the tertiary sector. It is held that the growth of the role of services in an industrial economy reduces cyclical fluctuations as services are less subject to variations in final demand, have a lesser effect (negative or positive) on employment and hence are more stable. This argument combines on two facts which, in my opinion, are completely independent of each other.

The first is the growing importance of the tertiary sector in economies which is shown by all the indicators: the weight of employment, value-added, consumption habits, etc. The growing tertiary sector is, to a large extent, the specialisation of services which were once part of the industrial sector: just as industry derived from agriculture (through the specialisation of textile and food activities which were once part of agricultural activities), so the tertiary sector derives from industry (it is sufficient to recall the many functions of commercialisation, marketing, computers and data management, engineering, etc.). Since this is a tendential — or long-term — process which has economic growth potential (as was the case with the process of industrialization) it is no surprise that the growth of services experiences lesser oscillations than industrial activity since it in fact mitigates the cyclical fluctuations and helps the GDP "avoid" quarterly downturns. Nonetheless, the steady growth of services is often accompanied by a certain decline (statistical) in industry and so in the long run the two phenomena tend to compensate each other; in addition, this is a specific phase which is drawing to a close. The evidence for this lies in the strong employment difficulties (of a cyclical nature) in countries where the tertiary sector has seen a strong growth such as the United Kingdom, where the credit and insurance sector now has a cyclical behaviour just like industry.

The second reason for the service sector's 'thick skin' *vis-à-vis* the short-term economic cycle is the result of how the service sector is measured in the industrial countries and in Italy in particular; a long-standing custom of inattention to surveying the added-value of services has ended up by linking, in an almost automatic manner, the estimate of GDP to that of employment in the service sector, on the assumption that each person employed should be apportioned an average gross product, generally increasing from year to year. This assumption is not proven, but is derived by analogy with the industrial sector: it results in a presumable overestimation of the gross product for the service sector, an inability to separate prices from the quality of services and, above all, their insensitiveness to cyclical fluctuations which does not derive from actual surveys but rather from the method of measurement employed.

In fact, the growth of the tertiary sector and its insensitivity to cyclical fluctuations are open to study and they cannot be proven today on the basis of the statistics available which are unable to translate reality into figures, given that they (the statistics) derive not from a survey but more often than not from an unverified hypothesis.

Finally, the third, and most complex, argument which is supposed to prove the demise of the business cycle. The argument is based on the assumption that change in the production processes has led to a strong change in the business cycle. In fact, cyclical fluctuations have been to a large extent attributed to the time lag between the economic variables and, in particular, the variable investments, as regards both its fixed component, which goes to increase or replace capital to adjust production capacities, and also its variable component stocks. Investments are decided on the basis of past trends (credit, demand conditions, etc.) but they affect the future (supply capacity, productivity, etc.) and hence generate cyclical fluctuations because they have an impact on new economic conditions.

Stocks and fixed investments have changed over the past years under the pressure of technology. Real-time production has strongly reduced the role of stocks just as it has abolished their role of a demand-supply cushion. The cost of storage has engendered a more active inventory management and hence it has become difficult to ascertain the role played by this variable in the business cycle.

Even fixed investments, which in J. Hick's multiplier-accelerator model stimulated the Keynesian cyclical fluctuations, have modified their behaviour. Present-day production technology allows production capacity to be adapted to demand almost down to the millimeter, so it is difficult to imagine expansionary phases characterised by an excess of investments which leads to a surplus of production capacity, hence a fall in prices and profits which is followed by an adjustment of investments and then a recession according to traditional models. A world which functions in "real time" has little room for Tinbergen's spider's web theorems or A. Aftallion's stoves. Even M. Kalecki's theoretical construction shows its limitations if decisions regarding investment, realisation and availability of production capacity are coincident moments.

Whatever the approach chosen, it is unarguable that cyclical fluctuations have lost that "irrregular regularity" so dear to Schumpeter and those who studied the business cycle as an independent phenomenon and not merely as an economy's capacity to fluctuate.

3. - The Real Business Cycle and Short-term Economic Analysis

However, economists have been more interested not so much in the form of the cycle but rather in the economy's capacity to vary in the short term, a capacity which has always existed even though it appears difficult to define these variations as a cycle, that is to say a regular phenomenon. In fact, increasingly complex statistical, operations are needed in order to succeed in identifying a regular cyclical variation in the mass of information available.

It is precisely to this worthwhile attempt to identify a regular cycle, attributing all the residual irregularities to the trend, that the most promising theory in the field of short-term economic analysis is due: the real business cycle theory derived from the works of C. Nelson, C.I. Plosser, R.G. King and S.T. Rebelo in the early 1980s.

The theory has been refined and now uses the permanent shock components, even transient, to determine a stochastic trend, that is to say a tendency which varies continually under the pressure of specific and random events to set against a deterministic trend such as the unchangeable trend which was an obligatory reference for economists in previous years.

Leaving aside the theoretical motivations and statistical specifications employed to define a stochastic trend which is variable even in the short term, we would emphasise here that the real business cycle theory's attempt to reconstruct a regular cycle (as a deviation of the present data from a stochastic tendency which modifies continually and hence absorbs many of the cycle's irregularities) does not resolve the problem of the different variability of the present cycle but merely moves it, locating the greater variability in the tendency.

If we assume that the real business cycle is more comprehensible than the "classical" cycle given that its profile is more regular and hence easier to interpret, it is also true that in the end this cyclical component plays an increasingly small and hence increasingly marginal and insignificant part in explaining why the economy has experienced a variation. In other words, the real business cycle theory makes short-term fluctuations more comprehensible but less useful for an overall understanding of the economy given that most of the residual fluctuation is explained by the trend. The economist's interest therefore moves to understanding why the tendency changed: it becomes important to explain why they vary in such an erratic manner even in the short term. However, those who study economics are little interested in knowing if the cycle varies or if the trend varies but are rather called upon to furnish an explanation of why the short and medium-term components of the economy vary.

In an analysis of the application of the real business cycle to the Italian case by G. Pellegrini, it turns out that the stochastic trend explains 75% of the short-term movements, while only the remaining 25% can be attributed to the business cycle. In these conditions, one can understand why the observer's attention immediately shifts from the cycle to the trend, even for short-term movements.

In fact, this approach to business-cycle analysis has the advantage of emphasising the strong interrelations which exist between business cycle and trend, that is to say between short-term economic cycle and structure. If most of the short-term movements can be ascribed to the tendency which changes due to transitory phenomena and which can affect tendential behaviour through hysteresis, then it is difficult and perhaps unproductive to separate the business cycle from the trend.

This approach — which was espoused by Mitchell — ends up by

increasing the importance of the European approach to business cycle analysis: that of short-term economic analysis.

If the trend is no longer regular, but experiences strong variations of a random nature, then business-cycle analysis should not limit itself to studying regular fluctuations taken from irregular economic tendencies, but should favour what in Europe is called short-term economic analysis, i.e., analysing the economy's short-term movements and forget its aspiration to seek out irregularities and laws of behaviour, but rather attentively observe the reactions — both short and long-term, hence on the cycle and the tendency — of events which take place both exogenously and endogenously in an economic system.

In this sense, it can be said that short-term economic analysis does not limit itself to examining the business cycle, given that it is the structure (or tendency) which shapes the short-term economic cycle, which, in turn, ends up by influencing it in a sort of vicious circle. For this reason, the most recent theories of the business cycle can be more conveniently classified under the heading of short-term economic analysis; or else, if one wishes, with these new approaches, business-cycle analysis and short-term economic analysis end up by drawing closer to one another if not completely converging.

4. - The Implications for Economic Policy

The vicissitudes and peaks and troughs of the business cycle testify not only the impossibility of considering the business cycle dead, but also the variability of its manifestations: no longer recessions, even though regular, but rather brusque variations in intensity which differ according to circumstances.

The considerations of those who consider the business cycle part of the past mirror those who have enabled its rebirth, by separating it from a stochastic trend: the tendency and cycle influence one another so that it is no longer possible to consider them separately.

The theoretical conclusion is not without practical consequences as regards economic policy. If the cycle and trend are inseparable, short-term economic instruments cannot be separated from structural instruments and vice versa.

In other words, there can be no two-stage policy; first the more urgent short-term measures to right an economy and then the substantial ones, of a structural nature. Not because urgency is superfluous, but because short-term measures also have an effect on the structure, in the same way as structural measures have short-term repercussions.

In these conditions, those responsible for economic policy should realise (and be able to evaluate) that short-term measures have some influence on the tendency of the economy, an influence which increases with the frequency of such measures. Even today in Italy the measures taken by each government to reduce the budget deficit are denounced as short-term: after years of such short-term measures they have influenced the structure of the country both positively (budget policy is now viewed as constraint and as such perceived and accepted by economic players even though it does not always have the desired effect) and negatively: many reactions and changes in behaviour can be traced back to the economy's resistance to the repeated attempts to reduce the budget deficit. Furthermore the short-term use of monetary policy in the last fifteen years to reduce inflation has lead to a permanent rise in interest rates with structural repercussions on the debt and credit accounts. An example of this is the present rigidity of budget policies, burdened by an enormous debt service.

On the other hand, structural measures — as for example the moves toward European union in Europe — have had clear short-term effects, influencing the short-term economic cycle and, in some cases, resulting in short-term movements.

It is not intended that these concluding remarks should be too general, leaving the short-term economic cycle and structure, and also short and medium-term measures undefined, but rather that they stimulate a more profound reflection on the interrelations existing between the short and medium term in the fields of economic analysis and policy. We are convinced that the social sciences ill support rigid separations of fields and that the explanation of many problems rather lies precisely here, in the ambiguous and uncertain sphere of the mutual interrelations.

BIBLIOGRAPHY

[1] ARCELLI M. - DI GIORGIO G.: «Regole di credibilità della politica economica e discrezionalità», Roma, SIPI, *Rivista di politica economica*, n. 7-8, 1991.

[2] BRONSENBRENNER M. (ed.): *Is the Business Cycle Obsolete*, New York, Wiley Interscience, 1969.

[3] CIPOLLETTA I: *Congiuntura economica e previsione*, Bologna, il Mulino, 1992.

[4] KING R.G. - PLOSSER C.F. - REBELO S.T.: "Production, Growth and Business Cycle: the Basic Neoclassical Model", *Journal of Monetary Economics*, n. 21, 1988.

[5] LUCAS R.E. jr.: *Studies in Business Cycles Theory*, Boston, The Mit Press, 1983.

[6] MITCHELL W.C.: *Business Cycles: the Problem and its Setting*, New York, NBER, 1929.

[7] MOORE G.H.: *Indicators of Business Expansions and Contractions*, New York, NBER, 1950.

[8] NELSON C. - PLOSSER C.I.: "Trends and Random Walks in Macroeconomic Time Series", *Journal of Monetary Economics*, n. 10, 1982.

[9] ONOFRI P.: «Osservazione empirica e analisi economica: esperienze di indagine sulle fluttuazioni cicliche», paper presented at the workshop on *Crisi della teoria e crisi degli indicatori*, Società Italiana di Statistica, Giardini Naxos, 24-25 October 1991.

[10] PELLEGRINI G.: *Trend stocastico e ciclo economico nella produzione industriale*, (forthcoming), Roma, Banca d'Italia, 1990.

[11] SCHUMPETER J.A.: *Business Cycles: a Theoretical, Historical and Statistical Analysis of the Capital Process*, New York, Mc Graw Hill, 1939.

Index

Arrow-Debreu model 107–8, 111, 116n
Australia 184–5, 188–90, 199–200, 208–11
Austria 184–5, 188–90, 199, 208–11, 225

Barro, R. J. 106–10
Belgium 184–5, 188–90, 199–200, 208–11
Beveridge, S. 13, 17–18, 20, 22, 28, 66, 67, 69–72, 76–7, 150
Blanchard, O. 27–8, 34, 67n, 70, 75–6, 78, 80, 94, 96, 100, 123, 167n
Bulgaria 202, 212–16
Burns, Arthur F. 120, 141–2, 145, 163, 168, 287
business cycle analysis and industrial production forecasts 257–9
   future research 278–81
   models based on firm's expectations 266–78
   models based on quantitative indicators collected in real time 259–66
business cycle analysis, short-term 227–9
   econometric models for 229–52
   monthly model of the industrial sector (Italy) 228–52
business cycle analysis, use of cyclical indicators in 139–40, 267n
   and economic theory 168–75
   applications of time series analysis 154–62
   classical cycles 141–5
   classical methods of constructing 141–54
   composite indicators 152–4, 196–8
   economy of the leading indicators 171–5
   growth cycles 145–52
   measurement without theory 168–71
   OECD leading indicator system 181–225
   in Central and Eastern European Countries (CEECs) 181–2, 201–25
   probabilistic approach 162–5
   recent developments in 154–67
   recessions and recoveries 165–7, 169
business cycle theory 6–7
   implications for economic policy 295–6
   peaks and troughs 285–8
   reasons for demise 289–93
business surveys 187, 190, 211–22, 232
   see also industrial production forecasts

Canada 184–5, 188–90, 199–200, 208–10, 225
capital 112, 121, 146–7, 233–5
capital accumulation 12, 108–9, 114, 119
capital stock 114, 116–17, 120
Central and Eastern European countries (CEECs), leading indicators for business cycle analysis 181–2
   classification of existing indicators 205
   data needs and cyclical analysis 215
   development of new indicators 214–15
   potential leading indicators 205–14
   selection of indicators in the long-term 221–5
   selection of indicators in the short run 217–21
   selection of reference cycles 201–3
   statistical problems 203–4
competition 126–8, 233
consumption 47–55, 59–61, 112, 113, 116, 118, 121n, 123, 146–7, 154, 206–7, 211, 231, 260, 291
cyclical indicators in business cycle analysis 139–40, 267n
   and economic theory 168–75
   applications of time series analysis 154–62

cyclical indicators in business cycle analysis cont.

classical cycles 141–5
classical methods of constructing 141–54
composite indicators 152–6, 160–2, 164, 172–3
economy of the leading indicators 171–5
growth cycles 145–52
measurement without theory 168–71
OECD leading indicator system 181–225
in Central and Eastern European countries (CEECs) 181–2, 201–25
probabilistic approach 162–5
recent developments in 154–67
recessions and recoveries 165–7, 169
Czechoslovakia 202, 212–16

demand shocks 34, 41–6, 50–60, 77, 78–9, 86–7, 96, 128–9, 171–2, 228, 229, 239–51
Denmark 184–5, 188–90, 199–200, 208–11

econometrics 119–22, 131
analysis of GDP fluctuations 37–41
models for short-term economic cycle analysis 229–52
economic cycles
short-term analysis of 227–52
theory and measurement of 11–29
economic theory
cyclical indicators and 168–75
EEC 149, 183–5, 199, 231–2
Efron, B. 81, 94–5
EMS 251
ENEL (Ente nazionale per l'energia ellectrica) 259–61, 264, 279
equilibrium analysis 106–11, 126–7, 130–1
Evans, G. W. 27–8, 124
exchange rates 46, 230, 232

Finland 184–5, 188–90, 199, 201, 208–10
industrial production forecasting 270–3, 276–7

France
industrial production 77, 80–1, 101, 184–5
demand shocks 86, 92, 96
estimates of the permanent components of 96–100
forecasting 232, 270–1
labour supply shock 82, 88, 95–9
reflation (1981) 100
technology shock 84, 90, 95
leading indicators 188–90, 199, 208–11, 225
Frisch, Ragnar 106–7, 110–11, 122

Gavosto, A. 67, 70, 77, 80, 81, 100, 101
German Democratic Republic (GDR) 212–14
Germany
business surveys 232
industrial production 77, 80–1, 101, 184–5
demand shocks 87, 93, 96
estimates of the permanent components of 96–100
labour supply shocks 83, 89, 95–9
public debt 96
technology shocks 85, 91, 95
leading indicators 188–90, 199, 208–10, 225
Greece 184–5, 188–90, 199, 208–11
growth 33–41, 46–51, 55–61
cycles 145–52, 191–3, 287
growth theory and business cycle theory 105–7, 119–20, 130

Hungary 202, 212–16
Hymans, S. 155–9

industrial production cycle 149–50, 182–5
industrial production forecasts 257–9
future research 278–81
models based on firm's expectations 266–78
models based on quantitative indicators collected in real time 259–66
industrial production index 76–7, 153, 160, 182, 201–3, 257

Index

demand shocks 77, 78–9, 86–7, 96
labour supply shocks 78–9, 88–9, 95–9
oil shocks 77, 79, 80, 99
permanent components in 77–100
supply shocks 77, 79, 82–3
technology shocks 78–80, 84–5, 90–1, 95–6
see also industrial production forecasts
inflation 4, 7, 41, 59, 229, 241, 243, 246, 251, 288, 290
interest rates 187–91, 210, 211, 213–14, 220, 222, 229–30, 232
investment 47–55, 59–60, 109–10, 113, 118, 122–3, 130, 146–7, 154, 206–7, 211, 231, 292–3
Ireland 184–5, 188–90, 199, 208–10
Italy
  business cycles 144–5, 188–90, 199–200, 294
  consumption 47–55, 59–61
  GDP 36–44, 47–50, 59–60
  fluctuations of the economy 33–62
  industrial production 76–7, 80–1, 101, 184–5
    demand shocks 41–6, 86, 92, 96
    estimates of the permanent components of 96–100
    labour supply shocks 46, 59–60, 82, 88, 95–9
    technology shocks 84, 90, 95
  industrial production forecasting 258–81
    business survey results 268–70, 273–81
    electrical energy data 259–65, 269, 279
  investment 47–55, 59–60
  leading indicators 188–90, 208–10, 225
  monthly model of the industrial sector 228–52
  output 47–61
  service sector 291–2
  shocks 37, 40–6, 50–61, 82, 84, 86, 88, 90, 92, 95–9, 239–51

Japan 184–5, 188–90, 199, 208–11
Johansen, S. 35, 41, 52

Keynesianism 3, 66n, 105–7, 122, 126–31, 288, 289, 292
King, R. G. 34, 35, 59, 117n, 120, 126, 129, 163, 164, 293
Koopmans, T. C. 119, 168, 171
Kuhn-Tucker method 114n, 117n
Kydland, F. E. 19, 111, 120–5, 127, 131

labour 34–41, 46–52, 55–6, 112–18, 121, 125, 128–30, 232–8, 243, 245, 249
  supply shocks 46, 59–60, 78–9, 82–3, 88–9, 95–9
Lawson, Nigel 99
leading indicators
  OECD system 181–225
  in Central and Eastern European countries (CEECs) 181–2, 201–25
Lippi, M. 12n, 23, 25–6, 28, 33n, 67n, 68, 70, 74, 109n, 120, 151n, 278
Long, J. B. 111, 120, 121n, 124
Lucas, R. E. 106–11, 116n, 117n, 163, 175, 287
Luxembourg 184–5, 188–90, 199, 208–11

Mitchell, W. 120, 141–2, 145, 163, 168, 287, 294–5
money supply 108–10, 187, 206–9, 211, 213–14, 220, 222, 230
monthly models of the industrial sector 227–52
Morgentau, Henry 141

National Bureau of Economic Research (NBER) 141, 142n, 144–5, 148–9, 153, 156–8, 191, 267n, 287, 289
Nelson, C. R. 16–24, 28, 66, 67, 69–72, 76–7, 109, 120n, 150–1, 163n, 293
Nerlove, M. 231–2
Netherlands 184–5, 188–90, 199, 208–10, 225
New Classical Macroeconomics (NCM) 106–11, 287–8
New Keynesian Economics (NKE) 126–31
Norway 184–5, 188–90, 199–200, 208–10

OECD 141, 149, 153
  leading indicator system 181–225
    for Central and Eastern European
      countries (CEECs) 6, 181–2,
      201–25
oil shocks 77, 79, 80, 99, 123, 287
Onofri, P. 33n, 35, 37, 41, 59, 169
output 46–61, 78–80, 95, 109, 154, 287
  permanent components of 65–7
    in industrial production index 77–100
    multivariate decomposition model 77–100
    stochastic trend in 65–77
    survey of permanent and ransitory components 67–77
    variability 67–70, 76–7

Pareto Optimality 106–7, 112, 116n, 124
Paruolo, P. 33n, 35, 37, 41, 59
Pellegrini, G. 67, 70, 74n, 76, 77, 80, 81, 100, 101, 120, 294
permanent components
  in industrial production index 77–100
  of economic fluctuations 12–29
  of output 65–77
Plosser, C. I. 16–19, 24, 34, 35, 67, 109, 111, 117n, 120, 121n, 124, 126, 150–1, 163, 293
Poland 202, 212–16
population growth 12–13, 47, 50, 55, 60
Portugal 184–5, 188–90, 199–200, 208–11
Prescott, E. C. 19, 111, 116n, 119, 120–5, 127, 131
prices 13–14, 96, 108–10, 124, 229–30, 233, 241–3, 247, 252, 288, 290, 293
  and wages 106, 108, 126, 129, 235–6
  as indicators 146–7, 154, 156–7, 160, 172, 187–91, 204, 206–16, 220, 222, 224
productivity 14, 25–6, 59, 118, 121, 128, 129–30
profits 113, 142, 146–7, 156, 189, 206–7, 212, 224, 293
public sector 46, 124–5, 289–90

Quah, D. 25, 27–8, 34, 67n, 68, 70, 75–6, 78, 80, 94, 96, 100

raw materials 229, 233–5, 243, 246
Real Business Cycle (RBC) theory 19, 22, 60, 66, 105–7, 111–31, 288
  and short–term economic analysis 293–5
  growth theory and 119–20, 130
  innovatory features of 119–22
  link to NKE 126–31
  recent developments in 122–31
recession 3, 96, 141–2, 165–7, 169, 286–7, 288–90, 293, 295
recovery 141–2, 165–7
Reichlin, L. 12n, 17n, 23, 25–6, 28, 33n, 67n, 68, 70, 74, 109n, 120n, 151n
Romania 202, 212–16

Salituro, B. 33n, 35, 37, 41, 59
Scala Mobile indexation system 235–6
Schumpeter, J. A. 111, 122, 286–7, 293
Shapiro, M. D. 34, 35, 67n, 70, 79, 96
shocks 4–6, 11–13, 17–19, 21–2, 34, 37, 40, 66, 71–3, 76, 80–100, 108–12, 164, 293
  demand 34, 41–6, 50–60, 77, 78–9, 86–7, 96, 128–9, 171–2, 228, 229, 239–51
  labour supply 46, 59–60, 78–9, 82–3, 88–9, 95–9
  oil 77, 79, 80, 99, 123, 287
  permanent 50–60
  supply 37, 41–6, 50–61, 77, 79, 82–3, 172, 228, 239–51
  technology 19, 22, 46, 51, 78–80, 84–5, 90–1, 95–6, 111n, 117, 120, 121n, 123–4, 128, 229
  transitory 50–61
short-term economic cycle analysis 227–52
Slutzky, Eugene 11, 106, 110–11
Slutzky-Frisch approach 11, 106, 110–11
social planner (SP) 115–19, 120
Solow, R. 35–6, 79, 121, 124, 130
Spain 184–5, 188–90, 199–200, 208–11
stagflation 288
standard of living 52–3
statistics 119–22
Stock, J. H. 34, 35, 120, 140n, 163, 164, 165n, 173

Index

supply shocks 37, 41–6, 50–61, 77, 79, 82–3, 172, 228, 229, 239–51
Sweden 184–5, 188–90, 199–200, 208–10
Switzerland 184–5, 188–90, 199, 201, 208–10, 231, 232n

technical progress 12, 25–7, 29, 35–7, 47, 50, 59, 79, 95, 120
technology 37, 42, 52–3, 56, 61, 66, 74, 78, 99, 106, 107, 116, 118, 119, 120–1, 130, 292
  shocks 19, 22, 46, 51, 78–80, 84–5, 90–1, 95–6, 111n, 117, 120, 121n, 123–4, 128, 229
Thatcher, Margaret 99
Tibshirani, R. 94–5
time series analysis 11, 33, 65–7
  applications of 154–62
  decomposition into trend and cycle 20–5
  DS models for USA output 14–22, 25, 29
  multivariate models 27–8
  traditional decomposition into permanent and transitory component 12–29, 67–77
  TS models 15–20
trade unions 78
transitory components
  of economic fluctuations 12–29
  of output 65–77
trend 12–25, 288, 293–6
  in output
    decomposition between trend and cycle 77–100
    stochastic trends in 65–77
    Phase-Average Trend method (PAT) 149–51, 191–6

unemployment 7, 27, 41, 59, 80, 96, 107n, 146–7, 153, 154, 206–7, 210, 290
Unidentified Component ARIMA models (UC–ARIMA) 73–4, 76–7
United Kingdom 77, 291
  business surveys 232n
  industrial production 80–1, 101
    demand shock 87, 93, 96
    estimates of the permanent components of 96–100
    labour supply shock 83, 89, 95–9
    technology shock 85, 91, 95
  leading indicators 188–90, 199, 208–11, 225
United States of America 14–22, 27, 34, 74n, 109n, 121n, 123, 124, 141, 257
  cyclical indicators 144–7, 152–3, 155–62, 167
  industrial production cycles 183–5, 287–8
  leading indicators 188–90, 199–201, 208–11, 225
USSR 212–14

vector auto-regressive (VAR) analysis 5, 27, 37–46, 50–62, 75, 78–100, 169–70, 229

wages 106, 108, 126, 129–30, 235–6
Walrasian equilibrium 106–8, 126–7, 130
Watson, M. 34, 35, 67n, 70, 71–4, 79, 96, 120, 123, 140n, 151n, 163, 164, 165n, 167n, 173
wealth 79, 118
welfare economics 115
welfare state 289–90

Yugoslavia 184–5, 188–90, 199–200, 208–11